# Access Database Design & Programming

# Access Database Design
# & Programming

Steven Roman

**O'REILLY**™

*Cambridge · Köln · Paris · Sebastopol · Tokyo*

**Access Database Design & Programming**
by Steven Roman

Copyright © 1997 Steven Roman.  All rights reserved.
Printed in the United States of America.

Published by O'Reilly & Associates, Inc., 101 Morris Street, Sebastopol, CA 95472.

**Editor:** Ron Petrusha

**Production Editor:** Jane Ellin

**Printing History:**

June 1997:            First Edition

This book is printed on acid-free paper with 85% recycled content, 15% post-consumer waste.
O'Reilly & Associates is committed to using paper with the highest recycled content available
consistent with high quality.

ISBN:  1-56592-297-2

*To Donna*

# Table of Contents

# *Preface*

This book appears to be about two separate topics—database design and database programming. It is.

It would be misleading to claim that database design and database programming are intimately related. So why are they in the same book?

The answer is that while these two subjects are not related, in the sense that knowledge of one leads directly to knowledge of the other, they are definitely *linked*, by the simple fact that a power database user needs to know something about both of these subjects in order to effectively create, use, and maintain a database.

In fact, it might be said that creating and maintaining a database application in Microsoft Access is done in three broad steps—designing the database, creating the basic graphical interface (i.e., setting up the tables, queries, forms, and reports) and then getting the application to perform in the desired way.

The second of these three steps is fairly straightforward, for it is mostly a matter of becoming familiar with the relatively easy-to-use Access graphical interface. Help is available for this through Access's own online help system, as well as through the literally dozens of overblown 1000-page-plus tomes devoted to Microsoft Access. Unfortunately, none of the books that I have seen does any real justice to the other two steps. Hence this book.

To be a bit more specific, the book has two goals:

- To discuss the basic concepts of relational database theory and design.
- To discuss how to extract the full power of Microsoft Access, through programming in the Access Structured Query Language (SQL) and the Data Access Object (DAO) component of the Microsoft Jet database engine.

To accomplish the first goal, we describe the how and why of creating an efficient database system, explaining such concepts as:

- Entities and entity classes

- Keys, superkeys, and primary keys

- One-to-one, one-to-many, and many-to-many relationships

- Referential integrity

- Joins of various types (inner joins, outer joins, equi-joins, semi-joins, θ-joins, and so on)

- Operations of the relational algebra (selection, projection, join, union, intersection, and so on)

- Normal forms and their importance

Of course, once you have a basic understanding of how to create an effective relational database, you will want to take full advantage of that database, which can only be done through programming. In addition, many of the programming techniques we discuss in this book can be used to create and maintain a database from within other applications, such as Microsoft Visual Basic, Microsoft Excel, and Microsoft Word.

We should hasten to add that this book is not a traditional cookbook for learning Microsoft Access. For instance, we do not discuss forms and reports, nor do we discuss such issues as database security, database replication, and multiuser issues. This is why we have been able to keep the book to a (hopefully) readable few hundred pages.

This book is for Access users at all levels. It applies equally well to Access 2.0, Access 7.0, and Access 8.0 (which is a component of Microsoft Office 97). We will assume that you have a passing acquaintance with the Access development environment, however. For instance, we assume that you already know how to create a table or a query.

Throughout the book, we will use a specific modest-sized example to illustrate the concepts that we discuss. The example consists of a database called LIBRARY that is designed to hold data about the books in a certain library. Of course, the amount of data we will use will be kept artificially small—just enough to illustrate the concepts.

## *The Book's Audience*

Most books on Microsoft Access focus primarily on the Access interface and its components, giving little attention to the more important issue of database design. After all, once the database application is complete, the interface components play only a small role, whereas the design continues to affect the usefulness of the application.

In attempting to restore the focus on database design, this book aspires to be a kind of "second course" in Microsoft Access—a book for Access users who have mastered the basics of the interface, are familiar with such things as creating tables and designing queries, and now want to move beyond the interface to create programmable Access applications. This book provides a firm foundation on which you can begin to build your database application development skills.

At the same time that this book is intended primarily as an introduction to Access for aspiring database application developers, it also is of interest to more experienced Access programmers. For the most part, such topics as normal forms or the details of the relational algebra are almost exclusively the preserve of the academic world. By introducing these topics to the mainstream Access audience, *Access Database Design & Programming* offers a concise, succinct, readable guide that experienced Access developers can turn to whenever some of the details of database design or SQL statements escape them.

# *Organization of This Book*

*Access Database Design & Programming* consists of 11 chapters that can informally be divided into three parts. In addition, there are four appendixes.

Chapter 1, *Introduction*, examines the problems involved in using a flat database—a single table that holds all of an application's data—and makes a case for using instead a relational database design consisting of multiple tables. But because relational database applications divide data into multiple tables, it is necessary to be able to reconstitute that data in ways that are useful—that is, to piece data back together from their multiple tables. Hence, the need for query languages and programming, which are in many ways an integral part of designing a database.

The first part of the book then focuses on designing a database—that is, on the process of decomposing data into multiple tables.

Chapter 2, *The Entity-Relationship Model of a Database*, introduces some of the basic concepts of relational database management, like entities, entity classes, keys, superkeys, and one-to-many and many-to-many relationships.

Chapter 3, *Implementing Entity-Relationship Models: Relational Databases*, shows how these general concepts and principles are applied in designing a real-world database. In particular, the chapter shows how to decompose a sample flat database into a well-designed relational database.

Chapter 4, *Database Design Principles*, continues the discussion begun in Chapter 3 by focusing on the major problem of database design, that of eliminating data redundancy without losing the essential relationships between items of data. The chapter introduces the notion of functional dependencies and examines each of the major forms for database normalization.

Once a database is properly normalized, or its data are broken up into discrete tables, it must, almost paradoxically, be pieced back together again in order to be of any value at all. The second part of the book focuses on the query languages that are responsible for doing this.

Chapter 5, *Query Languages and the Relational Algebra*, introduces procedural query languages based on the relational algebra and nonprocedural query languages based on the relational calculus, then focuses on the major operations— like unions, intersections, and inner and outer joins—that are available using the relational algebra.

Chapter 6, *Access Structured Query Language (SQL)*, shows how the relational algebra is implemented in Microsoft Access, both in the Access Query Design window and in Access SQL. Interestingly, the Access Query Design window is really a front end that constructs Access SQL statements, which ordinarily are hidden from the user or developer. However, it does not offer a complete replacement for Access SQL—a number of operations can only be performed using SQL statements, and not through the Access graphical interface. This makes a basic knowledge of Access SQL important.

While SQL is a critical tool for getting at data in relational database management systems and returning recordsets that offer various views of their data, it is also an unfriendly tool. The Access Query Design window, for example, was developed primarily to hide the implementation of Access SQL from both the user and the programmer. But Access SQL, and the graphical query facilities that hide it, do not form an integrated environment that the database programmer can rely on to shield the user from the details of an application's implementation. Instead, creating this integrated application environment is the responsibility of a programming language (Visual Basic for Applications or VBA) and an interface between the programming language and the database engine (DAO). The final portion of the book examines these two tools for application development.

Chapter 7, *Database System Architecture*, describes the role of programming in database application development, and introduces the major tools and concepts needed to create an Access application.

Chapter 8, *The Basics of Programming in VBA*, provides a quick overview of Visual Basic for Applications that focuses on its data types, commonly used intrinsic functions, and flow control statements.

Chapter 9, *Programming DAO: Overview*, introduces Data Access Objects, or DAO. DAO provides the interface between Visual Basic for Applications and the Jet database engine used by Access. The chapter provides an overview of working with objects in VBA before examining the DAO object model and the Microsoft Access object model.

Chapter 10, *Programming DAO: Data Definition Language*, focuses on the subset of DAO that is used to define basic database objects. The chapter discusses operations such as creating tables, indices, and query definitions under program control.

Chapter 11, *Programming DAO: Data Manipulation Language*, focuses on working with recordset objects and on practical record-oriented operations. The chapter discusses such topics as recordset navigation, finding records, and editing data.

Appendix A, *DAO 3.0/3.5 Collections, Properties, and Methods*, is intended as a quick reference guide to DAO 3.0 (which is included with Access for Office 95) and DAO 3.5 (which is included with Access for Office 97).

Appendix B, *The Quotient: An Additional Operation of the Relational Algebra*, examines one additional little-used query operation that was not discussed in Chapter 5.

Appendix C, *Obtaining or Creating the Sample Database*, contains instructions for either downloading a copy of the sample files from the book or creating them yourself.

Appendix D, *Suggestions for Further Reading*, lists some of the major works that provide in-depth discussion of the issues of relational database design and normalization.

## *Conventions in This Book*

Throughout this book, we've used the following typographic conventions:

*UPPERCASE*

indicates a database name (e.g., LIBRARY) or the name of a table within a database (e.g., BOOKS). Keywords in SQL statements (e.g., SELECT) also appear in uppercase, as well as types of data (e.g., LONG), commands (e.g., CREATE VALUE), options (HAVING), etc.

`Constant width`

indicates a code example.

*Italic*

is used in normal text to introduce a new term and to indicate object names (e.g., *QueryDef*), the names of entity classes (e.g., the *Books* entity class), and VBA keywords.

# Obtaining Updated Information

The sample tables in the LIBRARY database, as well as the sample programs presented in the book, are available online from the Internet and can be freely downloaded. Alternately, if you don't have access to the Internet either by using a web browser or a file transfer protocol (FTP) client, and if you don't use an email system that allows you to send and receive email from the Internet, you can create the database file and its tables yourself. For details, see Appendix C.

Updates to the material contained in the book, along with other Access-related developments, are available from our web site, *http://www.ora.com/*. Simply follow the links to the Windows section.

# Request for Comments

As a reader of this book, you can help us to improve the next edition. If you find errors, inaccuracies, or typos anywhere in the book, please let us know about them. Also, if you find any misleading statements or confusing explanations, let us know. Send your bug reports and comments to:

> O'Reilly & Associates, Inc.
> 101 Morris Street
> Sebastopol, CA  95472
> 1-800-998-9938 (in the U.S. or Canada)
> 1-707-829-0515 (international/local)
> 1-707-829-0104 (FAX)
> *bookquestions@ora.com*

Please let us know what we can do to make the book more helpful to you. We take your comments seriously, and will do whatever we can to make this book as useful as it can be.

# Acknowledgments

My thanks to Ron Petrusha, editor at O'Reilly & Associates, for making many useful suggestions that improved this book.

Also thanks to the production staff at O'Reilly & Associates, including Jane Ellin, the Production Editor, Edie Freedman for the cover design, Nancy Priest for interior design, Mike Sierra for Tools support, Chris Reilley and Rob Romano for the illustrations, David Futato and Sheryl Avruch for quality and sanity control, and Seth Maislin for the index.

1

# *Introduction*

## *Database Design*

As mentioned in the Preface, one purpose of this book is to explain the basic concepts of modern relational database theory and show how these concepts are realized in Microsoft Access. Allow me to amplify on this rather lofty goal.

To take a very simple view, which will do nicely for the purposes of this introductory discussion, a *database* is just a collection of related data. A *database management system*, or DBMS, is a system that is designed for two main purposes:

*   To add, delete, and update the data in the database

*   To provide various ways to view (on screen or in print) the data in the database

If the data are simple, and there is not very much data, then a database can consist of a single table. In fact, a simple database can easily be maintained even with a word processor! ·

To illustrate, suppose you want to set up a database for the books in a library. Purely for the sake of illustration, suppose the library contains 14 books. The same discussion would apply to a library of perhaps a few hundred books. Table 1-1 shows the LIBRARY_FLAT database in the form of a single table.

LIBRARY_FLAT (Table 1-1) was created using Microsoft Word. For such a simple database, Word has enough power to fulfill the two goals mentioned earlier. Certainly, adding, deleting, and editing the table presents no particular problems (provided we know how to manage tables in Word). In addition, if we want to sort the data by author, for example, we can just select the table and choose *Sort* from the *Table* menu in Microsoft Word. Extracting a portion of the data in the

Table 1-1. The LIBRARY_FLAT Sample Database

| ISBN | Title | AuID | AuName | AuPhone | PubID | PubName | PubPhone | Price |
|---|---|---|---|---|---|---|---|---|
| 1-1111-1111-1 | C++ | 4 | Roman | 444-444-4444 | 1 | Big House | 123-456-7890 | $29.95 |
| 0-99-999999-9 | Emma | 1 | Austen | 111-111-1111 | 1 | Big House | 123-456-7890 | $20.00 |
| 0-91-335678-7 | Faerie Queene | 7 | Spenser | 777-777-7777 | 1 | Big House | 123-456-7890 | $15.00 |
| 0-91-045678-5 | Hamlet | 5 | Shakespeare | 555-555-5555 | 2 | Alpha Press | 999-999-9999 | $20.00 |
| 0-103-45678-9 | Iliad | 3 | Homer | 333-333-3333 | 1 | Big House | 123-456-7890 | $25.00 |
| 0-12-345678-9 | Jane Eyre | 1 | Austen | 111-111-1111 | 3 | Small House | 714-000-0000 | $49.00 |
| 0-99-777777-7 | King Lear | 5 | Shakespeare | 555-555-5555 | 2 | Alpha Press | 999-999-9999 | $49.00 |
| 0-555-55555-9 | Macbeth | 5 | Shakespeare | 555-555-5555 | 2 | Alpha Press | 999-999-9999 | $12.00 |
| 0-11-345678-9 | Moby Dick | 2 | Melville | 222-222-2222 | 3 | Small House | 714-000-0000 | $49.00 |
| 0-12-333433-3 | On Liberty | 8 | Mill | 888-888-8888 | 1 | Big House | 123-456-7890 | $25.00 |
| 0-321-32132-1 | Balloon | 13 | Sleepy | 321-321-1111 | 3 | Small House | 714-000-0000 | $34.00 |
| 0-321-32132-1 | Balloon | 11 | Snoopy | 321-321-2222 | 3 | Small House | 714-000-0000 | $34.00 |
| 0-321-32132-1 | Balloon | 12 | Grumpy | 321-321-0000 | 3 | Small House | 714-000-0000 | $34.00 |
| 0-55-123456-9 | Main Street | 10 | Jones | 123-333-3333 | 3 | Small House | 714-000-0000 | $22.95 |
| 0-55-123456-9 | Main Street | 9 | Smith | 123-222-2222 | 3 | Small House | 714-000-0000 | $22.95 |
| 0-123-45678-0 | Ulysses | 6 | Joyce | 666-666-6666 | 2 | Alpha Press | 999-999-9999 | $34.00 |
| 1-22-233700-0 | Visual Basic | 4 | Roman | 444-444-4444 | 1 | Big House | 123-456-7890 | $25.00 |

Columns labeled AuID and PubID are included for identitification purposes, i.e., to uniquely identify an author or a publisher. In any case, their presence or absence will not affect the current discussion.

table (i.e., creating a view) can be done by making a copy of the table and then deleting appropriate rows and/or columns.

## *Why Use a Relational Database Design?*

Thus, maintaining a simple, so-called *flat database* consisting of a single table does not require much knowledge of database theory. On the other hand, most databases worth maintaining are quite a bit more complicated than that. Real-life databases often have hundreds of thousands or even millions of records, with data that are very intricately related. This is where using a full-fledged relational database program becomes essential. Consider, for example, the Library of Congress, which has over 16 million books in its collection. For reasons that will become apparent soon, a single table simply will not do for this database!

### *Redundancy*

The main problems associated with using a single table to maintain a database stem from the issue of unnecessary repetition of data, that is, *redundancy*. Some repetition of data is always necessary, as we will see, but the idea is to remove as much unnecessary repetition as possible.

The redundancy in the LIBRARY_FLAT table (Table 1-1) is obvious. For instance, the name and phone number of Big House publishers is repeated six times in the table, and Shakespeare's phone number is repeated thrice.

In an effort to remove as much redundancy as possible from a database, a database designer must split the data into multiple tables. Here is one possibility for the LIBRARY_FLAT example, which splits the original database into four separate tables.

- A BOOKS table, shown in Table 1-2, in which each book has its own record
- An AUTHORS table, shown in Table 1-3, in which each author has his or her own record
- A PUBLISHERS table, shown in Table 1-4, in which each publisher has its own record

We will explain the purpose of the BOOK/AUTHOR table (which appears in Table 1-5) a bit later.

*Table 1-2. The BOOKS Table from the LIBRARY_FLAT Database*

| ISBN | Title | PubID | Price |
|---|---|---|---|
| 0-555-55555-9 | Macbeth | 2 | $12.00 |
| 0-91-335678-7 | Faerie Queene | 1 | $15.00 |
| 0-99-999999-9 | Emma | 1 | $20.00 |

*Table 1-2. The BOOKS Table from the LIBRARY_FLAT Database (continued)*

| ISBN | Title | PubID | Price |
|---|---|---|---|
| 0-91-045678-5 | Hamlet | 2 | $20.00 |
| 0-55-123456-9 | Main Street | 3 | $22.95 |
| 1-22-233700-0 | Visual Basic | 1 | $25.00 |
| 0-12-333433-3 | On Liberty | 1 | $25.00 |
| 0-103-45678-9 | Iliad | 1 | $25.00 |
| 1-1111-1111-1 | C++ | 1 | $29.95 |
| 0-321-32132-1 | Balloon | 3 | $34.00 |
| 0-123-45678-0 | Ulysses | 2 | $34.00 |
| 0-99-777777-7 | King Lear | 2 | $49.00 |
| 0-12-345678-9 | Jane Eyre | 3 | $49.00 |
| 0-11-345678-9 | Moby Dick | 3 | $49.00 |

*Table 1-3. The AUTHORS Table from the LIBRARY_FLAT Database*

| AuID | AuName | AuPhone |
|---|---|---|
| 1 | Austen | 111-111-1111 |
| 12 | Grumpy | 321-321-0000 |
| 3 | Homer | 333-333-3333 |
| 10 | Jones | 123-333-3333 |
| 6 | Joyce | 666-666-6666 |
| 2 | Melville | 222-222-2222 |
| 8 | Mill | 888-888-8888 |
| 4 | Roman | 444-444-4444 |
| 5 | Shakespeare | 555-555-5555 |
| 13 | Sleepy | 321-321-1111 |
| 9 | Smith | 123-222-2222 |
| 11 | Snoopy | 321-321-2222 |
| 7 | Spenser | 777-777-7777 |

*Table 1-4. The PUBLISHERS Table from the LIBRARY_FLAT Database*

| PubID | PubName | PubPhone |
|---|---|---|
| 1 | Big House | 123-456-7890 |
| 2 | Alpha Press | 999-999-9999 |
| 3 | Small House | 714-000-0000 |

*Table 1-5. The BOOK/AUTHOR Table from the LIBRARY_FLAT Database*

| ISBN | AuID |
|---|---|
| 0-103-45678-9 | 3 |
| 0-11-345678-9 | 2 |
| 0-12-333433-3 | 8 |
| 0-12-345678-9 | 1 |
| 0-123-45678-0 | 6 |
| 0-321-32132-1 | 11 |
| 0-321-32132-1 | 12 |
| 0-321-32132-1 | 13 |
| 0-55-123456-9 | 9 |
| 0-55-123456-9 | 10 |
| 0-555-55555-9 | 5 |
| 0-91-045678-5 | 5 |
| 0-91-335678-7 | 7 |
| 0-99-777777-7 | 5 |
| 0-99-999999-9 | 1 |
| 1-1111-1111-1 | 4 |
| 1-22-233700-0 | 4 |

Note that now the name and phone number of Big House appears only once in the database (in the PUBLISHERS table), as does Shakespeare's phone number (in the AUTHORS table).

Of course, there are still some duplicated data in the database. For instance, the PubID information appears in more than one place in these tables. As mentioned earlier, we cannot eliminate all duplicate data and still maintain the relationships between the data.

To get a feel for the reduction in duplicate data achieved by the four-table approach, imagine (as is reasonable) that the database also included the address of each publisher. Then Table 1-1 would need a new column containing 14 addresses—many of which are duplicates. On the other hand, the four-table database needs only one new column in the PUBLISHERS table, adding a total of three distinct addresses.

To drive the difference home, consider the 16-million-book database of the Library of Congress. Suppose the database contains books from 10,000 different publishers. A publisher's address column in a flat database design would contain 16 million addresses, whereas a multitable approach would require only 10,000 addresses. Now, if the average address is 50 characters long, then the multitable approach would save

$$(16,000,000 - 10,000) \leftrightarrow 50 = 79.9 \text{ million characters}$$

Assuming that each character takes 2 bytes (in the Unicode that is used internally by Microsoft Access), the single-table approach wastes about 160 megabytes of space, just for the address field!

Indeed, the issue of redundancy alone is quite enough to convince a database designer to avoid the flat database approach. However, there are several other problems with flat databases, which we now discuss.

### Multiple-value problems

It is clear that some books in our database are authored by multiple authors. This leaves us with three choices in a single-table flat database:

- We can accommodate multiple authors with multiple rows—one for each author, as in the LIBRARY_FLAT table (Table 1-1) for the books *Balloon* and *Main Street*.

- We can accommodate multiple authors with multiple columns in a single row—one for each author.

- We can include all authors' names in one column of the table.

The problem with the multiple-row choice is that all of the data about a book must be repeated as many times as there are authors of the book—an obvious case of redundancy. The multiple column approach presents the problem of guessing how many Author columns we will ever need, and creates a lot of wasted space (empty fields) for books with only one author. It also creates major programming headaches.

The third choice is to include all authors' names in one cell, which can lead to trouble of its own. For example, it becomes more difficult to search the database for a single author. Worse yet, how can we create an alphabetical list of the authors in the table?

### Update anomalies

In order to update, say, a publisher's phone number in the LIBRARY_FLAT database (Table 1-1), it is necessary to make changes in every row containing that number. If we miss a row, we have produced a so-called *update anomaly*, resulting in an unreliable table.

### Insertion anomalies

Difficulties will arise if we wish to insert a new publisher in the LIBRARY_FLAT database (Table 1-1), but we do not yet have information about any of that publisher's books. We could add a new row to the existing table and place NULL values in all but the three publisher-related columns, but this may lead to trouble. (A NULL is a value intended to indicate a missing or unknown value for a field.) For instance, adding several such publishers means that the ISBN column, which should contain unique data, will contain several NULL values. This general problem is referred to as an *insertion anomaly.*

### Deletion anomalies

In contrast to the preceding problem, if we delete all book entries for a given publisher, for instance, then we will also lose all information about that publisher. This is a *deletion anomaly.*

This list of potential problems should be enough to convince us that the idea of using a single-table database is generally not smart. Good database design dictates that the data be divided into several tables, and that relationships be established between these tables. Such a database is called a *relational database.* On the other hand, relational databases do have their complications. Here are a few examples.

### Avoiding data loss

One complication in designing a relational database is figuring out how to split the data into multiple tables so as not to lose any information. For instance, if we had left out the BOOK/AUTHOR table (Table 1-5) in our previous example, there would be no way to determine the authors of each book. In fact, the sole purpose of the BOOK/AUTHOR table is so that we do not lose the book/author relationship!

### Maintaining relational integrity

We must be careful to maintain the integrity of the various relationships between tables when changes are made. For instance, if we decide to remove a publisher from the database, it is not enough just to remove that publisher from the PUBLISHERS table, for this would leave *dangling references* to that publisher in the BOOKS table.

### Creating views

When the data are spread throughout several tables, it becomes more difficult to create various views of the data. For instance, we might want to see a list of all publishers that publish books priced under $10.00. This requires gathering data from more than one table. The point is that, by breaking data into separate tables, we must often go to the trouble of piecing the data back together in order to get a comprehensive view of those data!

## Summary

In summary, it is clear that, to avoid redundancy problems and various unpleasant anomalies, a database needs to contain multiple tables, with relationships defined between these tables. On the other hand, this raises some issues, such as how to design the tables in the database without losing any data, and how to piece together the data from multiple tables to create various views of that data. The main goal of the first part of this book on database design is to explore these fundamental issues.

# Database Programming

The motivation for learning database programming is quite simple—power. If you want to have as much control over your databases as possible, you will need to do some programming. In fact, even some simple things require programming. For instance, there is no way to retrieve the list of fields of a given table using the Access graphical interface—you can only get this list through programming. (You can view such a list in the table design mode of the table but you cannot get access to this list in order to, for example, present the end-user with the list and ask if he or she wishes to make any changes to it.)

In addition, programming may be the only way to access and manipulate a database from within another application. For instance, if you are working in Microsoft Excel, you can create and manipulate an Access database with as much power as if you were working with Access itself, but only through programming! The reason is that Excel does not have the capability to render graphical representations of database objects. Instead you can create the database within Access and then manipulate it programmatically from within Excel.

It is also worth mentioning that programming can give you a great sense of satisfaction. There is nothing more pleasing than watching a program that you have written step through the rows of a table and make certain changes that you have requested. It is often easier to write a program to perform an action such as this, than trying to remember how to perform the same action using the graphical interface. In short, programming is not only empowering, but it also sometimes provides the simplest route to a particular end.

And let us not forget that programming can be just plain fun!

# 2

# The Entity-Relationship Model of a Database

Let us begin our discussion of database design by looking at an informal database model called the *entity-relationship model*. This model of a relational database provides a very useful perspective, especially for the purposes of the initial design of the database.

We will illustrate the general principles of this model with our LIBRARY database example, which we will carry through the entire book. This example database is designed to hold data about the books in a certain library. The amount of data we will use will be kept artificially small—just enough to illustrate the concepts. (In fact, at this point, you may want to take a look at the example database. For details on downloading it from the Internet, or on using Microsoft Access to create it yourself, see Appendix C, *Obtaining or Creating the Sample Database.*) In the next chapter, we will actually implement the entity-relationship (E/R) model for our LIBRARY database.

## What Is a Database?

A *database* may be defined as a collection of *persistent* data. The term persistent is somewhat vague, but is intended to imply that the data has a more-or-less independent existence, or that it is *semipermanent*. For instance, data that are stored on paper in a filing cabinet, or stored magnetically on a hard disk, CD-ROM, or computer tape are persistent, whereas data stored in a computer's memory are generally not considered to be persistent. (The term "permanent" is a bit too strong, since very little in life is truly permanent.)

Of course, this is a very general concept. Most real-life databases consist of data that exist for a specific purpose, and are thus related.

# *Entities and Their Attributes*

The purpose of a database is to store information about certain types of objects. In database language, these objects are called *entities*. For example, the entities of the LIBRARY database include books, authors, and publishers.

It is very important at the outset to make a distinction between the entities that are contained in a database at a given time and the world of all possible entities that the database might contain. The reason this is important is that the contents of a database are constantly changing and we must make decisions based not just on what is contained in a database at a given time, but on what might be contained in the database in the future.

For example, at a given time, our LIBRARY database might contain 14 book entities. However, as time goes on, new books may be added to the database and old books may be removed. Thus, the entities in the database are constantly changing. If, for example, based on the fact that the 14 books currently in the database have different titles, we decide to use the title to uniquely identify each book, we may be in for some trouble when, later on, a different book arrives at the library with the same title as a previous book.

The world of all possible entities of a specific type that a database might contain is referred to as an *entity class*. We will use italics to denote entity classes. Thus, for instance, the world of all possible books is the *Books* entity class and the world of all possible authors is the *Authors* entity class.

We emphasize that an entity class is just an *abstract description* of something, whereas an entity is a *concrete example* of that description. The entity classes in our very modest LIBRARY example database are (at least so far):

- *Books*
- *Authors*
- *Publishers*

The set of entities of a given entity class that are in the database at a given time is called an *entity set*. To clarify the difference between entity set and entity class with an example, consider the BOOKS table in the LIBRARY database, which is shown in Table 2-1.

*Table 2-1. The BOOKS Table from the LIBRARY Database*

| ISBN | Title | Price |
|------|-------|-------|
| 0-12-333433-3 | On Liberty | $25.00 |
| 0-103-45678-9 | Iliad | $25.00 |
| 0-91-335678-7 | Faerie Queene | $15.00 |

*Table 2-1. The BOOKS Table from the LIBRARY Database (continued)*

| ISBN | Title | Price |
|------|-------|-------|
| 0-99-999999-9 | Emma | $20.00 |
| 1-22-233700-0 | Visual Basic | $25.00 |
| 1-1111-1111-1 | C++ | $29.95 |
| 0-91-045678-5 | Hamlet | $20.00 |
| 0-555-55555-9 | Macbeth | $12.00 |
| 0-99-777777-7 | King Lear | $49.00 |
| 0-123-45678-0 | Ulysses | $34.00 |
| 0-12-345678-9 | Jane Eyre | $49.00 |
| 0-11-345678-9 | Moby Dick | $49.00 |
| 0-321-32132-1 | Balloon | $34.00 |
| 0-55-123456-9 | Main Street | $22.95 |

The entities are books, the entity class is the set of all possible books, and the entity set (at this moment) is the specific set of 14 books listed in the BOOKS table. As mentioned, the entity set will change as new books (book entities) are added to the table, or old ones are removed. However, the entity class does not change.

Incidentally, if you are familiar with object-oriented programming concepts, you will recognize the concept of a *class*. In object-oriented circles, we would refer to an entity class simply as a class, and an entity as an *object*.

The entities of an entity class possess certain properties, which are called *attributes*. We usually refer to these attributes as attributes of the entity class itself. It is up to the database designer to determine which attributes to include for each entity class. It is these attributes that will correspond to the fields in the tables of the database.

The attributes of an entity class serve three main purposes:

- Attributes are used to include *information* that we want in the database. For instance, we want the title of each book to be included in the database, so we include a Title attribute for the *Books* entity class.

- Attributes are used to help uniquely identify individual entities within an entity class. For instance, we may wish to include a publisher's ID number attribute for the *Publishers* entity class, to uniquely identify each publisher. If combinations of other attributes (such as the publisher's name and publisher's address) will serve this purpose, the inclusion of an identifying attribute is not strictly necessary, but it can still be more efficient to include such an attribute, since often we can create a much shorter identifying attribute. For instance, a combination of title, author, publisher, and copyright date would make a very awkward and inefficient identifying attribute for the *Books* entity class—much more so than the ISBN attribute.

- Attributes are used to describe *relationships* between the entities in different entity classes. We will discuss this subject in more detail later.

For now, let us list the attributes for the LIBRARY database that we need to supply information about each entity and to uniquely identify each entity. We will deal with the issue of describing relationships later. Remember that our example is kept deliberately small—in real life we would no doubt include many other attributes.

The attributes of the entity classes in the LIBRARY database are:

*Books* attributes
    Title
    ISBN
    Price

*Authors* attributes
    AuName
    AuPhone
    AuID

*Publishers* attributes
    PubName
    PubPhone
    PubID

Let us make a few remarks about these attributes.

- From these attributes alone, there is no direct way to tell who is the author of a given book, since there is no author-related attribute in the *Books* entity class. A similar statement applies to determining the publisher of a book. Thus, we will need to add more attributes in order to describe these relationships.

- The ISBN (International Standard Book Number) of a book serves to uniquely identify the book, since no two books have the same ISBN (at least in theory). On the other hand, the Title alone does not uniquely identify the book, since many books have the same title. In fact, the sole purpose of ISBNs (here and in the real world) is to uniquely identify books. Put another way, the ISBN is a quintessential identifying attribute!

- We may reasonably assume that no two publishers in the world have the same name and the same phone number. Hence, these two attributes together uniquely identify the publisher. Nevertheless, we have included a publisher's ID attribute to make this identification more convenient.

Let us emphasize that an entity class is a description, not a set. For instance, the entity class *Books* is a description of the attributes of the entities that we identify as books. A *Books* entity is the "database version" of a book. It is not a physical book, but rather a book as defined by the values of its attributes. For instance, the following is a *Books* entity:

```
Title = Gone With The Wind
ISBN = 0-12-345678-9
Price = $24.00
```

Now, there is certainly more than one physical copy in existence of the book *Gone With The Wind*, with this ISBN and price, but that is not relevant to our discussion. As far as the database is concerned, there is only one *Books* entity defined by:

```
Title = Gone With The Wind
ISBN = 0-12-345678-9
Price = $24.00
```

If we need to model multiple copies of physical books in our database (as a real library would do), then we must add another attribute to the *Books* entity class, perhaps called CopyNumber. Even still, a book entity is just a set of attribute values!

These matters emphasize the point that it is up to the database designer to ensure that the set of attributes for an entity uniquely identify the entity from among all other entities that may appear in the database (now and forever, if possible!). For instance, if the *Books* entity class included only the Title and Price attributes, there would certainly be cause to worry that someday we might want to include two books with the same title and price. While this is allowed in some database application programs, it can lead to great confusion, and is definitely not recommended. Moreover, it is forbidden by definition in a true relational database. In other words, no two entities can agree on all of their attributes. (This is allowed in Microsoft Access, however.)

## Keys and Superkeys

A set of attributes that uniquely identifies any entity from among all possible entities in the entity class that may appear in the database is called a *superkey* for the entity class. Thus, the set {ISBN} is a superkey for the *Books* entity class and the sets {PubID} and {PubName, PubPhone} are both superkeys for the *Publishers* entity class.

Note that there is a bit of subjectivity in this definition of superkey, since it depends ultimately on our decision about which entities may ever appear in the database, and this is probably something of which we cannot be absolutely certain. Consider, for instance, the *Books* entity class. There is no law that says all books must have an ISBN (and many books do not). Also, there is no law that says that two books cannot have the same ISBN. (The ISBN is assigned, at least in part, by the publisher of the book.) Thus, the set {ISBN} is a superkey only if we are willing to accept the fact that all books that the library purchases have distinct ISBNs, or that the librarian will assign a unique ersatz ISBN to any books that do not have a real ISBN.

It is important to emphasize that the concept of a superkey applies to entity classes, and not entity sets. Although we can define a superkey for an entity set, this is of limited use, since what may serve to uniquely identify the entities in a particular entity set may fail to do so if we add new entities to the set. To illustrate, the Title attribute does serve to uniquely identify each of the 14 books in the BOOKS table. Thus, {Title} is a superkey for the entity *set* described by the BOOKS table. However, {Title} is not a superkey for the *Books* entity class, since there are many distinct books with the same title.

We have remarked that {ISBN} is a superkey for the *Books* entity class. Of course, so is {Title, ISBN}, but it is wasteful and inefficient to include the Title attribute purely for the sake of identification.

Indeed, one of the difficulties with superkeys is that they may contain more attributes than is absolutely necessary to uniquely indentify any entity. It is more desirable to work with superkeys that do not have this property. A superkey with the property that no proper subset of it is also a superkey is called a *key*. Thus, a key is a superkey with the property that, if we remove an attribute, the resulting set is no longer a superkey. Put more succinctly, a key is a minimal superkey. Sometimes keys are called *candidate keys*, since it is usually the case that we want to select one particular key to use as an identifier. This particular choice is referred to as the *primary key*. The primary keys in the LIBRARY database are ISBN, AuID, and PubID.

We should remark that a key may contain more than one attribute, and different keys may have different numbers of attributes. For instance, it is reasonable to assume that both {SocialSecurityNumber} and {FullName, FullAddress, DateofBirth} are both keys for a *US Citizens* entity class.

## *Relationships Between Entities*

If we are going to model a database as a collection of entity sets (tables), then we need to also describe the *relationships* between these entity sets. For instance, an author relationship exists between a book and the authors who wrote that book. We might call this relationship *WrittenBy*. Thus, Hamlet is *WrittenBy* Shakespeare.

It is possible to draw a diagram, called an *entity-relationship diagram,* or *E/R diagram,* to illustrate the entity classes in a database model, along with their attributes and relationships. Figure 2-1 shows the LIBRARY E/R diagram, with an additional entity class called *Contributors* (a contributor may be someone who contributes to or writes only a very small portion of a book, and thus may not be accorded all of the rights of an author, such as a royalty).

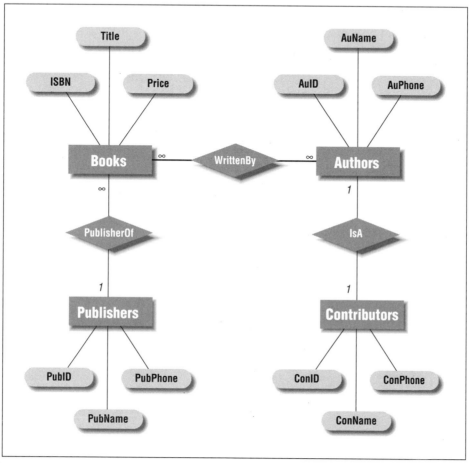

*Figure 2-1. The LIBRARY entity-relationship diagram*

Note that each entity class is denoted by a rectangle, and each attribute by an ellipse. The relations are denoted by diamonds. We have included the *Contributors* entity class in this model merely to illustrate a special type of relationship. In particular, since a contributor is considered an author, there is an *IsA* relationship between the two entity classes.

The model represented by an E/R diagram is sometimes referred to as a *semantic model,* since it describes much of the meaning of the database.

## Types of Relationships

Referring to Figure 2-1, the symbols 1 and ∞ represent the type of relationship between the corresponding entity classes. (The symbol ∞ is read "many.") Relationships can be classified into three types. For instance, the relationship between *Books* and *Authors* is *many-to-many,* meaning that a book may have many authors and an author may write many books. On the other hand, the relationship from *Publishers* to *Books* is *one-to-many,* meaning that one publisher may publish many books, but a book is published by at most one publisher (or so we will assume).

*One-to-one* relationships, where each entity on each side is related to at most one entity on the other side of the relationship, are fairly rare in database design. For instance, consider the *Contributors-Authors* relationship, which is one-to-one. We could replace the *Contributors* class by a *contributor* attribute of the *Authors* class, thus eliminating the need for a separate class and a separate relationship. On the other hand, if the *Contributors* class had several attributes that are not shared by the *Authors* class, then a separate class may be appropriate.

In Chapter 3, *Implementing Entity-Relationship Models: Relational Databases,* we will actually implement the full E/R model for our LIBRARY database.

*3*

# Implementing Entity-Relationship Models: Relational Databases

An E/R model of a database is an abstract model, visualized through an E/R diagram. For this to be useful, we must translate the abstract model into a concrete one. That is, we must describe each aspect of the model in the concrete terms that a database program can manipulate. In short, we must *implement* the E/R model. This requires implementing several things:

- The entities

- The entity classes

- The entity sets

- The relationships between the entity classes

The result of this implementation is a *relational database*.

As we will see, implementing the relationships usually involves some changes to the entity classes, perhaps by adding new attributes to existing entity classes or by adding new entity classes.

## Implementing Entities

As we discussed in the previous chapter, an entity is implemented (or described in concrete terms) simply by giving the values of its attributes. Thus, the following is an implementation of a *Books* entity:

```
Title = Gone With The Wind
ISBN = 0-12-345678-9
Price = $24.00
```

## Implementing Entity Classes—Table Schemes

Since the entities in an entity class are implemented by giving their attribute values, it makes sense to implement an entity class by the set of attribute names. For instance, the *Books* entity class can be identified with the set:

    {ISBN,Title,Price}

(We will add the PubID attribute name later, when we implement the relationships.)

Since attribute names are usually used as column headings for a table, a set of attribute names is called a *table scheme*. Thus, entity classes are implemented as table schemes. For convenience, we use notation such as:

    *Books*(ISBN,Title,Price)

which shows not only the name of the entity class, but also the names of the attributes in the table scheme for this class. You can also think of a table scheme as the column headings row (the top row) of any table that is formed using that table scheme. (We will see an example of this in a minute.)

We have defined the concepts of a superkey and a key for entity classes. These concepts apply equally well to table schemes, so we may say that the attributes {A,B} form a key for a table scheme, meaning that they form a key for the entity class implemented by that table scheme.

## Implementing Entity Sets—Tables

In a relational database, each entity set is modeled by a table. For example, consider the BOOKS table shown in Table 3-1, and note the following:

- The first row of the table is the table scheme for the *Books* entity class.
- Each of the other rows of the table implements a *Books* entity.
- The set of all rows of the table, except the first row, implements the entity set itself.

*Table 3-1. The BOOKS Table from the LIBRARY Database*

| ISBN | Title | Price |
|------|-------|-------|
| 0-12-333433-3 | On Liberty | $25.00 |
| 0-103-45678-9 | Iliad | $25.00 |
| 0-91-335678-7 | Faerie Queene | $15.00 |
| 0-99-999999-9 | Emma | $20.00 |
| 1-22-233700-0 | Visual Basic | $25.00 |
| 1-1111-1111-1 | C++ | $29.95 |

*Table 3-1. The BOOKS Table from the LIBRARY Database (continued)*

| ISBN | Title | Price |
|------|-------|-------|
| 0-91-045678-5 | Hamlet | $20.00 |
| 0-555-55555-9 | Macbeth | $12.00 |
| 0-99-777777-7 | King Lear | $49.00 |
| 0-123-45678-0 | Ulysses | $34.00 |
| 0-12-345678-9 | Jane Eyre | $49.00 |
| 0-11-345678-9 | Moby Dick | $49.00 |
| 0-321-32132-1 | Balloon | $34.00 |
| 0-55-123456-9 | Main Street | $22.95 |

More formally, a table T is a rectangular array of elements with the following properties:

1. The top of each column is labeled with a distinct *attribute name* $A_i$. The label $A_i$ is also called the *column heading*.

2. The elements of the ith column of the table T come from a single set $D_i$, called the *domain* for the ith column. Thus, the domain is the set of all *possible* values for the attribute. For instance, for the BOOKS table in Table 3-1, the domain $D_1$ is the set of all possible ISBNs and the domain $D_2$ is the set of all possible book titles.

3. No two rows of the table are identical.

Let us make some remarks about the concept of a table.

- A table may (but is not required to) have a name, such as BOOKS, which is intended to convey the meaning of the table as a whole.

- The number of rows of the table is called the *size* of the table and the number of columns is called the *degree* of the table. For example, the BOOKS table shown in Table 3-1 has size 14 and degree 3. The attribute names are ISBN, Title, and Price.

- As mentioned earlier, to emphasize the attributes of a table, it is common to denote a table by writing $T(A_1,...,A_n)$; for example, we denote the BOOKS table by:

  BOOKS(ISBN,Title,Price)

- The order of the rows of a table is not important, and so two tables that differ only in the order of their rows are thought of as being the same table. Similarly, the order of the columns of a table is not important as long as the headings are thought of as part of their respective columns. In other words, we may feel free to reorder the columns of a table, as long as we keep the headings with their respective columns.

- Finally, there is no requirement that the domains of different columns be different. (For example, it is possible for two columns in a single table to both use the domain of integers.) However, there is a requirement that the attribute names of different columns be different. Think of the potential confusion that would otherwise ensue, in view of the fact that we may rearrange the columns of a table!

Now that we have defined the concept of a table, we can say that it is common to define a relational database as a finite collection of tables. However, this definition belies the fact that the tables also model the relationships between the entity classes, as we will see.

# A Short Glossary

To help keep the various database terms clear, let us collect their definitions in one place.

*Entity*
: An object about which the database is designed to store information. Example: a book; that is, an ISBN, a title, and a price, as in:

```
0-12-333433-3, On Liberty, $25.00
```

*Attribute*
: A property that (partially or completely) describes an entity. Example: title.

*Entity Class*
: An abstract group of entities, with a common description. Example: the entity class *Books*, representing all books in the universe.

*Entity Set*
: The set of entities from a given entity class that are currently in the database. Example: the following set of 14 books:

```
0-12-333433-3, On Liberty, $25.00
0-103-45678-9, Iliad, $25.00
0-91-335678-7, Faerie Queene, $15.00
0-99-999999-9, Emma, $20.00
1-22-233700-0, Visual Basic, $25.00
1-1111-1111-1, C++, $29.95
0-91-045678-5, Hamlet, $20.00
0-555-55555-9, Macbeth, $12.00
0-99-777777-7, King Lear, $49.00
0-123-45678-0, Ulysses, $34.00
0-12-345678-9, Jane Eyre, $49.00
0-11-345678-9, Moby Dick, $49.00
0-321-32132-1, Balloon, $34.00
0-55-123456-9, Main Street, $22.95
```

*Superkey*

A set of attributes for an entity class that serves to uniquely identify an entity from among all possible entities in that entity class. Example: the set {Title, ISBN} for the *Books* entity class.

*Key*

A minimal superkey; that is, a key with the property that, if we remove an attribute, the resulting set is no longer a key. Example: the set {ISBN} for the *Books* entity class.

*Table*

A rectangular array of attribute values whose columns hold the attribute values for a given attribute and whose rows hold the attribute values for a given entity. Tables are used to implement entity sets. Example: the BOOKS table shown earlier in Table 3-1.

*Table Scheme*

The set of all attribute names for an entity class. Example:

```
{ISBN,Title,Price}
```

Since this is the table scheme for the entity class *Books*, we can use the notation *Books*(ISBN,Title,Price).

*Relational Database*

A finite collection of tables that provides an implementation of an E/R database model.

# Implementing the Relationships in a Relational Database

Now let us now discuss how we might implement the relationships in an E/R database model. For convenience, we repeat the E/R diagram for the LIBRARY database in Figure 3-1.

## Implementing a One-to-Many Relationship— Foreign Keys

Implementing a one-to-many relationship, such as the *PublisherOf* relationship, is fairly easy. To illustrate, since {PubID} is a key for the *Publishers* entity class, we simply add this attribute to the *Books* entity class. Thus, the *Books* entity class becomes:

```
Books(ISBN,Title,PubID,Price)
```

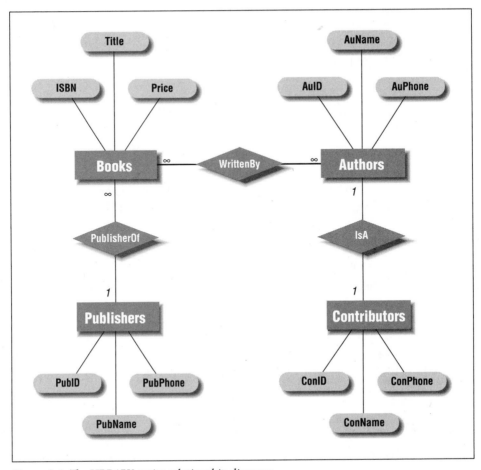

*Figure 3-1. The LIBRARY entity-relationship diagram*

The *Books* table scheme is now:

    {ISBN,Title,PubID,Price}

and the BOOKS table now appears as shown in Table 3-2 (sorted by PubID).

*Table 3-2. The BOOKS Table Sorted by PubID*

| ISBN | Title | PubID | Price |
|------|-------|-------|-------|
| 0-12-333433-3 | On Liberty | 1 | $25.00 |
| 0-103-45678-9 | Iliad | 1 | $25.00 |
| 0-91-335678-7 | Faerie Queene | 1 | $15.00 |
| 0-99-999999-9 | Emma | 1 | $20.00 |
| 1-22-233700-0 | Visual Basic | 1 | $25.00 |
| 1-1111-1111-1 | C++ | 1 | $29.95 |

*Table 3-2. The BOOKS Table Sorted by PubID (continued)*

| ISBN | Title | PubID | Price |
|------|-------|-------|-------|
| 0-91-045678-5 | Hamlet | 2 | $20.00 |
| 0-555-55555-9 | Macbeth | 2 | $12.00 |
| 0-99-777777-7 | King Lear | 2 | $49.00 |
| 0-123-45678-0 | Ulysses | 2 | $34.00 |
| 0-12-345678-9 | Jane Eyre | 3 | $49.00 |
| 0-11-345678-9 | Moby Dick | 3 | $49.00 |
| 0-321-32132-1 | Balloon | 3 | $34.00 |
| 0-55-123456-9 | Main Street | 3 | $22.95 |

The PubID attribute in the *Books* entity class is referred to as a *foreign key*, because it is a key for a foreign entity class; that is, for the *Publishers* entity class.

Note that the value of the foreign key PubID in the BOOKS table provides a reference to the corresponding value in PUBLISHERS. Moreover, since {PubID} is a key for the *Publishers* entity class, there is at most one row of PUBLISHERS that contains a given value. Thus, for each book entity, we can look up the PubID value in the PUBLISHERS table to get the name of the publisher of that book. In this way, we have implemented the one-to-many *PublisherOf* relationship.

The idea just described is pictured in more general terms in Figure 3-2. Suppose that there is a one-to-many relationship between the entity classes (or, equivalently, table schemes) S and T. Figure 3-2 shows two tables S and T based on these table schemes. Suppose also that {A2} is a key for table scheme S (the one side of the relationship). Then we add this attribute to the table scheme T (and hence to table T). In this way, for any row of the table T, we can identify the unique row in table S to which it is related.

The attribute set {A2} in table S is a key for the table scheme S. For this reason, the attribute set {A2} is also called a foreign key for the table scheme T. More generally, a set of attributes of a table scheme T is a foreign key for T if it is a key for some other table scheme S. Note that a foreign key for T is not a key for T—it is a key for another table scheme. Thus, the attribute set {PubID} is a key for *Publishers*, but a foreign key for *Books*.

As with our example, a foreign key provides a reference to the entity class (table scheme) for which it is a key. The table scheme T is called the *referencing table scheme* and the table scheme S is called the *referenced table scheme*. The key that is being referenced in the referenced table scheme is called the *referenced key*.

Note that adding a foreign key to a table scheme does create some duplicate values in the database, but we must expect to add some additional information to the database in order to describe the relationships.

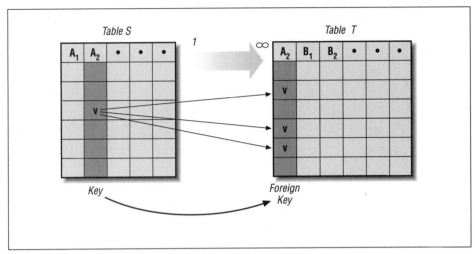

*Figure 3-2. A one-to-many relationship shown in tables S and T*

## Implementing a One-to-One Relationship

Of course, the procedure of introducing a foreign key into a table scheme works equally well for one-to-one relationships as for one-to-many relationships. For instance, we only need to rename the ConID attribute to AuID to make ConID into a foreign key that will implement the *Authors-Contributors IsA* relationship.

## Implementing a Many-to-Many Relationship—New Entity Classes

The implementation of a many-to-many relationship is a bit more involved. For instance, consider the *WrittenBy* relationship between *Books* and *Authors*.

At first glance, we might think of just adding foreign keys to each table scheme, thinking of the relationship as two distinct one-to-many relationships. However, this approach is not good, since it requires duplicating table rows. For example, if we add the ISBN key to the *Authors* table scheme and the AuID key to the *Books* table scheme, then each book that is written by two authors must be represented by *two* rows in the BOOKS table, so we can have two AuIDs. To be specific, since the book *Main Street* is written by Smith and Jones, we would need two rows in the BOOKS table:

```
TITLE: Main Street, ISBN 0-55-123456-9, Price: $22.95 AuID: Smith
TITLE: Main Street, ISBN 0-55-123456-9, Price: $22.95 AuID: Jones
```

It is clear that this approach will bloat the database with redundant information.

The proper approach to implementing a many-to-many relationship is to add a new table scheme to the database, in order to break the relationship into two one-to-many relationships. In our case, we add a *Book/Author* table scheme, whose attributes consist precisely of the foreign keys ISBN and AuID:

```
Book/Author(ISBN,AuID)
```

To get a pictorial view of this procedure, Figure 3-3 shows the corresponding E/R diagram. Note that it is not customary to include this as a portion of the original E/R diagram, since it belongs more to the implementation of the design than to the design itself.

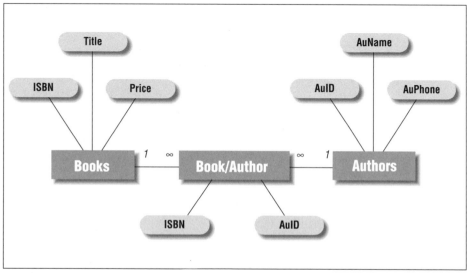

*Figure 3-3. A many-to-many relationship in the BOOK/AUTHOR table*

## Referential Integrity

There are a few important considerations that we must discuss with regard to using foreign keys to implement relationships. First, of course, is the fact that each value of the foreign key must have a matching value in the referenced key. Otherwise, we would have a so-called dangling reference. For instance, if the PubID key in a BOOKS table did not match a value of the PubID key in the PUBLISHERS table, we would have a book whose publisher did not exist in the database; that is, a dangling reference to a nonexistent publisher.

The requirement that each value in the foreign key is a value in the referenced key is called the *referential constraint*, and the problem of ensuring that there are no dangling references is referred to as the problem of ensuring *referential integrity*.

There are several ways in which referential integrity might be compromised. First, we could add a value to the foreign key that is not in the referenced key. This would happen, for instance, if we added a new book entity to the BOOKS table, whose publisher is not listed in the PUBLISHERS table. Such an action will be rejected by a database application that has been instructed to protect referential integrity. More subtle ways to affect referential integrity are to change or delete a value in the referenced key—the one that is being referenced by the foreign key. This would happen, for instance, if we deleted a publisher from the PUBLISHERS table, but that publisher had at least one book listed in the BOOKS table.

Of course, the database program can simply disallow such a change or deletion, but there is sometimes a preferable alternative, as we discuss next.

## Cascading Updates and Cascading Deletions

Many database programs allow the option of performing *cascading updates*, which simply means that, if a value in the referenced key is changed, then all matching entries in the foreign key are automatically changed to match the new value. For instance, if cascading updates are enabled, then changing a publisher's PubID in a PUBLISHERS table, say from 100 to 101, would automatically cause all values of 100 in the PubID foreign key of the referencing table BOOKS to change to 101. In short, cascading updates keep everything "in sync."

Similarly, enabling *cascading deletions* means that if a value in the referenced table is deleted by deleting the corresponding row in the referenced table, then all rows in the referencing table that refer to that deleted key value will also be deleted! For instance, if we delete a publisher from a PUBLISHERS table, all book entries referring to that publisher (through its PubID) will be deleted from the BOOKS table automatically. Thus, cascading deletions also preserve referential integrity, at the cost of performing perhaps massive deletions in other tables. Thus, cascading deletions should be used with circumspection.

As you may know, Microsoft Access allows the user to enable or disable both cascading updates and cascading deletions. We will see just how to do this in Access later.

# The LIBRARY Relational Database

We can now complete the implementation of the LIBRARY relational database (without the CONTRIBUTORS entity class) in Microsoft Access. If you open the LIBRARY database in Microsoft Access, you will see four tables:

- AUTHORS
- BOOK/AUTHOR

- BOOKS

- PUBLISHERS

(The LIBRARY_FLAT table is not used in the relational database.)

These four tables correspond to the following four entity classes (or table schemes):

- *Authors*(AuID,AuName,AuPhone)

- *Book/Author*(ISBN,AuID)

- *Books*(ISBN,Title,PubID,Price)

- *Publishers*(PubID, PubName, PubPhone)

The actual tables are shown in Tables 3-3 through 3-6.

*Table 3-3. The AUTHORS Table from the Access LIBRARY Database*

| AuID | AuName | AuPhone |
|------|--------|---------|
| 1 | Austen | 111-111-1111 |
| 10 | Jones | 123-333-3333 |
| 11 | Snoopy | 321-321-2222 |
| 12 | Grumpy | 321-321-0000 |
| 13 | Sleepy | 321-321-1111 |
| 2 | Melville | 222-222-2222 |
| 3 | Homer | 333-333-3333 |
| 4 | Roman | 444-444-4444 |
| 5 | Shakespeare | 555-555-5555 |
| 6 | Joyce | 666-666-6666 |
| 7 | Spenser | 777-777-7777 |
| 8 | Mill | 888-888-8888 |
| 9 | Smith | 123-222-2222 |

*Table 3-4. The BOOK/AUTHOR Table from the LIBRARY Database*

| ISBN | AuID |
|------|------|
| 0-103-45678-9 | 3 |
| 0-11-345678-9 | 2 |
| 0-12-333433-3 | 8 |
| 0-12-345678-9 | 1 |
| 0-123-45678-0 | 6 |
| 0-321-32132-1 | 11 |
| 0-321-32132-1 | 12 |
| 0-321-32132-1 | 13 |

*Table 3-4. The BOOK/AUTHOR Table from the LIBRARY Database (continued)*

| ISBN | AuID |
|------|------|
| 0-55-123456-9 | 9 |
| 0-55-123456-9 | 10 |
| 0-555-55555-9 | 5 |
| 0-91-045678-5 | 5 |
| 0-91-335678-7 | 7 |
| 0-99-777777-7 | 5 |
| 0-99-999999-9 | 1 |
| 1-1111-1111-1 | 4 |
| 1-22-233700-0 | 4 |

*Table 3-5. The BOOKS Table from the LIBRARY Database*

| ISBN | Title | PubID | Price |
|------|-------|-------|-------|
| 0-12-333433-3 | On Liberty | 1 | $25.00 |
| 0-103-45678-9 | Iliad | 1 | $25.00 |
| 0-91-335678-7 | Faerie Queene | 1 | $15.00 |
| 0-99-999999-9 | Emma | 1 | $20.00 |
| 1-22-233700-0 | Visual Basic | 1 | $25.00 |
| 1-1111-1111-1 | C++ | 1 | $29.95 |
| 0-91-045678-5 | Hamlet | 2 | $20.00 |
| 0-555-55555-9 | Macbeth | 2 | $12.00 |
| 0-99-777777-7 | King Lear | 2 | $49.00 |
| 0-123-45678-0 | Ulysses | 2 | $34.00 |
| 0-12-345678-9 | Jane Eyre | 3 | $49.00 |
| 0-11-345678-9 | Moby Dick | 3 | $49.00 |
| 0-321-32132-1 | Balloon | 3 | $34.00 |
| 0-55-123456-9 | Main Street | 3 | $22.95 |

*Table 3-6. The PUBLISHERS Table from the LIBRARY Database*

| PubID | PubName | PubPhone |
|-------|---------|----------|
| 1 | Big House | 123-456-7890 |
| 2 | Alpha Press | 999-999-9999 |
| 3 | Small House | 714-000-0000 |

Notice that we have included the necessary foreign key {PubID} in the BOOKS table in Table 3-5, to implement the *PublisherOf* relationship, which is one-to-many. Also, we have included the BOOK/AUTHOR table (Table 3-4) to implement the *WrittenBy* relationship, which is many-to-many.

Even though all relationships are established through foreign keys, we must tell Access that these foreign keys are being used to implement the relationships. Here are the steps.

## Setting Up the Relationships in Access

1. Just to illustrate a point, make the following small change in the BOOKS table: Open the table and change the PubID field for Hamlet to 4. Note that there is no publisher with PubID 4 and so we have created a dangling reference. Then close the BOOKS window.

2. Now choose Relationships from the Tools menu. You should get a window showing the table schemes in the database, similar to that in Figure 3-4. Relationships are denoted by lines between these table schemes. As you can see, there are as yet no relationships. Note that the primary key attributes appear in boldface.

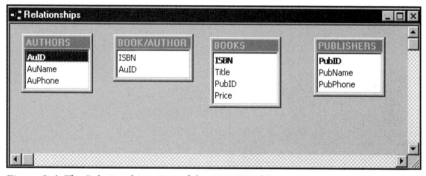

*Figure 3-4. The Relationships view of the BOOKS table*

3. To set the relationship between PUBLISHERS and BOOKS, place the mouse pointer over the PubID attribute name in the PUBLISHERS table scheme, hold down the left mouse button, and drag the name to the PubID attribute name in the BOOKS table scheme. You should get a window similar to Figure 3-5.

4. This window shows the relationship between PUBLISHERS and BOOKS, listing the key {PubID} in *Publishers* and the foreign key {PubID} in *Books*. (We did not need to call the foreign key PubID, but it makes sense to do so, since it reminds us of the purpose of the attribute.)

5. Now check the Enforce Referential Integrity box and click the *OK* button. You should get the message in Figure 3-6. The problem is, of course, the dangling reference that we created by changing the PubID field in the BOOKS table to refer to a nonexistent publisher.

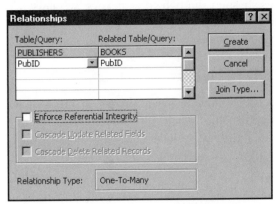

*Figure 3-5. Relationship between the PUBLISHERS and BOOKS table*

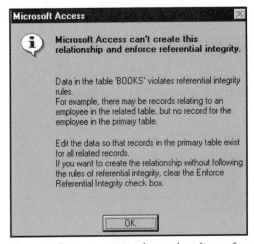

*Figure 3-6. Error message due to dangling reference*

6. Click the *OK* button, reopen the BOOKS table, and fix the offending entry (change the PubID field for *Hamlet* back to 2). Then close the BOOKS table and reestablish the relationship between PUBLISHERS and BOOKS. This time, check the Enforce Referential Integrity checkbox as well as the Cascade Update Related Fields checkbox. Do not check Cascade Delete Related Fields.

7. Next, drag the ISBN attribute name from the BOOKS table scheme to the ISBN attribute name in the BOOK/AUTHOR table scheme. Again check the Enforce Referential Integrity and Cascade Update Related Fields checkboxes.

8. Finally, drag the AuID attribute name from the AUTHORS table scheme to the AuID attribute name in the BOOK/AUTHOR table scheme. Check the Enforce Referential Integrity and Cascade Update Related Fields checkboxes. You

should now see the lines indicating these relationships, as shown in Figure 3-7. Note the small 1s and infinity signs, indicating the one side and many side of each relationship.

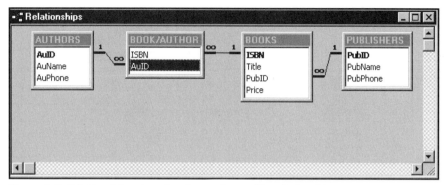

*Figure 3-7. Relationships view showing various table relationships*

9. To test the enforcement of referential integrity, try the following experiment: Open the BOOKS and PUBLISHERS tables and arrange them so that you can see both tables at the same time. Now change the value of PubID for Small House in the PUBLISHERS table from 3 to 4. As soon as you move the cursor out of the Small House row (which makes the change permanent), the corresponding PubID values in BOOKS should change automatically! When you are done, restore the PubID value in PUBLISHERS back to 3.

# *Index Files*

When a table is stored on disk, it is often referred to as a *file*. In this case, each row of the table is referred to as a *record* and each column is referred to as a *field*. (These terms are often used for any table.)

Since disk access is typically slow, an important goal is to reduce the amount of disk accesses necessary to retrieve the desired data from a file. Sequential searching of the data, record-by-record, to find the desired information may require a large number of disk accesses, and is very inefficient.

The purpose of an *index file* is to provide direct (also called *random*) access to data in a database file.

Figure 3-8 illustrates the concept of an index file. We have changed the Publishers data for illustration purposes, to include a city column. The file on the left is the index file and indexes the Publishers data file by the City field, which is therefore called the indexed field. The city file is called an *index* for the PUBLISHERS table. (The index file is not a table in the same sense as the PUBLISHERS table is a table. That is to say, we cannot directly access the index file—instead we use it indirectly.) The index file contains the cities for each publisher, along with a *pointer* to the corresponding data record in the Publishers file.

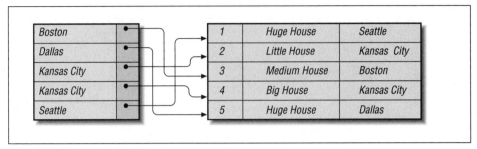

*Figure 3-8. Index file between City and Publisher*

An index file can be used in a variety of ways. For instance, to find all publishers located in Kansas City, Access can first search the alphabetical list of cities in the index file. Since the list is alphabetical, Access knows that the Kansas City entries are all together, and so once it reaches the first entry after Kansas City, it can stop the search. In other words, Access does not need to search the entire index file. (In addition, there are very efficient search algorithms for ordered tables.) Once the Kansas City entries are found in the index file, the pointers can be used to go directly to the Kansas City publishers in the indexed file.

Also, since the index provides a sorted view of the data in the original table, it can be used to efficiently retrieve a range of records. For instance, if the Books data were indexed on price, we could efficiently retrieve all books in the price range between $20.00 and $30.00.

A table can be indexed on more than one column; that is to say, a table can have more than one index file. Also, a table can be indexed on a combination of two or more columns. For instance, if the PUBLISHERS table also included a State column, we could index the table on a combination of City and State, as shown in Figure 3-9.

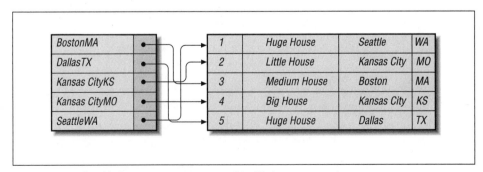

*Figure 3-9. Index file between City, State, and Publisher*

An index on a primary key is referred to as a *primary index*. Note that Microsoft Access automatically creates an index on a primary key. An index on any other column or columns is called a *secondary index*. An index based on a key (not necessarily the primary key) is called a *unique index*, since the indexed column contains unique values.

*Example*

To view the indexes for a given table in Microsoft Access, open the table in design view and then choose Indexes from the View menu. For the BOOKS table, you should see a window similar to Figure 3-10 (without the PubTitle entry).

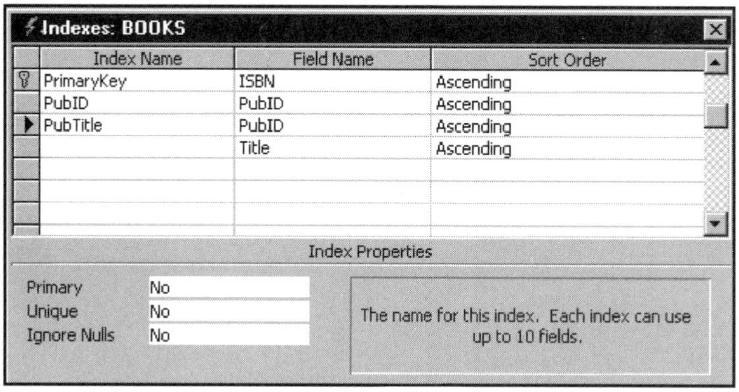

| Index Name | Field Name | Sort Order |
|---|---|---|
| PrimaryKey | ISBN | Ascending |
| PubID | PubID | Ascending |
| PubTitle | PubID | Ascending |
| | Title | Ascending |

Index Properties

| Primary | No |
| Unique | No |
| Ignore Nulls | No |

The name for this index. Each index can use up to 10 fields.

*Figure 3-10. Index View of the BOOKS table*

To add an index based on more than one attribute, you enter the multiple attributes on successive rows of the *Indexes* dialog box. We have done this in Figure 3-10, adding an index called PubTitle based on the PubID and the Title attributes. This index indexes the BOOKS entities first by PubID and then by Title (within each PubID).

# *NULL Values*

The question of NULLs can be very confusing to the database user, so let us set down the basic principles. Generally speaking, a NULL is a special value that is used for two reasons:

- To indicate that a value is missing or unknown
- To indicate that a value is not applicable in the current context

For instance, consider an author's table:

    AUTHORS(AuID,AuName,AuPhone)

If a particular author's phone number is unknown, it is appropriate for that value to be NULL. This is not to say that the author does not have a phone number, but simply that we have no information about the number—it may or may not exist. If we knew that the person had no phone number, then the information would no longer be unknown. In this case, the appropriate value of the AuPhone attribute would be the *empty string*, or perhaps the string "no phone," but not a NULL. Thus, the appropriateness of allowing NULL values for an attribute depends upon the context.

The issue of whether NULLs should appear in a key needs some discussion. The purpose of a key is to provide a means for uniquely identifying entities and so it would seem that keys and NULLs are incompatible. However, it is impractical to never allow NULLs in any keys. For instance, for the Publishers entity, this would mean not allowing a PubPhone to be NULL, since {PubName,PubPhone} is a key. On the other hand, the so-called *entity integrity rule* says that NULLs are not allowed in a primary key.

One final remark: The presence of a NULL as a foreign key value does not violate referential integrity. That is, referential integrity requires that every non-NULL value in a foreign key must have a match in the referenced key.

# 4

# *Database Design Principles*

In Chapter 1, *Introduction*, we tried to present a convincing case for why most databases should be modeled as relational databases, rather than single-table flat databases. We tried to make it clear why we split the single LIBRARY_FLAT table into four separate tables: AUTHORS, BOOKS, PUBLISHERS, and BOOK/AUTHOR.

However, for large real-life databases, it is not always clear how to split the data into multiple tables. As we mentioned in Chapter 1, the goal is to do this in such a way as to minimize redundancy, without losing any information.

The problem of effective database design is a complex one. Most people consider it an art rather than a science. This means that intuition plays a major role in good design. Nonetheless, there is a considerable theory of database design, and it can be quite complicated. Our goal in this chapter is to touch upon the general ideas, without becoming involved in the details. Hopefully, this discussion will provide a helpful guide to the intuition needed for database design.

## *Redundancy*

As we saw in Chapter 1, redundant data tends to inflate the size of a database, which can be a very serious problem for medium to large databases. Moreover, redundancy can lead to several types of anomalies, as discussed earlier. To understand the problems that can arise from redundancy, we need to take a closer look at what redundancy means.

Let us begin by observing that the attributes of a table scheme can be classified into three groups:

1. Attributes used strictly for identification purposes

2. Attributes used strictly for informational purposes

3. Attributes used for both identification and informational purposes

For example, consider the table scheme:

```
{PubID,PubName,PubPhone,YearFounded}
```

In this scheme, PubID is used strictly for identification purposes. It carries no informational content. On the other hand, YearFounded is strictly for informational purposes in this context. It gives the year that the publishing company was founded, but is not required for identification purposes.

Consider also the table scheme:

```
{Title,PubID,AuID,PageCount,CopyrightDate}
```

In this case, if we assume that there is only one book of a given title published by a given publisher and written by a given author, then {Title,PubID,AuID} is a key. Hence, each of these attributes is used (at least in part) for identification. However, Title is also an informational attribute.

We should hasten to add that these classifications are somewhat subjective, and depend upon the assumptions made about the entity class. Nevertheless, this classification does provide a useful intuitive framework.

We can at least pin down the strictly informational attributes a bit more precisely by making the following observation. The sign that an attribute is being used (at least in part) for identification purposes is that it is part of some key. Thus, an attribute that is not part of any key is being used, in that table scheme, strictly for informational purposes. Let us call such an attribute a *strictly informational attribute*.

Now consider the table shown in Table 4-1. In this case, both Title and PubName are strictly informational, since {ISBN} is the only key, and neither Title nor PubName is part of that key. However, the values of Title are not redundant (the fact that they are the same does not mean that they are not both required), whereas the values of PubName are redundant.

*Table 4-1. A Table with Two Informational Attributes*

| ISBN | Title | PubID | PubName |
|------|-------|-------|---------|
| 1-1111-1111-1 | C++ | 1 | Big House |
| 0-91-335678-7 | Faerie Queene | 1 | Big House |
| 1-011-22222-0 | C++ | 2 | ABC Press |

The reason that Title is not redundant is that there is no way to eliminate any of these titles. Each book entity must have its title listed somewhere in the database—one title per ISBN. Thus, the two titles C++ must both appear somewhere in the database.

On the other hand, PubName is redundant, as can easily be seen from the fact that the same PubName is listed twice without adding any new information to the database. To look at this another way, consider the table with two cells blank in Table 4-2. Can you fill in the title field for the last row? Not unless you call the publisher to get the title for that ISBN. In other words, some information is missing. On the other hand, you can fill in the blank PubName field.

*Table 4-2. A Table with Blank Cells to Illustrate Attribute Dependency*

| ISBN | Title | PubID | PubName |
|------|-------|-------|---------|
| 1-1111-1111-1 | Macbeth | 1 | Big House |
| 2-2222-2222-2 | Hamlet | 1 | |
| 5-555-55555-5 | | 2 | ABC Press |

The issue here is quite simple. The Title attribute depends only upon the ISBN attribute and {ISBN} is a key. In other words, Title depends only upon a key. However, PubName depends completely upon PubID, which is not a key for this table scheme. (Of course, PubName also depends on the key {ISBN}, but that is not relevant.)

Thus, we have seen a case where redundancy results from the fact that one attribute depends upon another attribute that is not a key. Armed with this observation, we can move ahead.

# *Normal Forms*

Those who make a study of database design have identified a number of special *forms*, or *properties*, or *constraints* that a table scheme may possess, in order to achieve certain desired goals, such as minimizing redundancy. These forms are called *normal forms*. There are six commonly recognized normal forms, with the inspired names:

- First normal form (or 1NF)
- Second normal form (or 2NF)
- Third normal form (or 3NF)
- Boyce Codd normal form (or BCNF)
- Fourth normal form (or 4NF)
- Fifth normal form (or 5NF)

We will consider the first four of these normal forms, but only informally. Each of these normal forms is stronger than its predecessors. Thus, for instance, a table scheme that is in third normal form is also in second normal form. While it is generally desirable for the table schemes in a database to have a high degree of normalization, as we will see in this chapter, the situation is not as simple as it may seem.

For instance, requiring that all table schemes be in BCNF may, in some cases, cause some loss of information about the various relationships between the table schemes. In general, it is possible to manipulate the data to achieve third normal form for all table schemes, but this may turn out to be far more work than it is worth!

The plain fact is that forcing all table schemes to be in a particular normal form may require some compromises. Each individual situation (database) must be examined on its own merit. It is impossible to make general rules that apply in all situations.

The process of changing a database design to produce table schemes in normal form is called *normalization.*

# *First Normal Form*

First normal form is very simple. A table scheme is said to be in first normal form if the attribute values are *indivisible.* To illustrate, we considered in Chapter 1 the question of including all the authors of a book in a single attribute, called Authors. Here is an example entity:

```
ISBN = 0-55-123456-9
Title = Main Street
Authors = Jones, H. and Smith, K.
Publisher = Small House
```

Since the table scheme in this case allows more than one author name for the Authors attribute, the scheme is not in first normal form. Indeed, one of the obvious problems with the Authors attribute is that it is impossible to sort the data by individual author name. It is also more difficult to, for instance, prepare a mailing label for each author, and so on.

Attributes that allow only indivisible values are said to be *scalar attributes* or *atomic attributes.* By contrast, an attribute whose values can be, for example, a list of items (such as a list of authors) is said to be a *structured attribute.* Thus, a table scheme is in first normal form if all of its attributes are atomic. Good database design almost always requires that all attributes be atomic, so that the table scheme is in first normal form.

In general, making the adjustments necessary to ensure first normal form is not hard and it is a good general rule that table schemes should be put in first normal form. However, as with the other normal forms (and even more so the higher up we go) each situation must be considered on its own merits. For instance, a single field might be designed to hold a street address, such as *1333 Bessemer Street*. Whether the house number and the street name should be separated into distinct attributes is a matter of context. Put another way, whether or not a street address is atomic depends upon the context. If there is reason to manipulate the street numbers apart from the street names, then they should certainly constitute their own attribute. Otherwise, perhaps not.

# *Functional Dependencies*

Before we can discuss the other normal forms, we need to discuss the concept of *functional dependency*, which is used to define these normal forms. This concept is quite simple, and we have actually been using it for some time now. As an example, we have remarked that, for the *Publishers* table scheme, the PubName attribute depends completely on the PubID attribute. (More properly, we should say that the *value* of the PubName attribute depends completely on the *value* of the PubID attribute, but the above shorthand is convenient.) Thus, we can say that the functional dependency from PubID to PubName, written:

> PubID → PubName

holds for the *Publishers* table scheme. This can be read *PubID determines PubName* or *PubName depends on PubID*.

More generally, suppose that $\{A_1,...,A_k\}$ are attributes of a table scheme and that $\{B_1,...,B_n\}$ are also attributes of the same table scheme. We do not require that the B's be different from the A's. Then the attributes $B_1,...,B_n$ *depend* on the attributes $A_1,...,A_k$, written:

> $\{A_1, ..., A_k\} \rightarrow \{B_1, ..., B_n\}$

if the values of $A_1,...,A_k$ completely determine the values of $B_1,...,B_n$. Our main interest is when there is only one attribute on the right:

> $\{A_1, ..., A_k\} \rightarrow \{B\}$

For instance, it is probably safe to say that:

> {PubName,PubPhone} → {PubID}

which is just another way of saying that there is only one publisher with a given name and phone number (including area code).

It is very important to understand that a functional dependency means that the attributes on the left completely determine the attributes on the right *for now and for all time to come, no matter what additional data may be added to the database.* Thus, just as the concept of a key relates to entity *classes* (table schemes) rather than individual entity sets (tables), so does functional dependency. Every table scheme has its set of associated functional dependencies, which are based on the meaning of the attributes.

Recall that a superkey is a set of attributes that uniquely determines an entity. Put another way, a superkey is a set of attributes upon which all other attributes of the table scheme are functionally dependent.

Some functional dependencies are obvious. For instance, an attribute functionally depends upon itself. Also, any set of attributes functionally determines any subset of these attributes, as in:

    {A,B,C} → {A,B}

This just says that if we know the values of A, B, and C, then we know the value of A and B! Such functional dependencies are not at all interesting, and are called *trivial dependencies*. All other dependencies are called *nontrivial*.

## *Second Normal Form*

Intuitively, a table scheme T is in second normal form, or 2NF, if all of the strictly informational attributes (attributes that do not belong to any key) are attributes of the entities in the table scheme, and not of some other class of entities. In other words, the informational attributes provide information specifically about the entities in *this* entity class and not about some other entities.

Let us illustrate with an example.

Consider a simplified table scheme designed to store house addresses. One possibility is:

    {City, Street, HouseNumber, HouseColor, CityPopulation}

The CityPopulation attribute is out of place here, because it is an attribute of cities, not house addresses. More specifically, CityPopulation is strictly an informational attribute (not for identification of houses) but it gives information not about house addresses, but about cities. Thus, this table scheme is *not* in second normal form.

We can be a little bit more formal about the meaning of second normal form as follows. Referring to the previous example, we have the dependency:

    {City} → {CityPopulation}

where CityPopulation does not belong to any key, and where City is a *proper* subset of a key, namely, the key {City, Street, HouseNumber}.

A table scheme is in second normal form, or 2NF, if it is not possible to have a dependency of the form:

    {A_1, ..., A_k} → {B}

where B does not belong to any key (is strictly informational) and $\{A_1,...,A_k\}$ is a *proper* subset of some key, and thus does not identify the entities of *this* entity class, but rather identifies the entities of some other entity class. (By proper subset, we mean a subset that is not the whole set.)

Let us consider another example of a table scheme that is not in second normal form.

Consider the following table scheme, and assume for the purposes of illustration that, while there may be many books with the same title, no two of them have the same publisher and author:

    {Title, PubID, AuID, Price, AuAddress}

Thus, {Title, PubID, AuID} is the only key. Now, AuAddress does not belong to any key, but it depends upon {AuID}, which is a proper subset of the key, in symbols:

    {AuID} → {AuAddress}

Hence, this table scheme is not in second normal form. In fact, AuAddress is not a piece of information about the entities modeled in the table scheme (i.e., books), but rather about *authors*. Of course, we could remove the AuAddress attribute to bring the table scheme into second normal form. (If each publisher charged a single price for all of its books, then Price would also cause a violation of second normal form, but this is not the case, of course.)

## *Third Normal Form*

Second normal form is good, but we can do better. We have seen that if a table scheme is in second normal form, then no strictly informational attribute depends on a proper subset of a key. However, there is another undesirable possibility. Let us illustrate with an example.

Consider the following table scheme and assume, for the purposes of illustration, that no two books with the same title have the same publisher:

    {Title,PubID,PageCount,Price}

The only key for this table scheme is {Title,PubID}. Both PageCount and Price are informational attributes only.

Now, let us assume that each publisher decides the price of its books based *solely* on the page count. First, we observe that this table is in second normal form. To see this, consider the proper subsets of the key. These are:

    {Title} and {PubID}

But none of the dependencies:

```
{Title} → {PageCount}
{Title} → {Price}
{PubID} → {PageCount}
{PubID} → {Price}
```

hold for this table scheme. After all, knowing the title does not determine the book, since there may be many books of the same title, published by different publishers. Hence, the table is in second normal form.

It is also not correct to say that:

```
{PageCount} → {Price}
```

holds, because different publishers may use different price schemes, based on page count. In other words, one publisher may price books over 1000 pages at one price, whereas another may price books over 1000 pages at a different price. However, it is true that:

```
{PubID,PageCount} → {Price}
```

holds. In other words, here we have an informational attribute (Price) that depends not on a proper subset of a key, but on a proper subset of a key (PubID) together with another informational attribute (PageCount).

This is bad, since it may produce redundancy. For instance, consider Table 4-3. Note that the price attribute is redundant. After all, we could fill in the Price value for the third row if it were blank, because we know that PubID 2 charges $34.95 for 500-page books.

*Table 4-3. Redundant Data in a Table*

| Title | PubID | PageCount | Price |
|-----------|-------|-----------|-------|
| Moby Dick | 1 | 500 | 29.95 |
| Giant | 2 | 500 | 34.95 |
| Moby Dick | 2 | 500 | 34.95 |

We can summarize the problem with the dependency:

```
{PubID,PageCount} → {Price}
```

by saying that the attribute Price depends upon a set of attributes:

```
{PubID,PageCount}
```

that is not a key, not a superkey, and not a proper subset of a key. It is a mix containing one attribute from the key {Title,PubID} and one attribute that is not in any key.

With this example in mind, we can now define third normal form. A table scheme is in third normal form, or 3NF, if it is not possible to have a dependency of the form:

$$\{A_1, \ldots, A_k\} \rightarrow \{B\}$$

where B does not belong to any key (is strictly informational) and $\{A_1, \ldots, A_k\}$ is not a superkey. In other words, third normal form does not permit any strictly informational attribute to depend upon anything *other than* a superkey. Of course, superkeys determine all attributes, including strictly informational attributes, and so all attributes depend on any superkey. The point is that, with third normal form, strictly informational attributes depend only on superkeys.

# *Boyce-Codd Normal Form*

It is possible to find table schemes that are in third normal form, but still have redundancy. Here is an example.

Consider the table scheme {City,StreetName,ZipCode}, with dependencies:

    {City,StreetName} → {ZipCode}

and:

    {ZipCode} → {City}

(Although in real life, a zip code may be shared by two different cities, we will assume otherwise for the purposes of illustration.) This table scheme is in third normal form. To see this, observe that the keys are {City,StreetName} and {ZipCode,StreetName}. Hence, no attribute is strictly informational and there is nothing to violate third normal form!

On the other hand, consider Table 4-4. We can fill in the blank city name because {ZipCode}→{City}.

*Table 4-4. A Table with Dependencies*

| City | StreetName | ZipCode |
|------|-----------|---------|
| Los Angeles | Hollywood Blvd | 95000 |
|  | Vine St | 95000 |

The problem here is with the dependency:

    {ZipCode}→{City}

which does not violate third normal form because, as we have mentioned, {City} is not strictly informational.

The previous example gives us the idea to strengthen the condition in the definition of third normal form, by dropping the requirement that B be strictly informational. Thus, we can define our last, and strongest, normal form. A table scheme is in Boyce-Codd normal form, or BCNF, if it is not possible to have a dependency of the form:

$$\{A_1, \ldots, A_k\} \rightarrow \{B\}$$

where $\{A_1, \ldots, A_k\}$ is not a superkey. In other words, BCNF form does not permit any attribute to depend upon anything other than a superkey.

As mentioned earlier, all attributes must depend on any superkey, by the very definition of superkey. Thus, BCNF is the strongest possible restriction of this type—it says that an attribute is not allowed to depend on anything other than a superkey.

# *Normalization*

As we mentioned earlier, the process of changing a database design to produce table schemes in normal form is called *normalization*.

As a very simple example, the table scheme:

```
{ISBN,Title,Authors}
```

is not even in first normal form, because the Authors attribute might contain more than one author and is therefore not atomic. By trading in this table scheme for the two schemes:

```
{ISBN,Title,AuID} and {AuID,AuName}
```

we have normalized the database into first normal form.

Here is another example involving the higher normal forms.

Recall from an earlier example that the table scheme {City,StreetName,ZipCode}, with dependencies:

```
{City,StreetName} → {ZipCode}
```

and:

```
{ZipCode} → {City}
```

is in third normal form. However, Table 4-5 shows that there is still some redundancy in the table scheme. The table scheme is not in BCNF. In fact, this was the example we used to motivate our definition of BCNF. (The example violates BCNF.)

*Table 4-5. A Table with Redundant Data*

| City | StreetName | ZipCode |
|------|-----------|---------|
| Los Angeles | Hollywood Blvd | 95000 |
|  | Vine St | 95000 |

However, we can split this table scheme into two schemes:

    {ZipCode,City}

and:

    {ZipCode,StreetName}

In this case, Table 4-5 gets split into two tables, Tables 4-6 and 4-7, and the redundancy is gone!

*Table 4-6. First Table Derived from Table 4-5 to Eliminate Redundancy*

| ZipCode | City |
|---------|------|
| 95000 | Los Angeles |

*Table 4-7. Second Table Derived from Table 4-5 to Eliminate Redundancy*

| ZipCode | StreetName |
|---------|-----------|
| 95000 | Hollywood Blvd |
| 95000 | Vine St |

Generally speaking, the design of a database may begin with an E/R diagram. This diagram can be implemented according to the principles that we discussed in Chapter 3, *Implementing Entity-Relationship Models: Relational Databases*. The result may very well be a perfectly satisfactory database design. However, if some of the table schemes have redundancies, it may be desirable to split them into smaller table schemes that satisfy a higher normal form, as in the previous example.

## Decomposition

Although the decomposition of a table scheme into smaller (hopefully normalized) table schemes is desirable from an efficiency point of view, in order to reduce redundancy and avoid various anomalies, it does carry with it some risk, which primarily comes in two forms:

- The possible loss of information
- The possible loss of dependencies

The following example illustrates the first problem—loss of information.

Consider the table scheme:

    {AuID, AuName, PubID}

The only dependency in this table scheme is:

    {AuID}  →  {AuName}

We could decompose this table scheme into the two schemes:

    {AuID, AuName} and {AuName, PubID}

Now consider Table 4-8, which has two different authors with the same name. The decomposition gives the two tables shown in Tables 4-9 and 4-10.

*Table 4-8. A Table with Two Identical Author Names*

| AuID | AuName | PubID |
|------|--------|-------|
| A1 | John Smith | P1 |
| A2 | John Smith | P2 |

*Table 4-9. Partial Decomposition of Table 4-8*

| AuID | AuName |
|------|--------|
| A1 | John Smith |
| A2 | John Smith |

*Table 4-10. Partial Decomposition of Table 4-8*

| AuName | PubID |
|--------|-------|
| John Smith | P1 |
| John Smith | P2 |

Unfortunately, if we were to ask Microsoft Access to show us the data for all authors named John Smith, we would get the table shown in Table 4-11, which is not the table we started with! Information has been lost, in the sense that we no longer know that both John Smiths together have published only two books, each author with a different publisher. (It may look as though we have more information, since the table is bigger, but in reality we have lost information.)

*Table 4-11. An Incorrect Reconstruction of Table 4-8*

| AuID | AuName | PubID |
|------|--------|-------|
| A1 | John Smith | P1 |
| A1 | John Smith | P2 |
| A2 | John Smith | P1 |
| A2 | John Smith | P2 |

The second problem we mentioned in connection with the decomposition of a table scheme is that of loss of dependencies. The issue is this: During the life of the database, we will be making changes (updates, insertions, and deletions) to the separate tables in the decomposition. Of course, we must be careful to preserve the functional dependencies that are inherited from the original table scheme. However, this does not necessarily guarantee that all of the original dependencies will be preserved!

Here is a simple example to illustrate the problem.

Consider the table scheme:

    {ISBN,PageCount,Price}

with dependencies:

    {ISBN}     → {PageCount}
    {PageCount} → {Price}

Consider the decomposition into the table schemes:

    {ISBN,PageCount} and {ISBN,Price}

Note that the key {ISBN} is in both schemes in the decomposition.

Unfortunately, the decomposition has caused us to lose the dependency {Page-Count}→{Price}, in the sense that these two attributes are not in the same table scheme of the decomposition. To illustrate, consider Table 4-12, which has two different books with the same page count and price. The decomposition of this table into two tables is shown in Tables 4-13 and 4-14.

*Table 4-12. Table Example to Show Further Decomposition*

| ISBN | PageCount | Price |
|------|-----------|-------|
| 0-111-11111-1 | 500 | $39.95 |
| 0-111-22222-2 | 500 | $39.95 |

*Table 4-13. Partial Decomposition of Table 4-12*

| ISBN | PageCount |
|------|-----------|
| 0-111-11111-1 | 500 |
| 0-111-22222-2 | 500 |

*Table 4-14. Partial Decomposition of Table 4-12*

| ISBN | Price |
|------|-------|
| 0-111-11111-1 | $39.95 |
| 0-111-22222-2 | $39.95 |

Now here is the problem. Looking at the second table, we have no indication that the original scheme required that PageCount determines Price. Hence, we might change the price of the second book to $12.50, as we've done in Table 4-15.

*Table 4-15. Decomposition Example Changing Price*

| ISBN | Price |
|---|---|
| 0-111-11111-1 | $39.95 |
| 0-222-22222-2 | $12.50 |

But putting the tables back together for a look at all of the data gives us Table 4-16, which reveals a violation of the requirement that PageCount determines Price. In fact, somebody at the publishing company is going to be very unhappy that the company is now selling a 500-page book at below cost!

*Table 4-16. Looking at Data by Combining Tables 4-12 Through 4-15*

| ISBN | PageCount | Price |
|---|---|---|
| 0-111-11111-1 | 500 | $39.95 |
| 0-222-22222-2 | 500 | $12.50 |

By contrast, consider the decomposition of the original table scheme into:

```
{ISBN,PubPhone} and {PubPhone,PubName}
```

Here, no dependency is lost, so we can update each separate table without fear.

The previous two examples illustrate the pitfalls in decomposing a table scheme into smaller schemes. If a decomposition does not cause any information to be lost, it is called a *lossless decomposition*. A decomposition that does not cause any dependencies to be lost is called a *dependency-preserving decomposition.*

Now it is possible to show that any table scheme can be decomposed, in a lossless way, into a collection of smaller schemes that are in the very nice BCNF form. However, we cannot guarantee that the decomposition will preserve dependencies. On the other hand, any table scheme can be decomposed, in a lossless way that also preserves dependencies, into a collection of smaller schemes that are in the almost-as-nice third normal form.

However, before getting too excited, we must hasten to add that the algorithms that we give do not always produce desirable results. They can, in fact, create decompositions that are less intuitive than we might do just using our intuition. Nevertheless, they can be relied upon to produce the required decomposition, if we can't do it ourselves.

We should conclude by saying that there is no law that says that a database is always more useful or efficient if the tables have a high degree of normalization. These issues are more subjective than objective and must be dealt with, as a design issue, on an ad hoc basis. In fact, it appears that the best procedure for good database design is to mix eight parts intuition and experience with two parts theory. Hopefully, our discussion of normalization has given you a general feeling for the issues involved, and will provide a good jumping-off place if you decide to study these somewhat complicated issues in greater depth. (See Appendix D, *Suggestions for Further Reading*, for some books for further study.)

# 5

*In this chapter:*
- *Query Languages*
- *Relational Algebra and Relational Calculus*
- *Details of the Relational Algebra*

# Query Languages and the Relational Algebra

In the first part of this book, we have tried to make a convincing argument that good database design is important to the efficient use of a database. As we have seen, this generally involves breaking the data up into separate pieces (tables). Of course, this implies that we need methods for piecing the data back together again in various forms.

After all, one of the main functions of a database program is to allow the user to view the data in a variety of ways. When data are stored in multiple tables, it is necessary to piece the data back together to provide these various views. For instance, we might want to see a list of all publishers that publish books priced under $10.00. This requires gathering data from more than one table. The point is that, by breaking data into separate tables, we must often go to the trouble of piecing the data back together in order to get a comprehensive view of those data.

Thus, we can state the following important maxim:

> As a direct consequence of good database design, we often need to use methods for piecing data from several tables into a single coherent form.

Many database applications provide the user with relatively easy ways to create comprehensive views of data from many tables. For instance, Microsoft Access provides a graphical interface to create queries for that purpose. Our goal in this chapter is to understand how a database application such as Access goes about providing this service.

The short answer to this is the following:

1. The user of a database application, such as Access, asks the application to provide a specific view of the data by creating a *query.*

2. The database application then converts this query into a statement in its query language, which in the case of Microsoft Access is *Access Structured Query Language*, or Access SQL. (This is a special form of standard SQL.)

3. Finally, a special component of Access (known as the *Jet Query Engine*, which we will discuss again in Chapter 7, *Database System Architecure*) executes the SQL statement to produce the desired view of the data.

In view of this answer, it is time that we turn away from a discussion of database design issues and turn toward a discussion of issues that will lead us toward database programming, and in particular, programming in query languages such as Access SQL.

We can now outline our plan for this and the next chapter. In this chapter, we will discuss the underlying methods involved in piecing together data from separate tables. In short, we will discuss methods for making new tables from existing tables. This will give us a clear understanding as to the general tasks that must be provided by a query language.

In the next chapter, we will take a look at Access SQL itself. We will see that SQL is much more than just a simple query language, for not only is it capable of manipulating the components of an existing database (into various views), but it also capable of creating those components in the first place.

# *Query Languages*

A query can be thought of as a request of the database, the response to which is a new table, which we will refer to as a *result table*. For instance, referring to the LIBRARY database, we might request the titles and prices of all books published by Big House that cost over $20.00. The result table in this case is shown in Table 5-1.

*Table 5-1. Books Published by Big House Costing Over $20.00*

| Title | Price | PubName |
|-------|-------|---------|
| On Liberty | $25.00 | Big House |
| Iliad | $25.00 | Big House |
| Visual Basic | $25.00 | Big House |
| C++ | $29.95 | Big House |

It is probably not necessary to emphasize the importance of queries, for what good is a database if we have no way to extract the data in meaningful forms?

Special languages that are are used to formulate queries, in other words, that are designed to create new tables from old ones, are known as *query languages*.

(There does not seem to be agreement on the precise meaning of the term "query language," so we have decided to use it in a manner that seems most consistent with the term "query.")

There are two fundamental approaches to query languages: one is based on algebraic expressions and the other is based on logical expressions. In both cases, an expression is formed that refers to existing tables, constants (i.e., values from the domains of tables), and operators of various types. How the expression is used to create the return table depends on the approach, as we will see.

Before proceeding, let us discuss a bit more terminology. A table whose data are actually stored in the database is called a *base table*. Base table data are generally stored in a format that does not actually resemble a table—but the point is that the data are stored. A table that is not stored, such as the result table of a query, is called a *derived table*. It is generally possible to save (i.e., store) a result table, which then would become a base table of the database. In Microsoft Access, this is done by creating a so-called *make-table query*.

Finally, a *view* is a query *expression* that has been given a name, and is stored in the database. For example, the expression

all titles where (PubName = Big House) and (Price > $20.00)

is a view. Note that it is the *expression* that is the view, not the corresponding result table (as might be implied by the name *view*).

Whenever the expression (or view) is executed, it creates a result table. Therefore, a view is often referred to as a *virtual table*. Again, it is important not to confuse a view with the result table that is obtained by executing the expression. The virtue of a virtual table (or view) is that an expression generally takes up far less room in storage than the corresponding result table. Moreover, the data in a result table are redundant, since the data are already in the base tables, even though not in the same logical structure.

# Relational Algebra and Relational Calculus

The most common algebraic query language is called the *relational algebra*. This language is *procedural*, in the sense that its expressions actually describe an explicit procedure for returning the results. Languages that use logic fall under the heading of the *relational calculus* (there is more than one such language in common use). These languages are *nonprocedural*, since their expressions represent statements that describe conditions that must be met for a row to be in the result table, without showing how to actually obtain those rows. Let us illustrate these ideas with an example.

Consider the following request, written in plain English:

> Get the names and phone numbers for publishers who publish books costing under $20.00.

For reference, let us repeat the relevant tables for this request. The BOOKS table appears in Table 5-2, while the PUBLISHERS table is shown in Table 5-3.

*Table 5-2. The BOOKS Table from the LIBRARY Database*

| ISBN | Title | PubID | Price |
|------|-------|-------|-------|
| 0-555-55555-9 | Macbeth | 2 | $12.00 |
| 0-91-335678-7 | Faerie Queene | 1 | $15.00 |
| 0-99-999999-9 | Emma | 1 | $20.00 |
| 0-91-045678-5 | Hamlet | 2 | $20.00 |
| 0-55-123456-9 | Main Street | 3 | $22.95 |
| 1-22-233700-0 | Visual Basic | 1 | $25.00 |
| 0-12-333433-3 | On Liberty | 1 | $25.00 |
| 0-103-45678-9 | Iliad | 1 | $25.00 |
| 1-1111-1111-1 | C++ | 1 | $29.95 |
| 0-321-32132-1 | Balloon | 3 | $34.00 |
| 0-123-45678-0 | Ulysses | 2 | $34.00 |
| 0-99-777777-7 | King Lear | 2 | $49.00 |
| 0-12-345678-9 | Jane Eyre | 3 | $49.00 |
| 0-11-345678-9 | Moby Dick | 3 | $49.00 |

*Table 5-3. The PUBLISHERS Table from the LIBRARY Database*

| PubID | PubName | PubPhone |
|-------|---------|----------|
| 1 | Big House | 123-456-7890 |
| 2 | Alpha Press | 999-999-9999 |
| 3 | Small House | 714-000-0000 |

Here is a procedure for executing this request. Don't worry if some of the terms do not make sense to you now; we will explain them later.

1. *Join* the BOOKS and PUBLISHERS tables, on the PubID attribute.

2. *Select* those rows (of the join) with Price attribute less than $20.00.

3. *Project* onto the columns PubName and PubPhone.

In the relational algebra, this would be translated into the following expression:

$$proj_{PubName,PubPhone}(sel_{Price<20.00}(BOOKS\ join\ PUBLISHERS))$$

The result table is shown in Table 5-4.

*Table 5-4. Publishers with Books Under $20.00*

| PubName | PubPhone |
|---------|----------|
| Big House | 123-456-7890 |
| Alpha Press | 999-999-9999 |

In a relational calculus, the corresponding expression might appear as

{(x,y) | PUBLISHERS(z,x,y) *and* BOOKS(a,b,z,c) *and* c < $20.00}

where the bar | is read "such that" and the entire expression is read:

The set of all pairs (x,y) such that (z,x,y) is a row in the PUBLISHERS table, (a,b,z,c) is a row in the BOOKS table, and c < $20.00.

Note that the variable z appears twice, and it must be the same for each appearance. This is precisely what provides the link between the BOOKS and PUBLISHERS tables. In other words, the row PUBLISHERS(z,x,y) in the PUBLISHERS table and the row BOOKS(a,b,z,c) in the BOOKS table have an attribute value in common (represented by the common letter z). This attribute, which is the first attribute in PUBLISHERS and the third attribute in BOOKS, is PubID.

As you can see from the previous example, the relational calculus is generally more complex (and perhaps less intuitive) than the relational algebra, and we will not discuss it further in this book, beyond making the following comments: First, it is important to at least be aware of the existence of the relational calculus, since there are commercially available applications, such as IBM's *Query-by-Example*, that use the relational calculus. Second, most relational calculus–based languages have exactly the same expressive power as the relational algebra. In other words, we get no more or less by using a relational calculus than we do by using the relational algebra.

## Details of the Relational Algebra

We are now ready to discuss the details of the relational algebra. The operations that are part of the relational algebra are described in this section. You should find most of these operations intuitive.

Before beginning, however, we should say a word about how Microsoft Access implements the operations of the relational algebra. Most of these operations can be implemented in Microsoft Access by creating a query. This is most easily done in Access's Query Design mode, which provides the graphical environment shown in Figure 5-1.

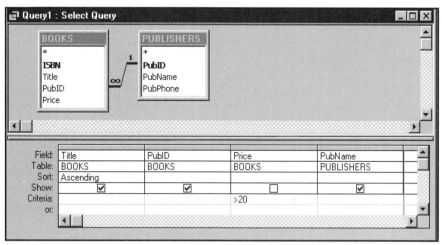

*Figure 5-1. The Access Query design window*

The user can add table schemes from the database to the upper portion of the Query Design window. From there, various attributes can be moved to the design grid. Note that the second row of the grid shows the table from whence the attribute comes, just in case two tables have attributes of the same name (which happens often).

The grid has options for sorting and for determining whether or not to display a particular attribute in the result table. It also has room for criteria used to filter out data from the query.

Note also that we do not need to include the PubID field from both tables in the lower portion of the design window. Microsoft Access takes care of forming the appropriate join based on the information in the upper portion of the window.

Microsoft Access translates the final query design into a statement in the query language known as *structured query language,* or SQL. We will discuss the details of Access SQL (which differs somewhat from standard SQL) in Chapter 6, *Access Structured Query Language (SQL)*, where the knowledge we gain here will prove very useful. We should also mention that Access SQL is more powerful than the Access Query Design interface, so some operations must be written directly in SQL. Fortunately, Access allows the user to write SQL statements.

Let us recall some notation used earlier in the book. In order to emphasize the attributes of a table (or table scheme), we use the notation $T(A_1,...,A_n)$. As an example, the BOOKS table can be written

BOOKS(ISBN,Title,PubID,Price)

and the *Books* table scheme can be written

*Books*(ISBN,Title,PubID,Price)

## Renaming

*Renaming* refers simply to changing the name of an attribute of a table. If a table T has an attribute named A, we will denote the table resulting from the operation of renaming A to B by

$ren_{A \to B}(T)$

For the table

| ISBN | Title | Price | PubID |
|------|-------|-------|-------|
| 0-103-45678-9 | The Firm | $24.95 | 1 |
| 0-11-345678-9 | Moby Dick | $49.00 | 2 |
| 0-12-333433-3 | War and Peace | $25.00 | 1 |

the result of performing

$ren_{ISBN \to BookID, Price \to Cost}(BOOKS)$

is shown in Table 5-5.

*Table 5-5. The BOOKS Table with Renamed Fields*

| BookID | Title | Cost | PubID |
|--------|-------|------|-------|
| 0-103-45678-9 | The Firm | $24.95 | 1 |
| 0-11-345678-9 | Moby Dick | $49.00 | 2 |
| 0-12-333433-3 | War and Peace | $25.00 | 1 |

## Union

If S and T are tables with the same attributes, then we may form the *union* $S \cup T$, which is just the table obtained by including all of the rows from both S and T.

*Example*

| A₁ | A₂ |
|---|---|
| a | b |
| c | d |
| e | f |

| A₁ | A₂ |
|---|---|
| g | h |
| i | j |

| A₁ | A₂ |
|---|---|
| a | b |
| c | d |
| e | f |
| g | h |
| i | j |

Note that if S and T do not have the same attributes, but do have the same *degree*—that is, the same number of columns, then we can first rename the attributes of one table to match the other, and then take their union. Of course, this will not always make sense, since it may result in combining attribute values from different domains into one column.

Let us consider an example of how to take a union in Microsoft Access.

Unions can be formed in one of two ways in Microsoft Access. The first is straightforward:

1. First, we need some expendable tables to use in this example. We can create these tables by copying the BOOKS table as follows. Highlight the BOOKS table in the Database Window and choose Copy from the Edit menu. Then choose Paste from the Edit menu. You will get the dialog box in Figure 5-2.

   Type the table name Union1 and click *OK.* Choose Paste a second time to create a table named Union2. Open Union1 and delete the last seven rows from the table. (Just highlight the rows and hit the Delete key.) Open Union2 and delete the first seven rows of the table. Thus, Union1 will consist of the first half of the BOOKS table and Union2 will consist of the second half of BOOKS.

2. The simplest way to take the union is to use the same *Copy...Paste* procedure that we used in Step 1. To illustrate, highlight Union2 and choose Copy from

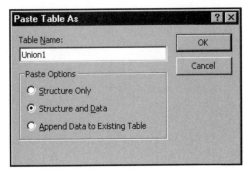

*Figure 5-2. The Access Paste Table dialog*

the Edit menu. Then choose Paste and enter the table name Union1. Select the Append Data to Existing Table option. If you then click *OK*, the rows of the copied table (Union2) will be appended to the rows of the table Union1. In other words, Union1 will now contain the union of the original Union1 table and the Union2 table, which in this case is the complete contents of BOOKS. In symbols

NewUnion1 = OriginalUnion1 $\cup$ Union2

Open Union1 to verify that it now has 14 rows. Then delete the last seven rows again to restore Union1 to its original condition.

Another way to create a union is to use an Append Query as follows:

1. From the Query tab in the Database window choose the New button. Select Design View and then add Union2 to the design window. Select Append from the Query menu to get the dialog in Figure 5-3.

*Figure 5-3. The Access Append dialog*

2. Click *OK* to get the window shown in Figure 5-4. Drag the asterisk (*) in the table scheme for Union2 to the first cell in the Field row of the design grid. This will fill in the first column of the design grid as shown in Figure 5-4. Run the query (choose Run from the Query menu). You will get a warning that

you are about to append seven rows and that the process cannot be undone. Click *OK* and then open the Union1 table to verify that it now has 14 rows.

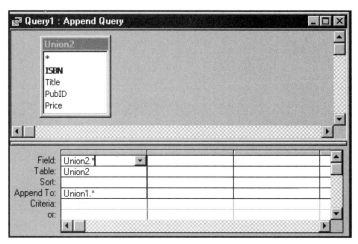

*Figure 5-4. The Access Append Query window*

## *Intersection*

The *intersection* S ∩ T of two tables S and T with the *same* attributes is the table formed by keeping only those rows that appear in *both* tables. Here is an example:

| A$_1$ | A$_2$ |
|-------|-------|
| a     | b     |
| c     | d     |
| e     | f     |

| A$_1$ | A$_2$ |
|-------|-------|
| c     | d     |
| i     | j     |
| e     | f     |

| A$_1$ | A$_2$ |
|-------|-------|
| c     | d     |
| e     | f     |

We will see an example of how to form an intersection in Microsoft Access when we discuss differences, in the next section.

# Difference

The *difference* S − T of two tables S and T with the same attributes is the table consisting of all rows of S that do *not* appear in T, as shown in the following tables:

| A₁ | A₂ |
|----|----|
| a  | b  |
| c  | d  |
| e  | f  |
| g  | h  |

| A₁ | A₂ |
|----|----|
| c  | d  |
| i  | j  |
| e  | f  |

| A₁ | A₂ |
|----|----|
| a  | b  |
| g  | h  |

Let us consider an example of how to take an intersection or difference in Microsoft Access.

1. First, we need some expendable tables. As in the first step of the example for creating a union, use the Copy and Paste features to create two tables named Diff1 and Diff2 that are exact copies of BOOKS. Open Diff1 and remove the last four rows. Open Diff2 and remove the first four rows. Thus, Diff1 contains the first ten books from BOOKS and Diff2 contains the last ten books from BOOKS.

2. Now switch to the Query tab and start a new query. Add both Diff1 and Diff2 to the query. You may notice a connecting line between the two ISBN attributes. If there is no such line, drag one ISBN name to the other to create a line. Now right click on the line and choose Join Properties from the popup menu. This should produce the dialog box shown in Figure 5-5. Select option 2, which will include all records (rows) from Diff1 and all rows of Diff2 that have a matching ISBN in Diff1. This is a so-called *left outer join*. We will discuss this in more detail later in this section. Click *OK*.

*Figure 5-5. The Access Join Properties dialog*

3. Drag the asterisk (*) from Diff1 to the design grid and then drag ISBN from Diff2 to the second column of the design grid. The Design Window should now appear as in Figure 5-6.

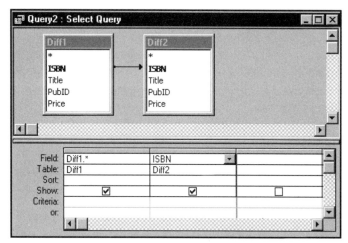

*Figure 5-6. The Access Select Query design window showing a join between two properties*

4. Now run the query. You should get a table as shown in Figure 5-7. This table contains the ten rows from Diff1, with an extra column that gives the matching ISBN from Diff2, if there is one. Otherwise, the column contains a NULL. We can see that the six rows that have a matching ISBN in column Diff2.ISBN form the intersection of the two tables. Also, the four rows that do not have a matching ISBN form the difference Diff1 − Diff2. Hence, we only need to add a simple criterion to the query to obtain either the intersection or the difference.

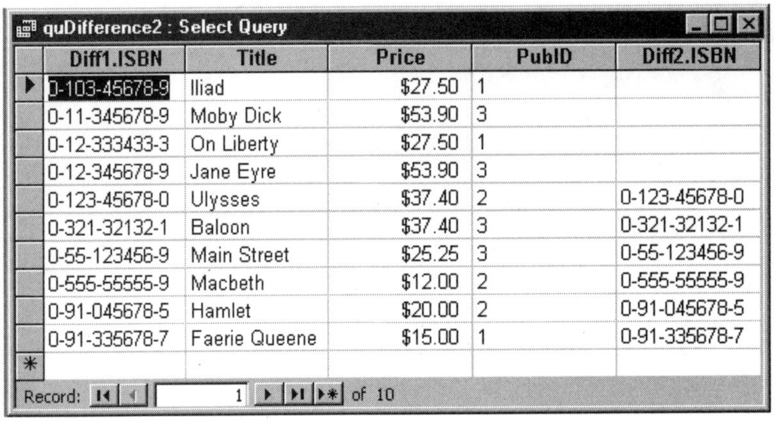

quDifference2 : Select Query

| Diff1.ISBN | Title | Price | PubID | Diff2.ISBN |
|---|---|---|---|---|
| 0-103-45678-9 | Iliad | $27.50 | 1 | |
| 0-11-345678-9 | Moby Dick | $53.90 | 3 | |
| 0-12-333433-3 | On Liberty | $27.50 | 1 | |
| 0-12-345678-9 | Jane Eyre | $53.90 | 3 | |
| 0-123-45678-0 | Ulysses | $37.40 | 2 | 0-123-45678-0 |
| 0-321-32132-1 | Baloon | $37.40 | 3 | 0-321-32132-1 |
| 0-55-123456-9 | Main Street | $25.25 | 3 | 0-55-123456-9 |
| 0-555-55555-9 | Macbeth | $12.00 | 2 | 0-555-55555-9 |
| 0-91-045678-5 | Hamlet | $20.00 | 2 | 0-91-045678-5 |
| 0-91-335678-7 | Faerie Queene | $15.00 | 1 | 0-91-335678-7 |

Record: 1 of 10

*Figure 5-7. The Access Select Query window showing the intersection of two tables*

5. To get the intersection Diff1 ∩ Diff2, return to the design view of the query and add the words *Is Not Null* under the Criteria row in the Diff2.ISBN column. Run the query.
6. To get the difference Diff1 – Diff2, return to the design view of the query and add the words *Is Null* under the Criteria row in the Diff2.ISBN column. Run the query.

## *Cartesian Product*

To define the Cartesian product of tables, we need to adjust the way we write attribute names, just in case both tables have an attribute of the same name. If a table T has an attribute named A, the *fully qualified attribute name* (or just *qualified attribute name*) is T.A. Thus, we may write BOOKS.ISBN or AUTHORS.AuID.

If $S(A_1,\ldots,A_n)$ and $T(B_1,\ldots,B_m)$ are tables then the *Cartesian product* $S \times T$ of S and T is the table whose attribute set contains the fully qualified attribute names of all attributes from S and T:

$$\{S.A_1,\ldots,S.A_n,T.B_1,\ldots,T.B_m\}$$

The rows of $S \times T$ are formed by combining *each* row s of S with each row t of T, to form a new row st. An example will help make this clear:

| $A_1$ | $A_2$ |
|---|---|
| a | b |
| c | d |
| e | f |

| $B_1$ | $B_2$ | $B_3$ |
|---|---|---|
| g | h | i |
| j | k | l |

| $S.A_1$ | $S.A_2$ | $T.B_1$ | $T.B_2$ | $T.B_3$ |
|---|---|---|---|---|
| a | b | g | h | i |
| a | b | j | k | l |
| c | d | g | h | i |
| c | d | j | k | l |
| e | f | g | h | i |
| e | f | j | k | l |

Notice that if S has $k$ rows and T has $j$ rows then the Cartesian product has $kj$ rows. Hence, the Cartesian product of two tables can be very large.

To form a Cartesian product of two tables in Microsoft Access, proceed as follows:

1. Create the two tables S and T in the previous example.

2. Create a new query and add the tables S and T. Make certain that there are no lines joining the two table schemes. (If there are, right click on the lines and choose Delete from the popup menu.)

3. Drag the asterisks from each table scheme to the design grid. You should now have a design window as shown in Figure 5-8. Run the query to get the Cartesian product.

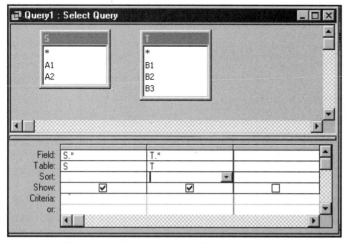

*Figure 5-8. The Access Query window illustrating a Cartesian product of two tables*

## *Projection*

Projection is a very simple concept. Intuitively, a projection of a table onto a subset of its attributes (columns) is the table formed by throwing away all other columns.

More formally, let $T(A_1,\ldots A_n)$ be a table, where $\mathcal{A} = \{A_1,\ldots,A_n\}$ is the attribute set. If $\mathcal{B}$ is a *subset* of $\mathcal{A}$ then the *projection* of T onto $\mathcal{B}$ is just the table obtained from T by keeping only those columns headed by the attribute names in $\mathcal{B}$. We denote this table by $proj_{\mathcal{B}}(T)$.

### *Example*

For the table:

| ISBN | Title | Price | PubID |
|------|-------|-------|-------|
| 0-103-45678-9 | The Firm | $24.95 | 1 |
| 0-11-345678-9 | Moby Dick | $49.00 | 2 |
| 0-12-333433-3 | War and Peace | $25.00 | 1 |

the projection $proj_{\text{ISBN,Price}}(\text{BOOKS})$ is:

| ISBN | Price |
|------|-------|
| 0-103-45678-9 | $24.95 |
| 0-11-345678-9 | $49.00 |
| 0-12-333433-3 | $25.00 |

Note that, if the projection produces two identical rows, the duplicate rows must be removed, since a table is not allowed to have duplicate rows. (This rule of relational databases is not enforced by all commercial database products. In particular, it is not enforced by Microsoft Access. That is, some products allow identical rows in a table. By definition, these products are not true relational databases—but that is not necessarily a flaw.)

The Query Design window in Microsoft Access was tailor-made for creating projections. Just add the table to the design window and drag the desired attribute names to the design grid. Run the query to get the projection. Figure 5-9 shows the Query Design window for computing the projection of *Books* onto the attributes ISBN and Price.

## *Selection*

Just as the operation of projection selects only a subset of the columns of a table, so the operation of *selection* selects a subset of the rows of a table. The first step

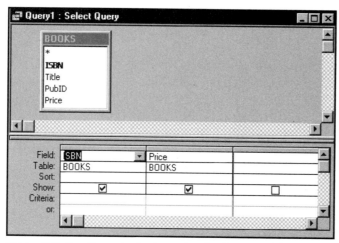

*Figure 5-9. Creating a projection using the BOOKS table*

in defining the operation of selection is to define a *selection condition* or *selection criterion* to be any legally formed expression that involves:

- Constants (i.e., members of any attribute domain)
- Attribute names
- Arithmetic comparison relations (=, ≠, <, ≤, >, ≥)
- Logical operators (*and, or, not*)

For example, the following are selection conditions:

- Price > $10.00
- Price ≤ $50.00 *and* AuName = "Bronte"
- (Price ≤ $50.00 *and* AuName = "Bronte") *or* (*not* AuName = "Austen")

If *condition* is a selection condition, then the result table obtained by applying the corresponding selection operation to a table T is denoted by:

$$sel_{condition}(T)$$

or sometimes by:

T where condition

and is the table obtained from T by keeping only those rows that satisfy the selection condition.

For example, for the BOOKS in the LIBRARY database:

| ISBN | Title | PubID | Price |
|------|-------|-------|-------|
| 0-103-45678-9 | Iliad | 1 | $25.00 |
| 0-11-345678-9 | Moby Dick | 3 | $49.00 |
| 0-12-333433-3 | On Liberty | 1 | $25.00 |
| 0-12-345678-9 | Jane Eyre | 3 | $49.00 |
| 0-123-45678-0 | Ulysses | 2 | $34.00 |
| 0-321-32132-1 | Balloon | 3 | $34.00 |
| 0-55-123456-9 | Main Street | 3 | $22.95 |
| 0-555-55555-9 | Macbeth | 2 | $12.00 |
| 0-91-045678-5 | Hamlet | 2 | $20.00 |
| 0-91-335678-7 | Faerie Queene | 1 | $15.00 |
| 0-99-777777-7 | King Lear | 2 | $49.00 |
| 0-99-999999-9 | Emma | 1 | $20.00 |
| 1-1111-1111-1 | C++ | 1 | $29.95 |
| 1-22-233700-0 | Visual Basic | 1 | $25.00 |

the table $sel_{\text{Price} \geq \$25.00}(\text{BOOKS})$ is:

| ISBN | Title | PubID | Price |
|------|-------|-------|-------|
| 0-12-345678-9 | Jane Eyre | 3 | $49.00 |
| 0-11-345678-9 | Moby Dick | 3 | $49.00 |
| 0-99-777777-7 | King Lear | 2 | $49.00 |
| 0-123-45678-0 | Ulysses | 2 | $34.00 |
| 1-1111-1111-1 | C++ | 1 | $29.95 |
| 0-321-32132-1 | Balloon | 3 | $34.00 |

Some authors refer to selection as *restriction*, which does seem to be a more appropriate term, and has the advantage that it is not confused with the SQL SELECT statement, which is much more general than just selection. However, it is less common than the term "selection," so we will use this term.

The Query Design window in Microsoft Access was also tailor-made for creating selections. We just use the *Criteria* rows to apply the desired restrictions. For example, Figure 5-10 shows the design window for the selection:

$$sel_{\text{Price} \geq \$25.00}(\text{BOOKS})$$

from the previous example.

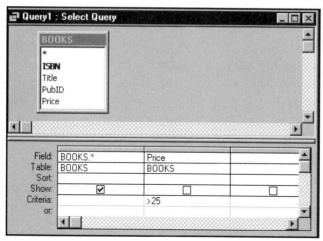

*Figure 5-10. Creating a selection in the Query Design window*

You will probably agree that the operations we have covered so far are pretty straightforward—union, intersection, difference, and Cartesian product are basic set-theoretic operations. Selecting rows and columns are clearly valuable table operations.

Actually, the six operations of renaming, union, difference, Cartesian product, projection, and selection are enough to form the complete relational algebra, by combining these operations with constants and attribute names to create relational algebra expressions.

However, it is very convenient to define some additional operations on tables, even though they can theoretically be expressed in terms of the six operations mentioned above. So let us proceed.

## Joins

The various types of joins are among the most important and useful of the relational algebra operations. Loosely speaking, joining two tables involves combining the rows of two tables based on comparing the values in selected columns.

### Equi-join

In an equi-join, rows are combined if there are equal attribute values in certain selected columns from each table.

To be specific, let S and T be tables and suppose that $\{C_1,\ldots,C_k\}$ are selected attributes of S and $\{D_1,\ldots,D_k\}$ are selected attributes of T. Each table may have additional attributes as well. Note that we select the same number of attributes from each table.

The equi-join of S and T on columns $\{C_1,...,C_k\}$ and $\{D_1,...,D_k\}$ is the table formed by combining a row of S with a row of T provided that corresponding columns have equal value, that is, provided that:

$$S.C_1 = T.D_1, S.C_2 = T.D_2, ..., S.C_k = T.D_k$$

*Example*

Consider the tables:

| $A_1$ | $A_2$ |
|---|---|
| 1 | 4 |
| 4 | 5 |
| 6 | 3 |

| $B_1$ | $B_2$ | $B_3$ |
|---|---|---|
| 2 | 3 | 4 |
| 6 | 7 | 3 |
| 1 | 1 | 4 |

To form the equi-join:

$$S \; equi\text{-}join_{A_2 = B_3} T$$

we combine rows for which

$$S.A_2 = T.B_3$$

This gives:

| $S.A_1$ | $S.A_2$ | $T.B_1$ | $T.B_2$ | $T.B_3$ |
|---|---|---|---|---|
| 1 | 4 | 2 | 3 | 4 |
| 1 | 4 | 1 | 1 | 4 |
| 6 | 3 | 6 | 7 | 3 |

Notice that the equi-join can be expressed in terms of the Cartesian product and the selection operation as follows:

$$S \; equi\text{-}join_{C_1 = D_1, ..., C_k = D_k} T = sel_{C_1 = D_1, ..., C_k = D_l}(S \times T)$$

This simply says that, to form the equi-join, we take the Cartesian product $S \times T$ of S and T (i.e., the set of *all* combinations of rows from S and T) and then select only those rows for which

$$S.C_1 = T.D_1, S.C_2 = T.D_2, ..., S.C_k = T.D_k$$

### Natural join

The natural join (*nat-join*) is a variation on the equi-join, based on the equality of all common attributes in two tables.

To be specific, suppose that S and T are tables and that the set of all common attributes between these tables is $\{C_1,...,C_n\}$. Thus, each table may have additional attributes, but no further attributes in common. The natural join of S and T, which we denote by:

S *nat-join* T

is formed in two steps:

1. Form the equi-join on the common attributes $\{C_1,...,C_n\}$

2. Remove the second set of common columns from the table

Consider these tables:

| $A_1$ | $A_2$ | $A_3$ | $A_4$ |
|-------|-------|-------|-------|
| a | b | c | d |
| e | f | g | h |
| i | j | k | l |
| m | n | o | p |

| $B_1$ | $A_2$ | $A_4$ | $B_4$ |
|-------|-------|-------|-------|
| a | b | c | d |
| c | j | l | f |
| f | b | d | g |
| x | y | z | h |
| s | j | l | j |

In this case, the set of common attributes is $\{A_2,A_4\}$. The corresponding columns are shaded for easier identification.

The equi-join on $A_2$ and $A_4$ is:

| S.A$_1$ | S.A$_2$ | S.A$_3$ | S.A$_4$ | T.B$_1$ | T.A$_2$ | T.A$_4$ | S.B$_4$ |
|---------|---------|---------|---------|---------|---------|---------|---------|
| a       | b       | c       | d       | f       | b       | d       | g       |
| i       | j       | k       | l       | c       | j       | l       | f       |
| i       | j       | k       | l       | s       | j       | l       | h       |

Deleting the second set of common columns (the columns that come from T, as shaded in the previous table) gives:

| S.A$_1$ | S.A$_2$ | S.A$_3$ | S.A$_4$ | T.B$_1$ | T.B$_4$ |
|---------|---------|---------|---------|---------|---------|
| a       | b       | c       | d       | f       | g       |
| i       | j       | k       | l       | c       | f       |
| i       | j       | k       | l       | s       | h       |

The importance of the natural join comes from the fact that, when there is a one-to-many relationship from S to T, we can arrange it, by renaming if necessary, so that the only common attributes are the key of S and the foreign key in T. In this case, the natural join S *nat-join* T is simply the table obtained by matching rows that are related through the one-to-many relationship.

For example, consider the following BOOKS and PUBLISHERS tables in Tables 5-6 and 5-7, respectively:

*Table 5-6. The BOOKS Table*

| ISBN          | Title          | Price    | PubID |
|---------------|----------------|----------|-------|
| 0-103-45678-9 | The Firm       | $24.95   | 1     |
| 0-11-345678-9 | Moby Dick      | $49.00   | 2     |
| 0-12-333433-3 | War and Peace  | $25.00   | 1     |
| 0-12-345678-9 | Jane Eyre      | $34.00   | 1     |
| 0-26-888888-8 | Persuasion     | $13.00   | 3     |
| 0-555-55555-9 | Emma           | $12.00   | 3     |
| 0-91-045678-5 | The Chamber    | $20.00   | 3     |
| 0-91-335678-7 | Partners       | $15.00   | 1     |
| 0-99-777777-7 | Triple Play    | $44.00   | 3     |
| 0-99-999999-9 | Mansfield Park | $18.00   | 1     |

*Table 5-7. The PUBLISHERS Table*

| PubID | PubName | PubPhone |
|---|---|---|
| 1 | Big House | 212-000-1212 |
| 2 | Little House | 213-111-1212 |
| 3 | Medium House | 614-222-1212 |

Then PUBLISHERS *nat-join* BOOKS is the table formed by taking each PUBLISHERS row and adjoining each BOOKS row with a matching PubID, as shown in Table 5-8.

*Table 5-8. The PUBLISHERS nat-join BOOKS Table*

| PubID | PubName | PubPhone | ISBN | Title | Price |
|---|---|---|---|---|---|
| 1 | Big House | 212-000-1212 | 0-103-45678-9 | The Firm | $24.95 |
| 1 | Big House | 212-000-1212 | 0-12-333433-3 | War and Peace | $25.00 |
| 1 | Big House | 212-000-1212 | 0-12-345678-9 | Jane Eyre | $34.00 |
| 1 | Big House | 212-000-1212 | 0-91-335678-7 | Partners | $15.00 |
| 1 | Big House | 212-000-1212 | 0-99-999999-9 | Mansfield Park | $18.00 |
| 2 | Little House | 213-111-1212 | 0-11-345678-9 | Moby Dick | $49.00 |
| 3 | Medium House | 614-222-1212 | 0-26-888888-8 | Persuasion | $13.00 |
| 3 | Medium House | 614-222-1212 | 0-555-55555-9 | Emma | $12.00 |
| 3 | Medium House | 614-222-1212 | 0-91-045678-5 | The Chamber | $20.00 |
| 3 | Medium House | 614-222-1212 | 0-99-777777-7 | Triple Play | $44.00 |

## θ-Join

The θ-join (read *theta join*, since θ is the Greek letter theta) is similar to the equi-join and is used when we need to make a comparison other than equality between column values. In fact, the θ-join can use any of these arithmetic comparison relations:

$$=, \neq, <, \leq, >, \geq$$

Let S and T be tables and suppose that $\{C_1,\ldots,C_k\}$ are selected attributes of S and $\{D_1,\ldots,D_k\}$ are selected attributes of T. Each table may have additional attributes as well. Note that we select the same number of attributes from each table. Let $\theta_1,\ldots,\theta_k$ be comparison relations. Then the θ-join of tables S and T on columns $C_1,\ldots,C_k$ and $D_1,\ldots,D_k$ is:

$$S \; \theta\text{-}join_{C_1\theta_1D_1, \ldots, C_k\theta_kD_k} T = sel_{C_1\theta_1D_1, \ldots, C_k\theta_kD_k}(S \times T)$$

Thus, to form the $\theta$-join we take the Cartesian product $S \times T$ of $S$ and $T$ and then select those rows for which the value in column $C_1$ stands in relation $\theta_1$ to the value in column $D_1$ and similarly for each of the other columns.

*Example*

Consider these tables:

| $A_1$ | $A_2$ |
|-------|-------|
| 1 | 2 |
| 4 | 5 |
| 6 | 3 |

| $B_1$ | $B_2$ | $B_3$ |
|-------|-------|-------|
| 2 | 3 | 4 |
| 6 | 7 | 3 |

To form the $\theta$-join:

$$S \ \theta\text{-}join_{A_2 \leq B_3} T$$

we keep only those rows of the Cartesian product of the two tables for which the value in column $A_2$ is $\leq$ the value in column $B_3$:

| $S.A_1$ | $S.A_2$ | $T.B_1$ | $T.B_2$ | $T.B_3$ |
|---------|---------|---------|---------|---------|
| 1 | 2 | 2 | 3 | 4 |
| 1 | 2 | 6 | 7 | 3 |
| 6 | 3 | 2 | 3 | 4 |
| 6 | 3 | 6 | 7 | 3 |

Notice that a $\theta$-join, where all relations $\theta_i$ are equality (=), is precisely the equi-join.

## Outer Joins

The natural join, equi-join, and $\theta$-join are referred to as *inner joins*. Each inner join has a corresponding *left outer join* and *right outer join*, which are formed by first taking the corresponding inner join and then including some additional rows.

In particular, for the left outer join, if s is a row of S that was not used in the inner join, we include the row s, filled out to the proper size with NULL values. An example may help to clarify this concept.

In an earlier example, we saw that the natural join of the tables:

| $A_1$ | $A_2$ | $A_3$ | $A_4$ |
|---|---|---|---|
| a | b | c | d |
| e | f | g | h |
| i | j | k | l |
| m | n | o | p |

| $B_1$ | $A_2$ | $A_4$ | $B_4$ |
|---|---|---|---|
| a | b | c | d |
| c | j | l | f |
| f | b | d | g |
| x | y | z | h |
| s | j | l | j |

is:

| $A_1$ | $A_2$ | $A_3$ | $A_4$ | $B_1$ | $B_4$ |
|---|---|---|---|---|---|
| a | b | c | d | f | g |
| i | j | k | l | c | f |
| i | j | k | l | s | h |

The corresponding left outer join is the same as the nat-join, but with a few extra rows:

| $A_1$ | $A_2$ | $A_3$ | $A_4$ | $B_1$ | $B_4$ |
|---|---|---|---|---|---|
| a | b | c | d | f | g |
| i | j | k | l | c | f |
| i | j | k | l | s | h |
| e | f | g | h | NULL | NULL |
| m | n | o | p | NULL | NULL |

In particular, the left outer join also contains the two rows of S that were not involved in the natural join, with NULL values used to fill out the rows. The right outer join is defined similarly, where the rows of T are included, with NULL values in place of the S values.

One of the simplest uses for an outer join is to help see what is not part of an inner join! For instance, the previous table shows us instantly that the second and fourth rows:

| e | f | g | h |
|---|---|---|---|
| m | n | o | p |

of table S are not involved in the natural join S *nat-join* T! Put another way, the values

$$A_2 = f, A_4 = h$$

and

$$A_2 = n, A_4 = p$$

are not present in any rows of table T.

## Implementing Joins in Microsoft Access

Now let us consider how to implement the various types of joins in Microsoft Access. The Access Query Design window makes it easy to create equi-joins. Of course, a natural join is easily created from an appropriate equi-join by using a projection. Let us illustrate this statement with an example.

Begin by creating the following two simple tables, S and T, shown in Tables 5-9 and 5-10.

*Table 5-9. The S Table*

| $A_1$ | $A_2$ |
|-------|-------|
| a | b |
| c | d |
| e | f |

*Table 5-10. The T Table*

| $B_1$ | $B_2$ | $B_3$ |
|-------|-------|-------|
| g | h | i |
| j | k | l |
| c | d | x |
| c | d | y |
| c | y | z |

Let us create the equi-join

$$S \ equi\text{-}join_{A_1 = B_1, A_2 = B_2} T$$

Open the Query Design window (by asking for a new query) and add these two tables. To establish the associations:

$$S.A_1 = T.B_1 \ \text{and} \ S.A_2 = T.B_2$$

drag the attribute name $A_1$ to $B_1$ and drag the attribute name $A_2$ to $B_2$. This should create the lines shown in Figure 5-11. Drag the two asterisks down to the first two columns of the design grid, as in Figure 5-11. (Access provides the asterisk as a quick way to drag all of the fields to the design grid. It is the same as dragging each field separately with one exception—changes to the underlying table design are reflected in the asterisk. In other words, if new fields are added to the underlying table, they will be included automatically in the query.)

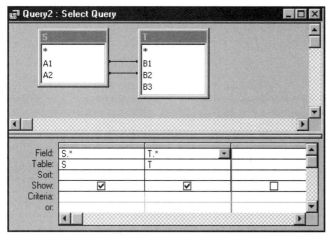

*Figure 5-11. Establishing associations in the Access Query Design window*

Now all we need to do is run the query. The result is shown in Table 5-11.

*Table 5-11. An Equi-Join of Tables S and T*

| $A_1$ | $A_2$ | $B_1$ | $B_2$ | $B_3$ |
|-------|-------|-------|-------|-------|
| c | d | c | d | y |
| c | d | c | d | x |

In other words, Microsoft Access uses the relationships defined graphically in the upper portion of the window to create an equi-join.

The Access Query Design window does not allow us to create a θ-join that does not use equality. However, we can easily create such a join from an equi-join by altering the corresponding SQL statement. We will discuss SQL in detail in Chapter 6. For now, let us modify the previous example to illustrate the technique.

From the Design view for the query in the previous example, select SQL from the View menu. You should see the window shown in Figure 5-12.

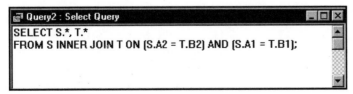

*Figure 5-12. The SQL statement generated from Figure 5-11*

This is the SQL statement that Access created from our query design for the previous example. Now, edit the two equal signs by changing each of them to <= (less than or equal to). Note that, for text, the less than or equal to sign refers to alphabetical order.

Now run the query. The result table should appear as shown in Table 5-12.

*Table 5-12. Result Table from a θ-join*

| $A_1$ | $A_2$ | $B_1$ | $B_2$ | $B_3$ |
|-------|-------|-------|-------|-------|
| a | b | g | h | I |
| a | b | j | k | l |
| a | b | c | d | x |
| a | b | c | d | y |
| a | b | c | y | z |
| c | d | g | h | I |
| c | d | j | k | l |
| c | d | c | d | x |
| c | d | c | d | y |
| c | d | c | y | z |
| e | f | g | h | i |
| e | f | j | k | l |

Notice that for each row of the table, $A_1$ precedes or equals $B_1$ in alphabetical order and $A_2$ precedes or equals $B_2$.

Finally, observe that if we try to return to the design view of this query, Access issues the message in Figure 5-13, because the design view cannot create θ-joins that are not based strictly on equality.

*Figure 5-13. Access error for attempting to create unequal θ-joins*

To create an outer join, return the SQL statement of the previous example back to its original form (with equal signs) and then return to design view. Click the right mouse button on one of the connecting lines between the table schemes and choose Join Properties from the popup menu. This should produce the dialog box shown in Figure 5-14.

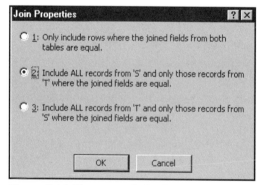

*Figure 5-14. The Access dialog box for joining properties*

Select option 2, which will produce a left outer join. (Option 1 creates an inner join, option 2 creates a left outer join, and option 3 creates a right outer join.) Do the same for the other connecting line. Take a peek at the SQL statement, which should appear as in Figure 5-15.

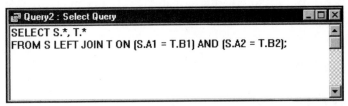

*Figure 5-15. The SQL statement illustrating a left outer join*

Now you can run the query, which should produce the result table in Table 5-13, where the empty cells contain the NULL value.

*Table 5-13. A Left Outer Join*

| $A_1$ | $A_2$ | $B_1$ | $B_2$ | $B_3$ |
|-------|-------|-------|-------|-------|
| a | b | | | |
| c | d | c | d | y |
| c | d | c | d | x |
| e | f | | | |

Of course, a right outer join is created similarly, by choosing option 3 in Figure 5-14.

## Semi-Joins

A *semi-join* is formed from an inner join (or θ-join) by projecting onto one of the tables that participated in the join. In other words, we first form the join

    S  θ-*join*T

and then just keep the columns that came from S or from T. Thus, the formula for the *left semi-join* is

$$S\ \textit{left-semi-join}_{C_1\theta_1D_1,\ ...,\ C_k\theta_kD_k}T = \textit{proj}_{\text{all columns of } S}(\text{sel}_{C_1\theta_1D_1,\ ...,\ C_k\theta_kD_k}(S \times T))$$

Similarly, the formula for the *right semi-join* is

$$S\ \textit{right-semi-join}_{C_1\theta_1D_1,\ ...,\ C_k\theta_kD_k}T = \textit{proj}_{\text{all columns of } T}(\text{sel}_{C_1\theta_1D_1,\ ...,\ C_k\theta_kD_k}(S \times T))$$

The concept of a semi-join occurs in relation to the DISTINCTROW keyword of the SELECT clause in Access SQL, which we will discuss in Chapter 6. For now, let us consider an example of the semi-join, which should indicate why semi-joins are useful.

Imagine that we add a new publisher to the PUBLISHERS table (Another Press in Table 5-14), but do not add any books for this publisher to the BOOKS table. Consider the inner join of the tables PUBLISHERS and BOOKS:

PUBLISHERS *join*<sub>PUBLISHERS.PubID=BOOKS.PubID</sub> BOOKS

For the LIBRARY database, the result table resulting from this join is shown in Table 5-15.

*Table 5-14. The PUBLISHERS (New) Table*

| PubID | PubName | PubPhone |
|-------|---------|----------|
| 1 | Big House | 123-456-7890 |
| 2 | Alpha Press | 999-999-9999 |
| 3 | Small House | 714-000-0000 |
| 4 | Another Press | 111-222-3333 |

*Table 5-15. Result Table from an Inner Join*

| PUBLISH-ERS. PubID | PubName | PubPhone | ISBN | Title | BOOKS .PubID | Price |
|--------------------|---------|----------|------|-------|--------------|-------|
| 3 | Small House | 714-000-0000 | 0-12-345678-9 | Jane Eyre | 3 | $49.00 |
| 3 | Small House | 714-000-0000 | 0-11-345678-9 | Moby Dick | 3 | $49.00 |
| 3 | Small House | 714-000-0000 | 0-321-32132-1 | Balloon | 3 | $34.00 |
| 3 | Small House | 714-000-0000 | 0-55-123456-9 | Main Street | 3 | $22.95 |
| 1 | Big House | 123-456-7890 | 0-12-333433-3 | On Liberty | 1 | $25.00 |
| 1 | Big House | 123-456-7890 | 0-103-45678-9 | Iliad | 1 | $25.00 |
| 1 | Big House | 123-456-7890 | 0-91-335678-7 | Faerie Queene | 1 | $15.00 |
| 1 | Big House | 123-456-7890 | 0-99-999999-9 | Emma | 1 | $20.00 |
| 1 | Big House | 123-456-7890 | 1-22-233700-0 | Visual Basic | 1 | $25.00 |
| 1 | Big House | 123-456-7890 | 1-1111-1111-1 | C++ | 1 | $29.95 |
| 2 | Alpha Press | 999-999-9999 | 0-91-045678-5 | Hamlet | 2 | $20.00 |
| 2 | Alpha Press | 999-999-9999 | 0-555-55555-9 | Macbeth | 2 | $12.00 |

*Table 5-15. Result Table from an Inner Join (continued)*

| PUBLISH-ERS. PubID | PubName | PubPhone | ISBN | Title | BOOKS .PubID | Price |
|---|---|---|---|---|---|---|
| 2 | Alpha Press | 999-999-9999 | 0-99-777777-7 | King Lear | 2 | $49.00 |
| 2 | Alpha Press | 999-999-9999 | 0-123-45678-0 | Ulysses | 2 | $34.00 |

If we now project onto the PUBLISHERS table, we get the left semi-join

PUBLISHERS *left-semi-join*$_{PUBLISHERS.PubID=BOOKS.PubID}$ BOOKS

for which the result table is shown in Table 5-16.

*Table 5-16. Result Table from a Semi-Join*

| PubID | PubName | PubPhone |
|---|---|---|
| 3 | Small House | 714-000-0000 |
| 1 | Big House | 123-456-7890 |
| 2 | Alpha Press | 999-999-9999 |

This is the set of all publishers that have book entries in the BOOKS database.

## Other Relational Algebra Operations

There is one more operation in the relational algebra that occurs from time to time, called the *quotient*. However, since this operation is less common, and a bit involved, we will cover it in Appendix B, *The Quotient: An Additional Operation of the Relational Algebra*. (You may turn to that appendix after finishing this chapter, if you are interested.)

## Optimization

Let us conclude this discussion with a brief remark about *optimization*. As we have discussed, statements in the relational algebra are *procedural;* that is, they describe a procedure for carrying out the operations. However, this procedure is often not very efficient. Let us illustrate with an extreme example.

Consider the two table schemes:

{ISBN,Title,Price} and {ISBN,PageCount}

If S is a table based on the first scheme and T is a table based on the second scheme, then the natural join is:

$$S \ join \ T = proj_{\text{S.ISBN,Title,Price,PageCount}} \ T(sel_{\text{S}.A_2 = \text{T}.A_2, \ \text{S}.A_4 = \text{T}.A_4}(S \times T))$$

According to this formula, the join is carried out in the following steps:

1. Form the Cartesian product
2. Take the appropriate selection
3. Take the appropriate projection

Now imagine two tables S and T, where S has 10,000 rows and T has 10,000 rows. Assume also that the tables have only one common attribute, for which no values are the same in both tables. In this case, according to the definition of natural join, the join is actually the empty table.

However, according to the procedure described by above, the first step in computing this join is to compute the product S × T, which has 10000 × 10000 = 100,000,000 rows; that is, one hundred million rows! Obviously, this is not the best procedure for computing the join!

Fortunately, database programs that use a procedural language have *optimization routines* to avoid problems like this. Such a routine looks at the task it is requested to perform, and tries to find an alternative procedure that will produce the same output with less computation. Thus, from a practical standpoint, procedural languages sometimes behave similarly to nonprocedural ones.

# 6

## Access Structured Query Language (SQL)

## Introduction to Access SQL

As we have said, Microsoft Access uses a form of query language referred to as Structured Query Language, or SQL. (I prefer to pronounce SQL by saying each letter separately, rather than saying "sequel." Accordingly, we will write "an SQL statement" rather than "a SQL statement.")

SQL is the most common database query language in use today. It is actually more than just a query language, as we have defined the term in the previous chapter. It is a complete database management system (DBMS) language, in that it has the capability not only to manipulate the components of a database, but also to create them in the first place. In particular, SQL has the following components:

1. A *data definition language*, or *DDL*, component, to allow the definition (creation) of database components, such as tables.

2. A *data manipulation language*, or *DML*, component, to allow manipulation of database components.

3. A *data control language*, or *DCL*, component, to provide internal security for a database.

We will discuss the first two components of SQL in some detail in this chapter.

SQL (also known as SEQUEL) was developed by IBM in San Jose, California. The current version of SQL is called SQL-92. However, Microsoft Access, like all other commercial products that support SQL, does not implement the complete SQL-92 standard, and in fact adds some additional features of its own to the language. Since this book uses Microsoft Access, we will discuss the Access version of SQL.

# Access Query Design

In Microsoft Access, queries can be defined in several different ways, but they all come down to an SQL statement in the end. The *Query Wizard* helps create a query by asking the user to respond to a series of questions. This approach is the most user-friendly, but also the least powerful. Access also provides a *Query Design window* with two different views. The *Design View* is shown in Figure 6-1.

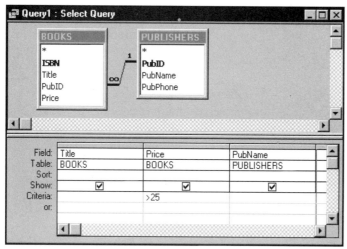

*Figure 6-1. The Access Query Design View*

Query Design View displays table schemes, along with their relationships, and allows the user to select columns to return (projection) and specify criteria for the returned data (selection). Figure 6-1 shows a query definition that joins the BOOKS and PUBLISHERS table and returns the Title, Publisher, and Price of all books whose price is over $25.00.

The Query Design window also has an *SQL View*. Switching to this view shows the SQL statement that corresponds to the Design View query. Figure 6-2 shows the corresponding SQL statement for the query in Figure 6-1.

*Figure 6-2. The Access SQL View of Figure 6-1*

In addition to using the Design View, users can enter SQL statements directly into the SQL View window. In fact, some constructions, such as directly creating the union of two tables in a third table, cannot be accomplished using Design View, and therefore must be entered in SQL View. However, such constructs are rare, and it is often possible to complete a project without the need to enter SQL statements directly.

# Access Query Types

Access supports a variety of query types. Here is a list, along with a brief description of each:

- *Select Query.* These queries return data from one or more tables and display the results in a result table. The table is (usually) *updatable*, which means that we can change the data in the table and the changes will be reflected in the underlying tables. Select queries can also be used to group rows and calculate sums, counts, averages, and other types of totals for these groups.

- *Action Queries.* These are queries that take some form of action. The action queries are:

  — *Make-Table Query.* A query that is designed to create a new table with data from existing tables.

  — *Delete Query.* A query that is used to delete rows from a given table or tables.

  — *Append Query.* A query that is used to append additional rows to the bottom of an existing table.

  — *Update Query.* A query that is used to make changes to one or more rows in a table.

- *SQL Queries.* These are queries that must be entered in SQL View. The SQL queries are:

  — *Union Query.* A query that creates the union of two or more tables.

  — *Pass-Through Query.* A query that passes the uninterpreted SQL statement through to an external database server. (We will not discuss these queries in this book.)

  — *Data-Definition Query.* These are queries that use the DDL component of SQL, such as CREATE TABLE or CREATE INDEX.

- *Crosstab Query.* This is a special type of select query that displays values in a spreadsheet format, with both row and column headings. For instance, we might wish to know how many books are published by each publisher at each price. This is most conveniently pictured as a crosstab query, as shown in Table 6-1.

*Table 6-1. A CROSSTAB Query*

| Price | Total | Big House | Medium House | Small House |
|-------|-------|-----------|--------------|-------------|
| $12.00 | 1 | | 1 | |
| $13.00 | 3 | 2 | 1 | |
| $15.00 | 1 | 1 | | |
| $18.00 | 1 | 1 | | |
| $20.00 | 6 | | 1 | 5 |
| $25.00 | 2 | 2 | | |
| $34.00 | 5 | 1 | 4 | |
| $44.00 | 1 | | 1 | |
| $49.00 | 6 | 1 | 4 | 1 |
| $99.00 | 1 | | 1 | |

- *Parameter Query.* For select or crosstab queries, we may choose to let the user supply certain data at run-time, by filling in a dialog box. This can be done in both Design View and SQL View. When the query asks for information from the user, it is referred to as a *parametrized query*, or *parameter query*.

Finally, we mention that Access allows a select or action query to contain another select query. This is done by nesting SQL SELECT statements, as we will see. The internal query is called a *subquery* of the external query. Access allows multiple levels of subqueries.

# *Why Use SQL?*

As you look through the syntax of the SQL statements in this chapter, you may be struck by the fact that SQL is not a particularly pleasant language. Moreover, as we have said, many features of SQL can be accessed through the Access Query Design Window. So why program in SQL at all?

Here are some reasons:

- There are some important features of SQL that cannot be reached through the Query Design Window. For instance, there is no way to create a union query, a subquery, or an SQL pass-through query (which is a query that passes through Access to an external database server, such as Microsoft SQL Server) using the Query Design Window.

- You cannot use the DDL component of SQL from within the Query Design Window. To use this component, you must write SQL statements directly.

- SQL can be used from within other applications, such as Microsoft Excel, Word, and Visual Basic, to run the Access SQL engine.

- SQL is an industry standard language for querying databases, and as such is useful outside of the Microsoft Access environment.

Despite these important reasons, we suggest that, on first reading, you go lightly over the SQL commands, to get a flavor for how they work. Then you can use this chapter as a reference whenever you need to actually write SQL statements yourself. Fortunately, SQL has relatively few actual commands, which makes it easy to get an overall picture of the language. (For instance, SQL is single-statement oriented. It does not have control structures such as *For... Next...* loops, nor conditional statements such as *If...Then...* statements.)

We should also mention that using the Query Design Window itself is a good way to learn SQL, for you can create a query in the Design Window and then switch to SQL View to see the corresponding SQL statement, obligingly created by Microsoft Access.

# Access SQL

SQL is a nonprocedural language, meaning, as we have seen, that expressions in SQL state what needs to be done, but not how it should be done. This frees the programmer to concentrate on the logic of the SQL program. The Access Query Engine takes care of optimization.

One way to experiment with SQL is to enter a query using Design View and then switch to SQL View to see how Access resolves the query into SQL. It is also worth mentioning that the Help system has complete details on the syntax and options of each SQL statement.

Incidentally, reading the definition of SQL statements can be tiresome. You may wish to just skim over the syntax of each statement and go directly to the examples. The main goal here is to get a reasonable feel for SQL statements and what they can do. You can then look up the correct syntax for the relevant statement when needed (as I do).

## Syntax Conventions

In looking at the SQL commands, we need to establish a consistent syntax. We will employ the following conventions:

- Uppercase words are SQL keywords, and should be typed in as written.

- Words in italics are intended to be replaced with something else. For instance, in the statement:

  CREATE TABLE *TableName*

  we must replace *TableName* with the name of a table.

- An item in square brackets [ ] is optional.

- Braces ({}) are used to (hopefully) clarify the syntax. They are *never* to be included in the statement proper.

- Parentheses should be typed as shown.

- The symbol ::= means "defined as" and the symbol | means *or*. For instance, the line:

  TableElement ::= ColumnDefinition | TableConstraint

  means that a table element is defined as either a column definition or a table constraint.

- The syntax *item, ...* means that you can repeat *item* as often as desired, separated by commas. For instance, in the line:

  CREATE TABLE TableName (TableElement, ...)

  you may repeat the *TableElement* as many times as desired but at least once, since it is not enclosed in square brackets, so it is not optional. (The parentheses must be included.) If a group of items may be repeated, then we use curly braces to enclose those items (for easier reading). For instance, the following expression means that you may repeat the clause *ColName* [ASC | DESC]:

  {*ColName* [ASC|DESC]}, ...

*Notes:*

- You may break the lines in an SQL statement at any point, which is useful for improving readability.

- Each SQL statement should end with a semicolon (although Access SQL does not require this).

- If a table name (or other name) contains a character that SQL regards as illegal, then the name must be enclosed in square brackets. For instance, the forward slash character is illegal in SQL and so the table name BOOK/AUTHOR is also illegal. Thus, it must be enclosed in square brackets: [BOOK/ AUTHOR]. This should not be confused with the use of square brackets to denote optional items in SQL syntax descriptions.

# The DDL Component of Access SQL

We begin by looking at the data definition commands in Access SQL. These commands do not have a counterpart in Query Design View (although, of course, you can perform these functions through the Access graphical environment). Access SQL supports these four DDL commands:

- CREATE TABLE
- ALTER TABLE
- DROP TABLE
- CREATE INDEX

We should mention now that there is some duplication of features in the DDL commands. For instance, you can add an index to a table using either the ALTER TABLE command or the CREATE INDEX command.

## The CREATE TABLE Statement

The CREATE TABLE command has the following syntax:

```
CREATE TABLE TableName
  (ColumnDefinition,...
  [,Multi-ColumnConstraint,...] );
```

In words, the parameters to the CREATE TABLE statement are a table name, followed by one or more column definitions, followed by one or more (optional) multicolumn constraints. Note that the parentheses are also part of the syntax.

### Column definition

A column definition is defined as follows:

```
ColumnDefinition ::= ColumnName
                     DataType[(Size)]
                          [Single-ColumnConstraint]
```

In words, a *ColumnDefinition* is a *ColumnName*, followed by a *DataType* (with size if appropriate), followed by a *Single-ColumnConstraint*.

There are several data types available in Access SQL. For comparison, the list in Table 6-2 includes the corresponding selection in the Access Table Design window. (We have not included all synonyms for the data types.) Note that the SQL type INTEGER corresponds with the Access data type *Long*. Note also that the *Size* option affects only TEXT columns, indicating the length of the field. (If it is omitted, the text length defaults to 255.)

*Table 6-2. Access SQL Data Types*

| SQL Data Type | Table Design Field Type |
|---|---|
| BOOLEAN, LOGICAL, or YES/NO | Yes/No |
| BYTE or INTEGER1 | Number, Field Size = Byte |
| COUNTER or AUTOINCREMENT | AutoNumber, Field Size = Long Integer |
| CURRENCY or MONEY | Currency |
| DATETIME, DATE, or TIME | Date/Time |
| SHORT, INTEGER2, or SMALLINT | Number, Field Size = Integer |
| LONG, INT, INTEGER, or INTEGER4 | Number, Field Size = Long |
| SINGLE, FLOAT4, or REAL | Number, Field Size = Single |
| DOUBLE, FLOAT, FLOAT8, NUMBER, or NUMERIC | Number, Field Size = Double |
| TEXT, ALPHANUMERIC, CHAR, CHARACTER, or STRING | Text |
| LONGTEXT, LONGCHAR, MEMO, or NOTE | Memo |
| LONGBINARY, GENERAL, or OLEOBJECT | (OLE) Object |
| GUID | AutoNumber, Field Size = Replication ID |

## Constraints

Constraint clauses can be used to:

- Designate a primary key

- Designate a foreign key, thus establishing a relationship between two tables

- Force a column to contain only unique values

(In SQL-92, this clauses has two other uses: to disallow NULLs and to restrict allowable values to a specified range.)

There are two types of constraint clauses in a CREATE TABLE command. The single-column constraint is used (as indicated in the syntax) within a column definition. Its syntax is:

```
Single-ColumnConstraint ::=
CONSTRAINT
 IndexName
 [PRIMARY KEY |
 UNIQUE |
    REFERENCES ReferencedTable [(ReferencedColumn,...)] ]
```

The first option designates the column as a primary key, and creates an index file of the name *IndexName* on that column. The second option designates the column as a (candidate) key, and creates a unique index file on that key, by the name *IndexName*. The third option designates the column as a foreign key that references the *ReferencedColumn,...* column(s) of the *ReferencedTable*. The *Refer-*

*encedColumn,...* clause is optional if the referenced table has a primary key, since that key will be the referenced key.

For multicolumn constraints, the CONSTRAINT clause must appear after all column definitions, and has the syntax:

```
Multi-ColumnConstraint ::=
CONSTRAINT
 IndexName
 [PRIMARY KEY (ColumnName,...) |
 UNIQUE (ColumnName,...) |
 FOREIGN KEY (ReferencingColumn,...)
    REFERENCES ReferencedTable [(ReferencedColumn,...)] ]
```

Here are some examples.

Create the *Publishers* table scheme:

```
CREATE TABLE PUBLISHERS
(PubID TEXT(10) CONSTRAINT PrimaryKeyName PRIMARY KEY,
PubName TEXT(100),
PubPhone TEXT(20));
```

Create the *Books* table scheme and link to *Publishers* using PubID as foreign key:

```
CREATE TABLE BOOKS
(ISBN TEXT(13) CONSTRAINT PrimaryKeyName PRIMARY KEY,
TITLE TEXT(100),
PRICE MONEY,
PubID TEXT(10) CONSTRAINT FOREIGN KEY PubID REFERENCES PUBLISHERS
(PubID) );
```

*Notes:*

- The CREATE TABLE statement does not provide a way to create an index with nonunique values. This can be done using the CREATE INDEX statement, however.

- In specifying a foreign key, the CREATE TABLE statement does enable referential integrity rules, but does not allow the option of enabling cascading updates or deletes. (This is one place where Access SQL is weaker than SQL-92, which has a FOREIGN KEY clause that allows the programmer to specify ON UPDATE CASCADE and/or ON DELETE CASCADE.)

## *The ALTER TABLE Statement*

The ALTER TABLE command is used to:

- Add a new column to the table

- Delete a column from a table

- Add or delete single- or multiple-column indices

The syntax for the ALTER TABLE command is:

```
ALTER TABLE
 TableName
 ADD COLUMN ColName ColType[(size)] [Single-ColumnConstraint] |
 DROP COLUMN ColName |
 ADD CONSTRAINT Multi-ColumnConstraint |
 DROP CONSTRAINT MultiColumnIndexName;
```

As you can see, the Single- and Multi-Column Constraint clauses (as defined earlier) can be used here to add or delete (DROP) an index.

*Notes:*

- New columns are added at the beginning of the table, immediately following any primary key columns.

- You cannot delete a column that is part of an index. The index must first be removed using a DROP CONSTRAINT statement (or DROP INDEX).

## The CREATE INDEX Statement

The CREATE INDEX command has the following syntax:

```
CREATE [ UNIQUE ] INDEX IndexName
ON TableName ({ColName [ASC|DESC]},...])
[WITH {PRIMARY | DISALLOW NULL | IGNORE NULL}]
```

where ASC stands for ascending and DESC for descending. Note that:

- The UNIQUE keyword prevents duplicate values in the index.

- WITH PRIMARY designates the primary key and creates a primary index file. In this case, the UNIQUE keyword is redundant.

- WITH DISALLOW NULL disallows NULL values in the key.

- WITH IGNORE NULL allows NULL values in the key, but does not include them in the index file. (Hence, they will be skipped in any searches that use the index.)

*Note:*

The CREATE INDEX command is specific to Access SQL and is not part of the SQL-92 standard.

## The DROP Statement

The syntax for the DROP statement, which is used for deleting tables and indices, is:

```
DROP TABLE TableName | DROP INDEX IndexName ON TableName
```

*Note:*

A table must be closed before it can be deleted or an index can be removed from the table.

# The DML Component of Access SQL

We now turn to the DML component of SQL. The commands we will consider are:

- SELECT
- UNION
- UPDATE
- DELETE
- INSERT INTO
- SELECT INTO
- TRANSFORM
- PARAMETER

Before getting to these statements, however, we must discuss a few relevant points.

## Updatable Queries

In many situations, a query is *updatable*, meaning that we may edit the values in the result table and the changes are automatically reflected in the underlying tables. The details of when this is permitted are fairly involved, but they are completely detailed in the Access Help facility. (This information is not easy to find, however. You can locate it by entering "updatable query" in the Access Answer Wizard and choosing "Determine when I can update data from a query.")

## Joins

Let's begin with a brief discussion of how Access SQL denotes joins. Note that a join clause is not an SQL statement by itself, but must be placed within an SQL statement.

### Inner joins

The INNER JOIN clause in Access SQL actually denotes a $\theta$-join on one or more columns. (See the discussion of joins in Chapter 5, *Query Languages and the Relational Algebra*.) In particular, the syntax is:

```
Table1 INNER JOIN Table2
  ON Table1.Column1 θ₁ Table2.Column1
  [{AND|OR ON Table1.Column2 θ₂ Table2.Column2},...]
```

where each $\theta$ is one of =,<,>,<=,>=, <> (not equal to).

## Outer joins

The syntax for an outer join clause is:

```
Table1 {LEFT [OUTER]} | {RIGHT [OUTER]} JOIN Table2
ON Table1.Column1 θ₁ Table2.Column1
[{AND|OR ON Table1.Column2 θ₂ Table2.Column2},...]
```

where $\theta$ is one of =,<,>,<=,>= or <>. Note that the word OUTER is optional.

## Nested joins

JOIN statements can be nested. Here is an example that joins the BOOKS, AUTHORS, PUBLISHERS, and BOOK/AUTHOR tables and then selects the Title, AuName, and PubName columns. We have indented some lines in the hope of increasing readability. (We will describe the SELECT statement soon.)

```
SELECT Title, AuName, PubName
FROM
AUTHORS INNER JOIN
 (PUBLISHERS INNER JOIN
 (BOOKS INNER JOIN [BOOK/AUTHOR]
 ON BOOKS.ISBN=[BOOK/AUTHOR].ISBN)
 ON PUBLISHERS.PubID = BOOKS.PubID)
 ON AUTHORS.AuID = [BOOK/AUTHOR].AuID;
```

To see how this was constructed, it helps to look at the relationships between the tables involved. Figure 6-3 shows a portion of the relationships window in Access.

*Figure 6-3. A portion of the Relationships window in Access*

One way to create the join statement above is to work from the inside out. We first join BOOKS and BOOK/AUTHOR by the statement:

```
(BOOKS INNER JOIN [BOOK/AUTHOR]
      ON BOOKS.ISBN=[BOOK/AUTHOR].ISBN)
```

We then join this to PUBLISHERS on the PubID column:

```
(PUBLISHERS INNER JOIN
 (BOOKS INNER JOIN [BOOK/AUTHOR]
 ON BOOKS.ISBN=[BOOK/AUTHOR].ISBN)
 ON PUBLISHERS.PubID = BOOKS.PubID)
```

and finally we join this to AUTHORS on the AuID column.

### Self-joins

A table can be joined to itself, resulting in a self-join. In order to do this, SQL requires the use of the AS *AliasName* syntax. For instance, we can write

```
BOOKS INNER JOIN BOOKS AS BOOKS2 ON ...
```

The least confusing way to think of this statement is as though Access creates a second copy of the BOOKS table and calls it BOOKS2. We can now refer to the columns of BOOKS as BOOKS.*ColumnName* or BOOKS2.*ColumnName*.

### Notes:

- An outer join may be nested inside an inner join, but an inner join may not be nested inside an outer join.

- We may use Access expressions, which involve functions (such as *Left$*, *Len*, *Trim$*, and *Instr*) in SQL statements (even though the "official" syntax does not describe this).

- In Access, we can define relationships between tables. However, these relationships have no effect on SQL statements. Thus, an INNER JOIN statement does not require that a relationship already exist between the participating tables. Relationships are used in Design View, however, and translate into INNER JOIN statements. For example, if we add BOOKS and PUBLISHERS to the Query Design View window, move Title and PubName to the Design grid and then view the SQL equivalent, we will see an INNER JOIN clause in the SQL statement.

## The SELECT Statement

The SELECT statement is the workhorse of SQL commands (as you can tell by the length of our discussion on this statement). The statement returns a table, and can perform both of the relational algebra operations *selection* and *projection*. The syntax of the SELECT statement is:

```
SELECT [predicate] ReturnColumnDescription,...
FROM TableExpression
[WHERE RowCondition]
[GROUP BY GroupByCriteria]
[HAVING GroupCriteria]
[ORDER BY OrderByCriteria]
```

Let us describe the various components of this statement. We note immediately that the keyword SELECT is in some ways unfortunate, since it denotes the relational algebra operation of projection, not selection! It is the WHERE clause that performs selection.

### Predicate

The *predicate* is used to describe how to handle duplicate return rows. It can have one of the following values: ALL, DISTINCT, DISTINCTROW, or TOP.

The (default) option ALL returns all qualifying rows, including duplicates. If there is more than one qualifying row with the same values in all of the columns that are requested in the *ReturnColumnDescription*, then the option DISTINCT returns only the first such row. The

```
TOP number [PERCENT]
```

or

```
TOP percent [PERCENT]
```

option returns the top number (or percent) of rows in the sort order determined by the ORDER BY clause.

The DISTINCTROW option can be a bit confusing, so let us see if we can straighten it out. The Access Help system says that the DISTINCTROW option "Omits data based on entire duplicate records, not just duplicate fields." It doesn't say how this is done. Microsoft Technet is a bit less vague:

> In contrast, DISTINCTROW is unique to Microsoft Access. It causes a query to return unique records, not unique values. For example, if 10 customers are named Jones, a query based on the SQL statement "SELECT DISTINCTROW Name FROM Customers" returns all 10 records with Jones in the Name field. The major reason for adding the DISTINCTROW reserved word to Microsoft Access SQL is to support updatable semi-joins, such as one-to-many joins in which the output fields all come from the table on the "one" side. DISTINCTROW is specified by default in Microsoft Access queries and is ignored in queries in which it has no effect. You should not delete the DISTINCTROW reserved word from the SQL dialog box.

The intended purpose of DISTINCTROW is simple. DISTINCTROW applies only when the FROM clause involves more than one table. Consider this statement:

```
SELECT ALL PubName
FROM PUBLISHERS INNER JOIN BOOKS
ON PUBLISHERS.PubID = BOOKS.PubID;
```

Since there are many books published by the same publisher, the result table tblALL shown in Table 6-3 has many duplicate publisher names.

*Table 6-3. The tblALL Table*

| PubName |
| --- |
| Small House |
| Small House |
| Small House |

*Table 6-3. The tblALL Table (continued)*

| PubName |
|---|
| Small House |
| Big House |
| Big House |
| Big House · |
| Big House |
| Big House |
| Big House |
| Alpha Press |
| Alpha Press |
| Alpha Press |
| Alpha Press |

To remove duplicate publisher names, we can include the DISTINCT keyword. Thus, the statement

```
SELECT DISTINCT PubName
FROM PUBLISHERS INNER JOIN BOOKS
ON PUBLISHERS.PubID = BOOKS.PubID;
```

produces the table tblDISTINCT that is shown in Table 6-4.

*Table 6-4. The tblDISTINCT Table*

| PubName |
|---|
| Alpha Press |
| Big House |
| Small House |

Now consider what happens if the PUBLISHERS table is changed, by adding a new publisher with the same name as an existing publisher (but a different PubID and phone), as we have done in Table 6-5. The previous DISTINCT statement will give the same result table as before, thus leaving out the new publisher.

*Table 6-5. The PUBLISHERS (Altered) Table*

| PubID | PubName | PubPhone |
|---|---|---|
| 1 | Big House | 123-456-7890 |
| 2 | Alpha Press | 999-999-9999 |
| 3 | Small House | 714-000-0000 |
| 4 | Small House | 555-123-1111 |

What is called for is a selection criterion that will return both publisher names simply because they come from different rows of the PUBLISHERS table. This is the purpose of DISTINCTROW. Thus, the statement:

```
SELECT DISTINCT PubName
FROM PUBLISHERS INNER JOIN BOOKS
ON PUBLISHERS.PubID = BOOKS.PubID;
```

produces the result table tblDISTINCTROW shown in Table 6-6 (note that we also had to add a book to the BOOKS table, with PubID 4).

*Table 6-6. The tblDISTINCTROW Table*

| PubName |
| --- |
| Small House |
| Big House |
| Alpha Press |
| Small House |

We can now describe how DISTINCTROW works. Consider the following SQL skeleton:

```
SELECT DISTINCTROW ColumnsRequested
FROM TablesClause
```

Here *ColumnsRequested* is a list of columns requested by the statement and *TablesClause* is a join of tables. Let us refer to a table mentioned in *TablesClause* as a *return table* if at least one of its columns is mentioned in *ColumnsRequested*. Thus, in the statement:

```
SELECT DISTINCTROW PubName
FROM PUBLISHERS INNER JOIN BOOKS
ON PUBLISHERS.PubID = BOOKS.PubID;
```

PUBLISHERS is a return table but BOOKS is not. Here is how DISTINCTROW works:

1. Form the join(s) described in *TablesClause*.

2. Project the resulting table onto all of the columns from all return tables (not just the columns requested). Put another way, remove all columns that are not part of a return table.

3. Remove all duplicate rows, where two rows are considered duplicates if they are composed of the same rows from each result table. It is not the values that are compared, but the actual rows. It is necessary to add this because two different rows may have identical values in an Access table.

Let us illustrate with a simple example.

Consider the following tables:

| $A_1$ | $A_2$ |
|---|---|
| a1 | x |
| a2 | link |
| a3 | link |

| $B_1$ | $B_2$ | $B_3$ |
|---|---|---|
| b1 | y | z |
| b2 | link | link2 |

| $C_1$ | $C_2$ | $C_3$ |
|---|---|---|
| c1 | t | link2 |
| c2 | v | link2 |
| c3 | a | x |

The statement

```
SELECT *
FROM
(Temp1 INNER JOIN Temp2 ON Temp1.A2 = Temp2.B2)
INNER JOIN Temp3 ON Temp2.B3 = Temp3.C3;
```

gives the result table tblALL:

| $A_1$ | $A_2$ | $B_1$ | $B_2$ | $B_3$ | $C_1$ | $C_2$ | $C_3$ |
|---|---|---|---|---|---|---|---|
| a3 | link | b2 | link | link2 | c2 | v | link2 |
| a3 | link | b2 | link | link2 | c1 | t | link2 |
| a2 | link | b2 | link | link2 | c2 | v | link2 |
| a2 | link | b2 | link | link2 | c1 | t | link2 |

Now let us add the DISTINCTROW keyword and select a single column from just tblA:

```
SELECT DISTINCTROW A1
FROM
(Temp1 INNER JOIN Temp2 ON Temp1.A2 = Temp2.B2)
INNER JOIN Temp3 ON Temp2.B3 = Temp3.C3;
```

Now we consider the projection onto the rows of the only return table (tblA):

| $A_1$ | $A_2$ |
|---|---|
| a3 | link |
| a3 | link |
| a2 | link |
| a2 | link |

It is clear that the first two rows of this table are the same row of tblA, so they produce only one row in the final result table. The same holds for the last two rows. Hence, the result table is:

| $A_1$ |
| --- |
| $a_2$ |
| $a_3$ |

Let us now change this by requesting a column from tblC, thus making it a return table as well:

```
SELECT DISTINCTROW A1,C1
FROM
(Temp1 INNER JOIN Temp2 ON Temp1.A2 = Temp2.B2)
INNER JOIN Temp3 ON Temp2.B3 = Temp3.C3;
```

The projection onto return table rows is now:

| $A_1$ | $A_2$ | $C_1$ | $C_2$ | $C_3$ |
| --- | --- | --- | --- | --- |
| a3 | link | c2 | v | link2 |
| a3 | link | c1 | t | link2 |
| a2 | link | c2 | v | link2 |
| a2 | link | c1 | t | link2 |

These row "pairs" are all distinct. In fact:

- Row 1 comes from row 1 of tblA and row 2 of tblC

- Row 2 comes from row 1 of tblA and row 1 of tblC

- Row 3 comes from row 2 of tblA and row 2 of tblC

- Row 4 comes from row 2 of tblA and row 1 of tblC

It follows that the return table includes all rows:

| $A_1$ | $C_1$ |
| --- | --- |
| a2 | c1 |
| a2 | c2 |
| a3 | c1 |
| a3 | c2 |

Finally, consider what happens if we change the third row of tblA to:

| $A_1$ | $A_2$ |
|-------|-------|
| a1    | x     |
| a2    | link  |
| a2    | link  |

Running the first DISTINCTROW statement:

```
SELECT DISTINCTROW A1
FROM
(Temp1 INNER JOIN Temp2 ON Temp1.A2 = Temp2.B2)
INNER JOIN Temp3 ON Temp2.B3 = Temp3.C3;
```

gives:

| $A_1$ |
|-------|
| a2    |
| a2    |

Comparing this to the previous result table DISTINCTROW A1 emphasizes the fact that, even though the second and third rows of tblNewA are identical in values, they are different rows, so they both contribute to the final result table. If we were to replace the DISTINCTROW keyword with the word DISTINCT, then the result table would have only one row, since then it is the values in each row that form the basis for comparison.

Of course, this would not be an issue if all tables had a key, since then the values in a row would determine the row. You may see now why, some time ago, we recommended against having two different rows with the same column values, even though Access permits this possibility (but true relational databases do not).

Notice what happens if all tables mentioned in the *TablesClause* are return tables. This would happen, for instance, if there is only one table in *TablesClause*. In this case, the projection does nothing and since each row of the *TablesClause* result table must come from a distinct combination of rows of the result tables, we deduce that DISTINCTROW has exactly the same effect as ALL, or, to put it another way, DISTINCTROW is ignored.

It is useful to compare DISTINCTROW and DISTINCT. We can see that the only difference is that a DISTINCT statement will return distinct values, rather than values from distinct rows. However, these will be the same if the requested columns from each return table uniquely identify their rows.

Let us illustrate with the PUBLISHERS example. Suppose we return a key (PubID) for PUBLISHERS, as in the statement:

```
SELECT DISTINCTROW PubID, PubName
FROM PUBLISHERS INNER JOIN BOOKS
ON PUBLISHERS.PubID = BOOKS.PubID;
```

Then the result table will return all PUBLISHERS rows that have at least one book in the BOOKS table, as Table 6-7 shows.

*Table 6-7. Publishers with at Least One Book in BOOKS*

| PubID | PubName |
|-------|-------------|
| 3 | Small House |
| 1 | Big House |
| 2 | Alpha Press |
| 4 | Small House |

This is, in fact, the semi-join

PUBLISHERS *semi-join*~PUBLISHERS.PubID=BOOKS.PubID~ BOOKS

Recall that the semi-join is the projection of the join onto one of the tables (in this case, the PUBLISHERS table). Thus, as Microsoft itself says, the purpose of the DISTINCTROW option is to return an updatable semi-join!

Of course, the same statement with DISTINCT in place of DISTINCTROW will return the same result table. However, there is one big difference. Since DISTINCT statements can completely hide the origin of the returned values, it would be disaster if Access allowed such a result table to be updatable—and indeed it does not. For instance, recall the table tblDISTINCT discussed earlier and shown in Table 6-8.

*Table 6-8. The tblDISTINCT Table*

| PubName |
|-------------|
| Alpha Press |
| Big House |
| Small House |

Changing the name of Small House in this result table would be disastrous, since we would not know which Small House was being affected!

On the other hand, the result table of the DISTINCTROW statement has a "representative" from each row of the PUBLISHERS table, as Table 6-9 shows. Hence, while it still may not be a good idea to change this particular table, since we cannot tell which Small House is which, it would be reasonable to make a change to both names, for instance.

*Table 6-9. The tblDISTINCTROW Table*

| PubName |
| --- |
| Small House |
| Big House |
| Alpha Press |
| Small House |

More generally, Access does not permit updating of the result table of a DISTINCT statement, but it does permit updating of the result table for a DISTINCTROW statement.

Finally, we mention that Microsoft Access includes the DISTINCTROW keyword by default when you create a query using the Access Query Design Window.

### ReturnColumnDescription

The *ReturnColumnDescription* describes the columns, or combination of columns, to return. It can be any of the following:

- \* (indicating all columns)
- The name of a column
- An expression involving column names, enclosed in brackets, along with strings and string operators; for example, [PubID] & "-" & [Title]

(Note that, according to the syntax of the SELECT statement, the *ReturnColumnDescription* can be repeated as many times as desired.)

When two returned columns (from different tables) have the same name, it is necessary to *qualify* the column names using the table names. For instance, to qualify the PubID column name, we write BOOKS.PubID and PUBLISHERS.PubID. We can also write BOOKS.\* to indicate all columns of the BOOKS table.

Finally, each *ReturnColumnDescription* can end with:

```
[AS AliasName]
```

to give the return column a (new) name.

For example, the following statement:

```
SELECT DISTINCTROW
[ISBN] & " from " & [PubName] AS [ISBN from PubName]
FROM PUBLISHERS INNER JOIN BOOKS ON PUBLISHERS.PubID = BOOKS.PubID;
```

returns a single column result table ISBN-PUB, as shown in Table 6-10.

*Table 6-10. The ISBN-PUB Table*

| ISBN from PubName |
|---|
| 0-12-345678-9 from Small House |
| 0-11-345678-9 from Small House |
| 0-321-32132-1 from Small House |
| 0-55-123456-9 from Small House |
| 0-12-333433-3 from Big House |
| 0-103-45678-9 from Big House |
| 0-91-335678-7 from Big House |
| 0-99-999999-9 from Big House |
| 1-22-233700-0 from Big House |
| 1-1111-1111-1 from Big House |
| 0-91-045678-5 from Alpha Press |
| 0-555-55555-9 from Alpha Press |
| 0-99-777777-7 from Alpha Press |
| 0-123-45678-0 from Alpha Press |

Not only does the AS *AliasName* option allow us to name a "compound column" as above, but it also allows us to rename duplicate column names without having to qualify the names.

### FROM TableExpression

The FROM clause specifies the tables (or queries) from which the SELECT statement is to take its rows. The expression *TableExpression* can be a single table name, several table names separated by commas, or a join clause. The *TableExpression* may also include the AS *AliasName* syntax for table name aliases.

When tables are separated by commas in the FROM clause, a Cartesian product is formed. For example, the statement:

```
SELECT *
FROM AUTHORS, PUBLISHERS;
```

will produce the Cartesian product of the two tables.

### WHERE RowCondition

The *RowCondition* is any Access expression that specifies which rows are included in the result table. Expressions can involve column names, constants, arithmetic (=, <, >, <=, >=, <>, BETWEEN) and logical (AND, OR, XOR, NOT, IMP) relations, as well as functions. Here are some examples:

- WHERE Title LIKE "F*"

- WHERE Len(Trim(Title)) > 10

- WHERE Instr(Title, "Wind") > 0 AND Len(Trim(Title)) > 10

- WHERE DateSold = #5/21/96#

Note that dates are enclosed in number signs (#) and the strings are enclosed in quotation marks (" ").

### GROUP BY GroupByCriteria

The GROUP BY option allows records to be grouped together for the purpose of computing the value of an *aggregate function* (*Avg, Count, Min, Max, Sum, First, Last, StDev, StDevP, Var,* and *VarP*). It is equivalent to creating a so-called *totals query*. The *GroupByCriteria* can contain the names of up to ten columns. The order of the column names in determines the grouping levels, from highest to lowest.

For example, the following statement lists each publisher by name, along with the minimum price of each publisher's books in the BOOKS table:

```
SELECT PUBLISHERS.PubName, MIN(Price) AS [Minimum Price]
FROM PUBLISHERS INNER JOIN BOOKS
ON PUBLISHERS.PubID = BOOKS.PubID
GROUP BY PUBLISHERS.PubName;
```

The result table appears in Table 6-11.

*Table 6-11. Each Publisher's Least Expensive Book*

| PubName | Minimum Price |
|---|---|
| Alpha Press | $12.00 |
| Big House | $15.00 |
| Small House | $22.95 |

### HAVING GroupCriteria

The HAVING option in used in conjunction with the GROUP BY option and allows us to specify a criterion, in terms of aggregate functions, for deciding which data to display.

For example, the following command is the same as the previous one, with the additional HAVING option that restricts the return table to those publishers whose minimum price is less than $20.00:

```
SELECT PUBLISHERS.PubName, SUM(Price)
FROM PUBLISHERS INNER JOIN BOOKS
ON PUBLISHERS.PubID = BOOKS.PubID
GROUP BY PUBLISHERS.PubName;
HAVING MIN(Price)<20.00
```

The result table is shown in Table 6-12.

*Table 6-12. Each Publisher's Cheapest Book Under $20.00*

| PubName | Minimum Price |
|---------|---------------|
| Alpha Press | $12.00 |
| Big House | $15.00 |

Note that the WHERE clause restricts which rows participate in the grouping, and hence contribute to the value of the aggregate functions, whereas the HAVING clause affects only which values are displayed.

### ORDER BY OrderByCriteria

The ORDER BY option describes the order in which to return the rows in the return table. The *OrderByCriteria* has the form:

```
OrderByCriteria ::= {ColumnName [ASC | DESC ]},...
```

In other words, it is just a list of columns to use in the ordering. Rows are sorted first by the first column listed, then rows with identical values in the first column are sorted by the values in the second column, and so on.

## *The UNION Statement*

The UNION statement is used to create the union of two or more tables. The syntax is:

```
[TABLE] Query
{UNION [ALL] [TABLE] Query},...
```

where *Query* is either a SELECT statement, the name of a stored query, or the name of a stored table preceded by the TABLE keyword. The ALL option forces Access to include all records. Without this option, Access does not include duplicate rows. The use of ALL increases performance as well, and is thus recommended even when there are no duplicate rows.

### Example

The following statement takes the union of all rows of BOOKS and those rows of NEWBOOKS that have Price > $25.00, sorting the result table by Title:

```
TABLE BOOKS
UNION ALL
SELECT * FROM NEWBOOKS WHERE Price > 25.00
ORDER BY Title;
```

*Notes:*

- All queries in a UNION operation must return the same number of fields. However, the fields do not need to have the same size or data type.

- Columns are combined in the union by their order in the query clauses, not by their names.

- Aliases may be used in the first SELECT statement (if there is one) to change the names of returned columns.

- An ORDER BY clause can be used at the end of the last Query to order the returned data. Use the column names from the first Query.

- GROUP BY and/or HAVING clauses can be used in each query argument to group the returned data.

- The result table of a UNION is not updatable.

- UNION is not part of SQL-92.

## *The UPDATE Statement*

The UPDATE statement is equivalent to an Update query, and is used for updating data in a table or tables. The syntax is:

```
UPDATE TableName | QueryName
SET NewValueExpression,...
WHERE Criteria;
```

The WHERE clause is used to restrict updating to qualifying rows.

### *Example*

The following example updates the Price column in the BOOKS table with new prices from a table called NEWPRICES that has an ISBN and a Price column:

```
UPDATE
BOOKS INNER JOIN NEWPRICES ON BOOKS.ISBN = NEWPRICES.ISBN
SET BOOKS.Price = NEWPRICES.Price
WHERE BOOKS.Price <> NEWPRICES.Price;
```

Note that UPDATE does not produce a result table. To determine which rows will be updated, first run a corresponding SELECT query, as in:

```
SELECT * FROM
BOOKS INNER JOIN NEWPRICES ON BOOKS.ISBN = NEWPRICES.ISBN
WHERE BOOKS.Price <> NEWPRICES.Price
```

# The DELETE Statement

The DELETE statement is equivalent to a Delete query and is used to delete rows form a table. Here is the syntax:

```
DELETE
FROM TableName
WHERE Criteria
```

*Criteria* is used to determine which rows to delete.

This command can be used to delete all data from a table, but it will not delete the structure of the table. Use DROP for that purpose.

You can use DELETE to remove records from tables that have a one-to-many relationship. If cascading delete is enabled when you delete a row from the one side of the relationship, all matching rows are deleted from the many side. The action of the DELETE statement is not reversable. Always make backups before deleting! You can run a SELECT operation before DELETE to see which rows will be affected by the DELETE operation.

# The INSERT INTO Statement

The INSERT INTO statement is designed to insert new rows into a table. This can be done by specifying the values of a new row using this syntax:

```
INSERT INTO Target [(FieldName,...)]
VALUES (Value1,...)
```

If you do not specify the *FieldName*(s), then you must include values for each field in the table.

Let's look at several examples of the INSERT INTO statement. The following statement inserts a new row into the BOOKS table:

```
INSERT INTO BOOKS
VALUES ("1-000-00000-0", "SQL is Fun",1,25.00);
```

The following statement inserts a new row into the BOOKS table. The Price and PubID columns have NULL values.

```
INSERT INTO BOOKS (ISBN,Title)
VALUES ("1-1111-1111-1","Gone Fishing");
```

To insert multiple rows, use this syntax:

```
INSERT INTO Target [(FieldName,...)]
SELECT FieldName,...
FROM TableExpression
```

In both syntaxes, *Target* is the name of the table or query into which rows are to be inserted. In the case of a query, that query must be updatable and all updates will be reflected in the underlying tables. *TableExpression* is the name of the table from which records are inserted, or the name of a saved query, or a SELECT statement.

Assume that NEWBOOKS is a table with three fields: ISBN, PubID, and Price. The following statement inserts rows from BOOKS into NEWBOOKS. It inserts only those books with Price > $20.00.

```
INSERT INTO NEWBOOKS
SELECT ISBN, PubID, Price
FROM BOOKS
WHERE Price>20;
```

*Note:*

Text field values must be enclosed in double quotation marks (" ").

## The SELECT... INTO Statement

The SELECT... INTO statement is equivalent to a MakeTable query. It makes a new table and inserts data from other tables. The syntax is:

```
SELECT FieldName,...
INTO NewTableName
FROM Source
WHERE RowCondition
ORDER BY OrderCondition
```

*FieldName* is the name of the field to be copied into the new table. *Source* is the name of the table from which data is taken. This can also be the name of a query or a join statement.

For example, the following statement creates a new table called EXPENSIVE-BOOKS and includes books from the BOOKS table that cost more than $45.00:

```
SELECT Title, ISBN
INTO EXPENSIVEBOOKS
FROM BOOKS
WHERE Price>45
ORDER BY Title;
```

*Notes:*

- This statement is unique to Access SQL.

- This statement does not create indicies in the new table.

# TRANSFORM

The TRANSFORM statement (which is not part of SQL-92) is designed to create crosstab queries. The basic syntax is:

```
TRANSFORM AggregateFunction
SelectStatement
PIVOT ColumnHeadingsColumn [IN (Value,...)]
```

The *AggregateFunction* is one of Access's aggregate functions (*Avg*, *Count*, *Min*, *Max*, *Sum*, *First*, *Last*, *StDev*, *StDevP*, *Var*, and *VarP*). The *ColumnHeadings-Column* is the column that is pivoted to give the column headings in the crosstab result table. The *Values* in the IN clause option specify fixed column headings.

The *SelectStatement* is a select statement that uses the GROUP BY clause, with some modifications. In particular, the select statement must have at least two GROUP BY columns and no HAVING clause.

As an example, suppose we wish to display the total number of books from each publisher by price. The SELECT statement:

```
SELECT PubName, Price, COUNT(Title) AS Total
FROM PUBLISHERS INNER JOIN BOOKS
  ON PUBLISHERS.PubID=BOOKS.PubID
  GROUP BY PubName, Price;
```

whose result table is shown in Table 6-13, doesn't really give the information in the desired form. For instance, it is difficult to tell how many books cost $20.00. (Remember, this small table is just for illustration.)

*Table 6-13. Book Prices by Publisher*

| PubName | Price | Total |
|---|---|---|
| Big House | $15.00 | 1 |
| Big House | $20.00 | 1 |
| Big House | $25.00 | 2 |
| Big House | $49.00 | 1 |
| Medium House | $12.00 | 2 |
| Medium House | $20.00 | 1 |
| Medium House | $34.00 | 1 |
| Medium House | $49.00 | 1 |
| Small House | $49.00 | 1 |

We can transform this into a crosstab query in two steps:

1. Add a TRANSFORM clause at the top and move the aggregate function whose value is to be computed to that clause.

2. Add a PIVOT line at the bottom and move the column whose values will form the column headings to that clause. Also, delete the reference to this column in the SELECT clause.

This gives:

```
TRANSFORM COUNT(Title)
SELECT Price
FROM PUBLISHERS INNER JOIN BOOKS
  ON PUBLISHERS.PubID=BOOKS.PubID
GROUP BY Price
PIVOT PubName;
```

with the result table shown in Table 6-14.

*Table 6-14. A Cross-Tablulation of Book Prices by Publisher*

| Price | Big House | Medium House | Small House |
|-------|-----------|--------------|-------------|
| $12.00 |          | 2            |             |
| $15.00 | 1        |              |             |
| $20.00 | 1        | 1            |             |
| $25.00 | 2        |              |             |
| $34.00 |          | 1            |             |
| $49.00 | 1        | 1            | 1           |

We can group the rows by the values in more than one than one column. For example, suppose that the BOOKS table also had a DISCOUNT column that gave the discount from the regular price of the book (as a percentage). Then by including the DISCOUNT column in the SELECT and GROUP BY clauses, we get

```
TRANSFORM COUNT(Title)
SELECT Price, Discount
FROM PUBLISHERS INNER JOIN BOOKS
  ON PUBLISHERS.PubID=BOOKS.PubID
GROUP BY Price, Discount
PIVOT PubName;
```

for which the result table is shown in Table 6-15.

*Table 6-15. Book Prices and Discount by Publisher*

| Price | Discount | Big House | Medium House | Small House |
|-------|----------|-----------|--------------|-------------|
| $12.00 | 30%     |           | 2            |             |
| $15.00 | 20%     | 1         |              |             |
| $20.00 | 20%     |           | 1            |             |
| $20.00 | 30%     | 1         |              |             |
| $25.00 | 10%     | 1         |              |             |

*Table 6-15. Book Prices and Discount by Publisher (continued)*

| Price | Discount | Big House | Medium House | Small House |
|-------|----------|-----------|--------------|-------------|
| $25.00 | 20% | 1 | | |
| $34.00 | 10% | | 1 | |
| $49.00 | 10% | 1 | | |
| $49.00 | 30% | | 1 | 1 |

In this case, each row represents a unique price/discount pair.

A crosstab can also include additional row aggregates by adding additional aggregate functions to the SELECT clause, as follows:

```
TRANSFORM COUNT(Title)
SELECT Price, COUNT(Price) AS Count, SUM(Price) AS Sum
FROM PUBLISHERS INNER JOIN BOOKS
  ON PUBLISHERS.PubID=BOOKS.PubID
GROUP BY Price
PIVOT PubName;
```

which gives the result table shown in Table 6-16.

*Table 6-16. Aggregating Results in a Crosstab Table*

| Price | Count | Sum | Big House | Medium House | Small House |
|-------|-------|-----|-----------|--------------|-------------|
| $12.00 | 2 | $24.00 | | 2 | |
| $15.00 | 1 | $15.00 | 1 | | |
| $20.00 | 2 | $40.00 | 1 | 1 | |
| $25.00 | 2 | $50.00 | 2 | | |
| $34.00 | 1 | $34.00 | | 1 | |
| $49.00 | 3 | $147.00 | 1 | 1 | 1 |

Finally, by including fixed column names, we can reorder or omit columns from the crosstab result table. For instance, the next statement is just like the previous one except for the PIVOT clause:

```
TRANSFORM COUNT(Title)
SELECT Price, COUNT(Price) AS Count, SUM(Price) AS Sum
FROM PUBLISHERS INNER JOIN BOOKS
  ON PUBLISHERS.PubID=BOOKS.PubID
GROUP BY Price
PIVOT PubName IN ("Small House", "Medium House");
```

The result table is shown in Table 6-17. Note that the order of the columns has changed and Big House is not shown.

*Table 6-17. Omitting Columns from a Crosstab Table*

| Price | Count | Sum | Small House | Medium House |
|---|---|---|---|---|
| $12.00 | 2 | $24.00 | | 2 |
| $15.00 | 1 | $15.00 | | |
| $20.00 | 2 | $40.00 | | 1 |
| $25.00 | 2 | $50.00 | | |
| $34.00 | 1 | $34.00 | | 1 |
| $49.00 | 3 | $147.00 | 1 | 1 |

## Subqueries

SQL permits the use of SELECT statements within the following:

- Other SELECT statements
- SELECT...INTO statements
- INSERT...INTO statements
- DELETE statements
- UPDATE statements

The internal SELECT statement is referred to as a *subquery*, and is generally used in the WHERE clause of the main query.

The syntax of a subquery takes three possible forms, described below.

### Syntax 1

```
Comparison [ANY | SOME | ALL] (SQLStatement)
```

where *Comparison* is an expression followed by a comparison relation that compares the expression with the return value(s) of the subquery. This syntax is used to compare a value against the values obtained from another query.

For example, the following statement returns all titles and prices of books from the BOOKS table, whose prices are greater than the maximum price of all books in the table BOOKS2:

```
SELECT Title, Price
FROM BOOKS
WHERE Price > (SELECT Max(Price) FROM BOOKS2);
```

Note that since the subquery returns only one value, we do not need to use any of the keywords ANY, SOME, or ALL.

The following statement selects all BOOKS titles and prices for books that are more expensive than ALL of the books published by Big House:

```
SELECT Title, Price
FROM BOOKS
WHERE Price > ALL
   (SELECT Price
   FROM PUBLISHERS INNER JOIN BOOKS ON PUBLISHERS.PubID =
   BOOKS.PubID
   WHERE PubName = "Big House");
```

Note that ANY and SOME have the same meaning and return all choices that make the comparison true for at least one value returned by the subquery. For example, if we were to replace ALL by SOME in the previous example, the return table would consist of all book titles and prices for books that are more expensive than the cheapest book published by Big House.

### Syntax 2

```
Expression [NOT] IN (SQLStatement)
```

This syntax is used to look up a column value in the result table of another query.

For example, the following statement returns all book titles from BOOKS that do *not* appear in the table BOOKS2:

```
SELECT Title
FROM BOOKS
WHERE Title NOT IN (SELECT Title FROM BOOKS2);
```

### Syntax 3

```
[NOT] EXISTS (SQLStatement)
```

This syntax is used to check whether an item exists (is returned) in the subquery.

For example, the following statement selects all publishers that do not have books in the BOOKS table:

```
SELECT PubName
FROM PUBLISHERS
WHERE NOT EXISTS
   (SELECT * FROM BOOKS WHERE BOOKS.PubID =
   PUBLISHERS.PubID);
```

Notice that the PUBLISHERS table is referenced in the subquery. This causes Access to evaluate the subquery once for each value of PUBLISHERS.PubID in the PUBLISHERS table.

*Notes:*

- When using Syntax 1 or 2, the subquery must return a single column or an error will occur.

- The SELECT statement that constitutes the subquery follows the same format and rules as any other SELECT statement. However, it must be enclosed in parentheses.

## Parameters

Access SQL allows the use of *parameters* to obtain information from the user when the query is run. The PARAMETERS line must be the first line in the statement, and has the syntax:

```
PARAMETERS Name DataType,...
```

An example will illustrate the technique.

The following statement will prompt the user for a portion of the title of a book, and return all books from BOOKS with that string in the title. Note the semicolon at the end of the PARAMETERS line.

```
PARAMETERS [Enter portion of title] TEXT;
SELECT *
FROM BOOKS
WHERE Instr(Title, [Enter portion of title]) > 0;
```

The function *Instr(Text1, Text2)* returns the first location of the text string *Text2* within the text string *Text1*. Note that *Name* is repeated in the WHERE clause, and will be filled in by the value that the user enters as a result of *Name* appearing in the PARAMETERS clause.

# 7

# *Database System Architecture*

## *Why Program?*

There is no doubt that SQL is a powerful language—as far as it goes. However, it is a somewhat unfriendly language and it lacks the sophisticated control structures of a more traditional language, such as *For...Next...* loops and *If...Then...* statements.

This is not really a problem, since SQL is designed for a very specific purpose, related to database component creation and manipulation. SQL is not designed to provide an overall programming environment for Microsoft Access itself. This role is played by Visual Basic for Applications, or VBA.

VBA is the macro, or scripting language, for all of the major Microsoft Office products: Microsoft Access, Excel, PowerPoint, and Word (starting with Word 97). It is a very powerful programming language that gives the programmer access to the full features of these applications, as well as the means to make the applications work together.

One of the major components of VBA is its support for the Data Access Objects model, or *DAO*. DAO is the programming language interface for the Jet database management system (DBMS) that underlies Microsoft Access. It provides a more-or-less object-oriented data definition language (DDL) and data manipulation language (DML), thereby allowing the VBA programmer to define the structure of a database and manipulate its data.

Of course, it is a natural question to wonder why you would want to use DAO, and VBA in general, rather than using the built-in graphical interface of Microsoft Access. The answer is simple. While the graphical interface is very easy to use, and is quite adequate for many purposes, it is simply not as powerful as the programming languages. The database creator gains more power and flexibility over the database by directly manipulating the basic objects of the database (such as the tables, queries, relationships, indexes, and so on) through programming.

As a simple example, there is no way to get a list of the fields of a given table (i.e., the table's *table scheme*) using the Access graphical interface. However, this is a simple matter using programming techniques. The following short program:

```
Dim db As DATABASE
Dim tdf As TableDef
Dim fld As Field

Set db = CurrentDb
Set tdf = db.TableDefs("BOOKS")
For Each fld In tdf.Fields
    Debug.Print fld.Name
Next
```

displays the following list of fields for the BOOKS table in the Debug window:

```
ISBN
Title
PubID
Price
```

This is a good place to discuss the relationship between DAO and SQL. The fact is that DAO both uses SQL and overlaps SQL. That is, there are many commands in DAO that can accept an SQL statement as an argument. For instance, the following VBA code opens a recordset (discussed later in the book) using an SQL statement to define the records in the recordset:

```
' Get current database
Set dbs = CurrentDb()

' Write SQL statement
strSelect = "Select * FROM Books WHERE Price=10"

' Open recordset using SQL statement
Set rsCheap = dbs.OpenRecordset(strSelect)
```

On the other hand, DAO overlaps SQL in the sense that many actions can be performed using either language. For instance, a table can be created using either the SQL statement CREATE TABLE or the DAO method *CreateTable*. The choice is up to the programmer.

Our main goal in the remaining portion of this book is to discuss the DAO model. Before doing so, however, we need to set the stage by discussing the overall architecture of a database management system, and of the Jet DMBS in particular, so we can put DAO in its proper context. We will do so in this chapter, and also take a quick peek at DAO programming. In Chapter 8, *The Basics of Programming in VBA*, we will present a brief introduction to programming in Visual Basic for Applications. Then we will turn to DAO itself in the remaining chapters of the book.

# Database Systems

A *database system* is often pictured as a three-level structure, as shown in Figure 7-1.

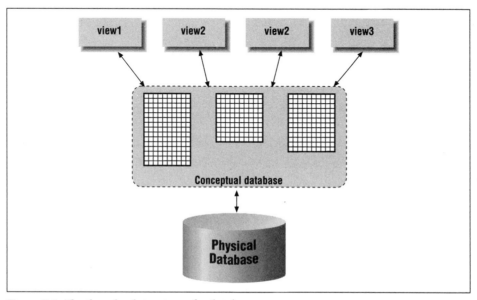

*Figure 7-1. The three-level structure of a database system*

At the lowest level of the structure is the *physical database*, which consists of the raw data existing on a physical object, such as a hard disk. At this level, the data have no logical meaning, as related to the database. However, the data do have a very definite physical structure, to allow efficient access. In other words, the data are more than just a string of bits.

In fact, there are a variety of structures in which the data might be stored, including hash tables, balanced trees, linked lists, nested records, and so on, and the choice of data structure is not a simple one. However, we will not pursue a discussion of the physical database in this book. Suffice it to say that, at the physical level, the data is viewed as a structured collection of bits and the sole purpose of the structure is to provide efficient access to the data. The physical level of a database is often referred to as the *internal level*.

The *conceptual database* is a conceptual view of the database, as a whole. It gives the data a *logical structure*. For instance, in a relational database system, the data are viewed as a collection of tables, with column headings describing the attributes of the corresponding entity class. Moreover, tables are related to one another through certain columns.

The conceptual model is intended to model the entire database. However, individual users may be interested in views of only specific portions of the data. For instance, in the LIBRARY database, a student using the library's online database catalog is probably not interested in the price of the book, but is interested in where it is located on the shelves. Thus, a single database, such as LIBRARY, may need different views for the student than for the librarian.

The highest level in the three-tier structure consists of the individual *views* of the data that may be held by users of the database. Views are also referred to as *subschemes*, and this level of the tier is also referred to as the *external level*.

As another example, we can think of the Microsoft Visual Basic programming language as providing an external view of the Jet Database Management System that is geared toward database programmers. We can think of Microsoft Access as providing an external view that is geared, not just to programmers, but also to high-level users of varying degrees of sophistication. After all, a user does not need to know anything about database programming to create a database in Microsoft Access, although he or she does need to have a familiarity with the conceptual level of a relational database.

Thinking of a database system as a three-tier structure has distinct advantages. One advantage is that it allows for a certain level of independence that permits the individual tiers to be changed or replaced without affecting the other tiers. For instance, if the database is moved to a new computer system that stores the data in hash tables rather than balanced trees, this should not affect the conceptual model of the data, nor the views of users of the database. Also, if we switch from the Visual Basic view of the database to the Access view, we can still use the same conceptual database model. Put more bluntly, a database table in Visual Basic is still a database table in Microsoft Access.

## *Database Management Systems*

A DBMS is a software system that is responsible for managing all aspects of a database, at all levels. In particular, a DBMS should provide the following features, and perhaps more:

- A mechanism for defining the structure of a database, in the form of a *data definition language*, or DDL.

- A mechanism for data manipulation, including data access, sorting, searching, and filtering. This takes the form of a *data manipulation language*, or DML.

- Interaction with a high-level *host language* or *host application*, allowing programmers to write database applications designed for specific purposes. The host language can be a standard programming language, such as C or Visual Basic, or a database application language, such as Microsoft Access.

- Efficient and correct multiuser access to the data.

- Effective data security.

- *Robustness*; that is, the ability to recover from system failures without data loss.

- A *data dictionary*, or *data catalog*. This is a database (in its own right) that provides a list of the definitions of all objects in the main database. For instance, it should include information on all entities in the database, along with their attributes and indexes. This "data about data" is sometimes referred to as *metadata*. The data dictionary should be accessible to the user of the database, so that he or she can obtain this metadata.

# *The Jet DBMS*

As the title of the book suggests, our primary interest is in the DBMS that underlies Microsoft Access (and also Visual Basic). Accordingly, we will take our examples from this DBMS, called the *Jet DBMS* or the *Jet Database Engine*. The relationship between the Jet DBMS and other database-related programs, including Microsoft Access and Visual Basic, can be pictured as in Figure 7-2.

Microsoft's application-level products *Visual Basic*, *Access*, and *Excel* play host to *Visual Basic for Applications* (or VBA), which is the underlying programming language (also called *scripting* or *macro* language) for these applications. (Microsoft Word Version 7 does not use VBA—it uses a similar language called *Word Basic*. However, Microsoft Word 97 does use VBA.) As expected, each of these applications integrates VBA into its environment in a specific way, since each application has a different purpose.

In turn, Visual Basic for Applications is the host language for the Jet DBMS. The Jet DBMS contains the *Data Access Object Component* (or DAO), which is the programming language interface for the Jet DBMS. The DAO provides a more-or-less object-oriented DDL and DML, thereby allowing the VBA programmer to define the structure of a database and manipulate its data.

The *Jet Database Engine* is a collection of components, generally in the form of dynamic link libraries (DLLs), designed to provide specific functions within the Jet DBMS. (A DLL is essentially a collection of functions for performing various tasks.) The *Jet Query Engine* handles the translation of database queries into

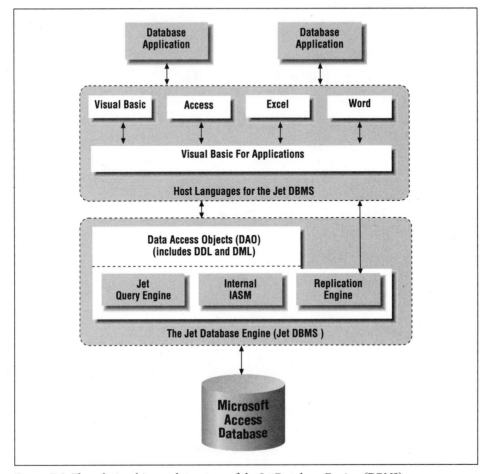

*Figure 7-2. The relationships and structure of the Jet Database Engine (DBMS)*

Access SQL (structured query language), and the subsequent compilation, optimization, and execution of these queries. In short, it handles queries. The *Internal ISAM Component* is responsible for storing and retrieving data from the physical database file. ISAM stands for *Indexed Sequential Access Method*, and is the method by which data are stored in a Jet database file. The *Replication Engine* allows exact duplicates of a database to coexist on multiple systems, with periodic synchronization.

The host languages for the Jet DBMS, such as Visual Basic and Access, are used by database programmers to create database applications for specific purposes. For instance, we might create a *Library* database application, which a library can use to maintain information about its books, or an *Order Entry* database application for a small business.

Incidentally, the Jet DBMS is also capable of interfacing with non-Access-formatted databases, such as those with format Xbase (dBase), Paradox, Btrieve, Excel, and delimited text formats. It can also interface with ODBC (ODBC stands for *open database connectivity*) to access server database applications across networks.

Let us take a closer look at the components of the Jet DBMS. We will study these components in much greater detail in separate chapters of the book.

# Data Definition Languages

We have already mentioned that a DBMS needs to provide a method for defining new databases. This is done by providing a data definition language, or DDL, to the programmer. A DDL is not a procedural language; that is, its instructions do not actually perform operations. Rather, a DDL is a definitional language.

## The Jet Data Definition Language

Example 7-1 illustrates the use of the Jet data definition language. The code will run in Visual Basic or in an Access code module, so feel free to key it in and try it yourself. (Use a new database in Access, since some of this code will conflict with the LIBRARY database that we have been working with in earlier chapters.) The purpose is to create a new database called LIBRARY, along with a table called BOOKS, containing two fields (ISBN and TITLE) and one index. (Don't worry if some portions of this code don't make sense to you at this point.) Note that Access uses a space followed by an underscore character ( _) to indicate that the next line is a continuation of the current line.

*Example 7-1. Use of the Jet Data Definition Language*

```
' Data Definition Language example

' Declare variables of the required types
Dim ws As Workspace
Dim dbLibrary As Database
Dim tblBooks As TableDef
Dim fldBooks As Field
Dim idxBooks As Index

' Use the default workspace, called Workspaces(0)
Set ws = DBEngine.Workspaces(0)

' Create a new database named LIBRARY
' in the default Workspace
Set dbLibrary =  _
ws.CreateDatabase("d:\dao\library.mdb",  _
dbLangGeneral)
```

*Example 7-1. Use of the Jet Data Definition Language (continued)*

```
dbLibrary.Name = "LIBRARY"

' Create a new table called BOOKS
Set tblBooks = dbLibrary.CreateTableDef("BOOKS")

' Define ISBN field and append to the
' table's Fields collection
Set fldBooks = tblBooks.CreateField("ISBN", dbText)
fldBooks.Size = 13
tblBooks.Fields.Append fldBooks

' Define Title field and append to the
' table's Fields collection
Set fldBooks = tblBooks.CreateField("Title", dbText)
fldBooks.Size = 100
tblBooks.Fields.Append fldBooks

' Add the table to the db's Tables collection
dbLibrary.TableDefs.Append tblBooks

' Create an index
Set idxBooks = tblBooks.CreateIndex("ISBNIdx")
idxBooks.Unique = False

' Indices need their own fields
Set fldBooks = idxBooks.CreateField("ISBN")

' Append to the proper collections
idxBooks.Fields.Append fldBooks
tblBooks.Indexes.Append idxBooks
```

As you can see, the clue that we are dealing with a DDL are the commands
*CreateDatabase, CreateTableDef, CreateField,* and *CreateIndex* (in boldface for
easier identification). You can also see from this code that the Jet DBMS uses the
collections to hold the properties of an object. For instance, the fields that we
create for a table must be appended to the *Fields* collection for that table. This
has the advantage that we don't need to keep a separate reference to each field—
the collection does that for us. This approach is typical of object-oriented
programming.

# Data Manipulation Languages

A DBMS must also provide a language designed to manipulate the data in a database. This language is called a database manipulation language, or DML. To the
database programmer, however, the distinction between a DDL and a DML may
be just a logical one, defined more by the purpose of the language than the
syntax.

# The Jet Data Manipulation Language

Example 7-2 is Jet DML code to add two records to the BOOKS table, set the index, and display the records.

*Example 7-2. Jet DML Code Altering the BOOKS Table*

```
' Data Manipulation Language example

Dim rsBooks As Recordset

' Open the database
Set dbLibrary = ws.OpenDatabase("d:\dao\library.mdb")

' Create a recordset for the BOOKS table
Set rsBooks = dbLibrary.OpenRecordset("BOOKS")

' Add two records
rsBooks.AddNew
rsBooks!ISBN = "0-99-345678-0"
rsBooks!Title = "DB Programming is Fun"
rsBooks.Update
rsBooks.AddNew
rsBooks!ISBN = "0-78-654321-0"
rsBooks!Title = "DB Programming isn't Fun"
rsBooks.Update

' Set index
rsBooks.Index = "ISBNIdx"

' Show the records
rsBooks.MoveFirst
MsgBox "ISBN: " & rsBooks!ISBN & "  TI: " & rsBooks!Title
rsBooks.MoveNext
MsgBox "ISBN: " & rsBooks!ISBN & "  TI: " & rsBooks!Title
```

As you can see even from this small example, the DML is designed to perform a variety of actions, such as:

- Moving through the data in the database

- Adding data to the database

- Editing or updating data in the database

- Deleting data from the database

- Querying the data and returning those portions of the data that satisfy the query

# Host Languages

Data are seldom manipulated without some intended purpose. For instance, consider a LIBRARY database consisting of information about the books in a library. If a student wishes to access these data, it is probably with the intention of finding a certain book, for which the student has some information, such as the title. On the other hand, if a librarian wishes to access the information, it may be for other purposes, such as determining when the book was added to the library, or how much it cost. These issues probably don't interest the student.

The point here is that a DBMS should supply an interface with a high-level language with which programmers can program the database to provide specific services; that is, with which programmers can create database applications. Thus, when a student logs onto a library's computer to search for a book, he or she may be accessing a different database application than the librarian might access. The language that is used for database application programming is the host language for the DBMS. As mentioned earlier, a host language may be a traditional programming language, such as C or COBOL, or it may be an application-level language, such as Microsoft Access or Visual Basic, as it is for the Jet DBMS.

In fact, the Jet DBMS is so tightly integrated into both of these applications that it is hard to tell where one leaves off and the other begins. Put another way, it sometimes seems as though Microsoft Access *is* the Jet DBMS, whereas it is more accurate to say that Access and Visual Basic are frontends, or host applications, for the Jet DBMS.

# The Client/Server Architecture

The client/server model of a database system is really very simple, but its meaning has evolved somewhat through popular usage. The client/server model is shown in Figure 7-3.

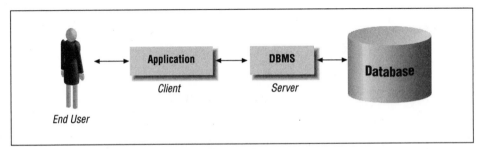

*Figure 7-3. The client/server mode example*

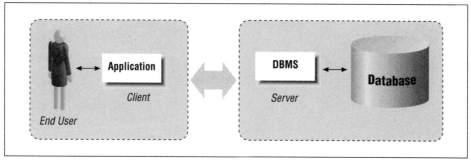

*Figure 7-4. The distributed client/server model example*

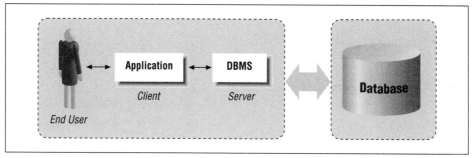

*Figure 7-5. The remote database example*

The server in a client/server model is simply the DBMS, whereas the client is the database application serviced by the DBMS. (We could also think of Visual Basic and Access as clients of the Jet DBMS server.)

The basic client/server model says nothing about the *location* of the various components. However, since the components are distinct, it is not uncommon to find them on different computers. The two most common configurations are illustrated below. The *distributed client/server model* (Figure 7-4), wherein the client is on one computer and the server and database are on another, is so popular that it is usually simply referred to as the *client/server model*. The *remote database* (Figure 7-5) model refers to the case where the client and server are on the same computer, but the database is on a remote computer.

# 8

*In this chapter:*
- *Constants and Variables*
- *Running a Program*
- *VBA Operators*
- *Some VBA Statements and Functions*

# The Basics of Programming in VBA

This chapter is intended to cover just enough of the basics of the Visual Basic for Applications, or VBA, programming language to allow you to follow the chapter on programming DAO. If you have some programming experience, this information may seem familiar to you. We will be deliberately brief here, since this is not a book on VBA programming. Even if you are familiar with Visual Basic, we suggest you skim quickly through this chapter.

A *program* is simply a set of instructions that an application can execute. Programs generally take the form of one or more *subroutines* and/or *functions*, referred to collectively as *procedures*. These can be thought of as code modules that are designed to accomplish a specific purpose. The difference between a subroutine and a function is that a function returns a value, whereas a subroutine does not. For instance, if you want to display some data on the screen, you would write a subroutine, since there is no need to return a value. On the other hand, if you want a procedure to take the sum of a collection of numbers, you would write a function, which can then return that sum.

In Microsoft Access, programs are written in the language called Visual Basic for Applications and are contained within code *modules*. A code module can be associated with a form, or it can be standalone. We will confine our code writing to a single standalone code module.

A new code module is created by choosing the *New* button from the Modules tab of the Database window. A window such as the one in Figure 8-1 should result. (If the line OPTION EXPLICIT does not appear in your new code module, then select the Module tab of the Options choice on the Tools menu and check the Require Variable Declaration option.)

The left-hand drop down list box in Figure 8-1 (which currently shows the word *General*) indicates to which object the code belongs. For instance, when a

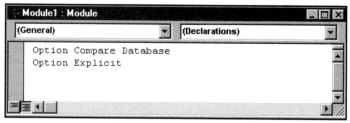

*Figure 8-1. A new code module window in Access*

module is associated with an Access form, the controls on the form are listed in this list box. Since our module is not associated with a form, our only choice is *General.* The right-hand list box contains a list of the different procedures in the module. For a new module, this list is empty, except for the (*Declarations*) option, which is where some variables may be declared.

We will use small code snippets to illustrate both the objects under consideration and the general techniques and syntax of programming the DAO. We suggest that you follow along on your personal computer (PC), from within the LIBRARY database. If you've downloaded the sample database, you will find many of the code examples in a module named *Examples.*

To start a new subroutine or function within a module, you have two choices. First, you can select Procedure from the Insert menu. This will produce the dialog box shown in Figure 8-2. Just type in the name and select Sub or Function, whichever is appropriate for the example.

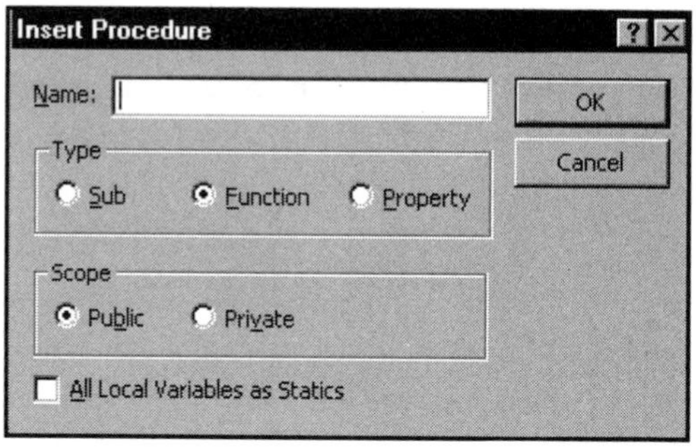

*Figure 8-2. The Insert Procedure dialog box in Access*

Alternatively, to create a new subroutine, you can just begin typing:

```
Sub SubName
```

or

```
Function FunctionName
```

in any other code window, after the *End Sub* statement, or in the *General* window. Access is smart enough to realize that you want to create a new subroutine.

# Constants and Variables

A *literal constant* (or *literal*, or sometimes just *constant*) is a specific value, such as a number, date, or text string, that does not change, and that is used exactly as written. String constants are enclosed in double quotes, as in:

```
"Donna Smith"
```

and date constants are enclosed between number signs, as in:

```
#1/1/96#
```

A *symbolic constant* (also sometimes referred to simply as a *constant*) is a name for a literal constant. For example, we can define a symbolic constant by writing:

```
Const FirstName = "Donna"
```

In this case, whenever we use the word *FirstName*, VBA will replace it by the string "Donna". Thus, *FirstName* is a constant, since it never changes value, but it is not a literal constant, since it is not used as written. The great virtue of using symbolic constants is that, if you decide later to change "Donna" to "Diane", you only need to change one line of the program:

```
Const FirstName = "Diane"
```

rather than searching through the entire program for every occurrence of the word "Donna."

VBA has a large number of *built-in symbolic constants*, which usually begin with the lowercase letters *vb*. We will encounter a few built-in constants as we proceed. For now, let us note the two very useful constants: *vbCrLf*, which is equivalent to a carriage return followed by a line feed, and *vbTab*, which is equivalent to the tab character. (Without these symbolic constants, you would have to enter Chr$(13) + Chr$(10) for the former constant and Chr$(9) for the latter.)

A *variable* is a memory location that can hold values of a specific type. The value in a variable may change during the life of the program. In VBA, each variable has a specific *type*, which indicates which type of data it may hold. For instance, a variable that holds text strings is called a *string variable*.

When the OPTION EXPLICIT option is enabled, all variables must be *declared* before they can be used. This tells VBA the type of that variable. Variables are declared with the *Dim* keyword (or with the keywords *Private* and *Public*, which we will discuss later in this chapter). Here are some examples:

```
Dim Name As String
Dim Holliday As Date
```

```
Dim Age As Integer
Dim Height As Single
Dim Money As Currency
```

The general syntax of a variable declaration is:

```
Dim VariableName As DataType
```

For reference, Table 8-1 shows the complete set of standard data types, along with the amount of memory that they consume and their range of values.

*Table 8-1. The VBA Standard Data Types*

| Type | Size in Memory | Range of Values |
|---|---|---|
| Byte | 1 byte | 0 to 255 |
| Boolean | 2 bytes | True or False |
| Integer | 2 bytes | -32,768 to 32,767 |
| Long (long integer) | 4 bytes | -2,147,483,648 to 2,147,483,647 |
| Single (single-precision real) | 4 bytes | Approximately -3.4E38 to 3.4E38 |
| Double (double-precision real) | 8 bytes | Approximately -1.8E308 to 4.9E324 |
| Currency (scaled integer) | 8 bytes | Approximately -922,337,203,685,477.5808 – 922,337,203,685,477.5807 |
| Date | 8 bytes | 1/1/100 to 12/31/9999 |
| Object | 4 bytes | Any Object reference |
| String | Variable length: 10 bytes + string length; Fixed length: string length | Variable length: <= about 2 billion (65,400 for Win 3.1); Fixed length: up to 65,400 |
| Variant | 16 bytes for numbers 22 bytes + string length | Number: same as Double; String: same as String |
| User-defined | Varies | |

It is generally good programming practice to include OPTION EXPLICIT in your modules. This tells VBA to require that all variables be explicitly declared. However, it is not absolutely necessary. If you omit OPTION EXPLICIT, then VBA will use the *Variant* data type for any undeclared variables. This is a catch-all data type designed to be able to hold data of any other type except fixed-length *String* data and user-defined types. The virtue of the *Variant* data type is that it frees you from having to declare the type of every variable. Its vice is that a *Variant* data type uses more memory than other data types. For instance, in the code:

```
Dim intAge as Integer
intAge = 25
```

the variable *intAge* takes 2 bytes of memory (according to Table 8-1). However, if the variable *varAge* is undeclared and you write:

```
varAge = 25
```

then VBA will assign the variable the *Variant* data type and thus give it 16 bytes of memory, even though it is only storing an integer.

You can also append a special character to variable names in order to tell VBA the type of the variable. In particular, VBA allows the *type-declaration suffixes* shown in Table 8-2.

*Table 8-2. Type-Declaration Suffixes Allowed in VBA*

| Suffix | Type |
|--------|------|
| % | integer variable |
| & | long integer variable |
| ! | single variable |
| # | double variable |
| @ | currency variable |
| $ | string variable |

For instance, the line:

```
Dim Name$
```

declares a variable named *Name$* of type *String*. We can then write:

```
Name$ = "Donna"
```

## *Arrays*

It is also possible to declare variables that hold arrays of data, called *array variables*. An array variable is essentially a collection of simple variables using the same name, but distinguished by an index value. For instance, if we want to store the ages of 10 people, we could declare an array variable as follows:

```
Dim intAges(1 To 10) As Integer
```

The array variable is *intAges*. It has *size* 10. Each of the variables *intAges(1)*, *intAges(2)*,..., *intAges(10)* are simple integer variables. Note that we may omit the first index in the declaration:

```
Dim intAges(10) As Integer
```

but then VBA will set the first index to be 0 and so the size of the array is then 11, with 11 integer variables *intAges(0)* through *intAges(10)*.

The virtue of declaring array variables, as opposed to individual variables, such as *intAges1*, *intAges2*, ..., *intAges10*, is easily seen when we want not just 10 variables, but 10,000 variables! In addition, as we will see, there are ways to work collectively with all of the elements in an array, using a few simple programming constructs.

## Naming Variables

It is good programming practice to develop a consistent naming convention for variable names. There are many such conventions and each programmer has his or her favorite. A programmer named Charles Simonyi had a very good idea for naming variables. In particular, he developed a scheme in which each name is prefixed with characters that describe the type of the variable. Also, capital letters are used to separate words, rather than spaces, which are not always allowed, or the underscore, which is awkward at best.

For example, we use the prefix *int* for integer variables, as in:

```
Dim intBookCount As Integer
```

and the prefix *str* for variables of type *String*, as in:

```
Dim strTitle As String
```

Table 8-3 shows the naming convention for standard variables, although we will use only a few of these in our examples. We shall give more complete tables in Chapter 9, *Programming DAO: Overview.*

*Table 8-3. Standard Variable Naming for VBA*

| Variable Type | Prefix |
| --- | --- |
| Boolean | bool, b, or f |
| Byte | byt |
| Currency | cur |
| Date | dte |
| Double | dbl |
| Integer | int |
| Long | lng |
| Object | obj |
| Single | sng |
| String | str |
| User-defined type | typ |
| Variant | var |

## The Scope of a Variable

Each variable has a *scope*, which indicates where in the program the variable is recognized. The variables that we declare have either *procedure-level scope* or *module-level scope.* Simply put, if a variable is declared within a procedure (subroutine or function), then it is visible only within that procedure. No other procedures will recognize that variable. This allows you to declare other variables of the same name in other procedures.

On the other hand, if the variable is declared in the (*Declarations*) section of the module, it has module-level scope, meaning that it is visible from every procedure in the module. Thus, for instance, the variable *intThisModuleOnly* declared in Figure 8-3 has module-level scope.

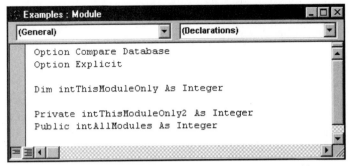

*Figure 8-3. Example module illustrating module-level variables*

When one is dealing with more than one code module, there is a further level of scope. Module-level variables declared using the keyword *Private* (or *Dim*) are visible only to the module in which they are declared, whereas module-level variables declared using the keyword *Public* can be seen in every module. These declarations are also illustrated in Figure 8-3.

# Running a Program

To run our sample programs in Access, we will use the *debug window*. (Programs can also be assigned to macros, using the *RunCode* command.) To make the debug window visible, hit Ctrl-G. The debug window is shown in Figure 8-4.

To run a subroutine, just type its name and hit the Enter key.

It is time we wrote a small program. Start a code module and enter the following subroutine:

```
Sub test()

MsgBox "Workspace Count: " & DBEngine.Workspaces.Count
MsgBox "Workspace Name: " & DBEngine.Workspaces(0).Name

End Sub
```

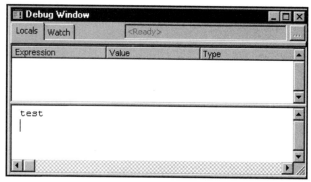

*Figure 8-4. The Access Debug Window*

Open the debug window and run this program by typing *test* and hitting the enter key. You will get two messages:

```
Workspace Count: 1
Workspace Name: #Default Workspace#
```

This tells us that there is one workspace currently open, whose name is #Default Workspace#.

# VBA Operators

VBA uses a handful of simple operators:

*Arithmetic Operators*
    Addition: +
    Subtraction: –
    Multiplication: *
    Division: /
    Exponentiation: ∧

*String Operator*
    Concatenation: &

*Logical Operations*
    AND
    OR
    NOT

*Comparison Operators*
    =
    <
    >
    <= (less than or equal to)

>= (greater than or equal to)
<> (not equal to)

String concatenation is the only operator that you might not have seen before. Here is an example:

```
"Donna " & "Smith"
```

is the same as:

```
"Donna Smith"
```

# Some VBA Statements and Functions

Now let us discuss a few of the most fundamental statements in VBA.

## The MsgBox Statement

The *MsgBox* statement is used to display a message and wait for the user to respond by pushing a button. There are many variations on this statement. For a complete description, please check the Access online help. We will use it in its simplest form:

```
MsgBox MessageString
```

For example, the code:

```
Dim strName as String
strName = "Donna"
MsgBox "Your name is: " & strName
```

will produce the message box shown in Figure 8-5.

*Figure 8-5. Example window illustrating the use of the MsgBox statement*

## The InputBox Function

The *InputBox* function is designed to get input from the user. Let us consider an example.

The following code requests the name of a database file on disk:

```
Sub exaInputBox()
```

```
Dim strResponse As String, strMsg As String

strMsg = "Please enter complete path name of database file"

strResponse = InputBox(strMsg)

If strResponse = "" Then
    Exit Sub
Else
    MsgBox strResponse
End If

End Sub
```

In response to the InputBox function, VBA will display the dialog box in Figure 8-6.

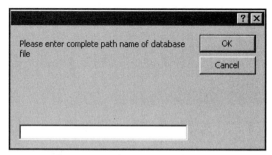

*Figure 8-6. An example InputBox function dialog box*

When the user hits the *OK* button, the string in the text box will be placed in the variable *strResponse*. If the user hits the *Cancel* button, then strResponse will be the empty string, denoted by " ".

The last portion of the code, beginning with the line:

```
If strResponse = "" Then
```

is used to detect whether or not *strResponse* is empty, If so, we simply exit the subroutine. If not, the value of *strResponse* is displayed to the user. We will discuss the *If ... Then* statement in detail a bit later.

## Some Useful String Functions

Here are a handful of useful functions that apply to strings (both constants and variables).

### The Len function

The *Len* function return the length of a string, that is, the number of characters in the string. Thus,

```
Len("Donna Smith")
```

returns the number 11.

### The UCase and LCase functions

These functions convert a string to all uppercase or all lowercase, respectively. The syntax is:

```
UCase(string)
LCase(string)
```

For instance,

```
MsgBox UCase(Donna)
```

will display the string: DONNA.

### The Left, Right, and Mid functions

These functions return a portion of a string. In particular,

```
Left(string, number)
```

returns the leftmost *number* characters in *string* and

```
Right(string, number)
```

returns the rightmost *number* characters in *string*. For instance,

```
MsgBox Right("Donna Smith", 5)
```

displays the string: Smith.

The syntax for *Mid* is:

```
Mid(string,start,length)
```

This function returns the first *length* number of characters of *string*, starting at character number *start*. For instance,

```
Mid("Library.mdb",9,3)
```

returns the string: mdb.

If the *length* parameter is missing, as in:

```
Mid("Library.mdb",9)
```

the function will return the rest of the string, starting at *start*.

### The Instr function

The syntax for this function is:

```
Instr(Start, StringToSearch, StringToFind)
```

The return value is the position of the first occurrence of *StringToFind* within *StringToSearch*, starting at *Start*. If *Start* is missing, then the function starts searching at the beginning of *StringToSearch*.

For instance,

```
MsgBox Instr("Donna Smith", "Smith")
```

displays the number 7.

### The Str and Val functions

The *Str* function converts a number to a string. For instance,

```
Str(123)
```

returns the *string* "123". Conversely, the *Val* function converts a string that represents a number into a number (so that we can do arithmetic with it, for instance). For example,

```
Val("4.5")
```

returns the number 4.5.

The *Val* function is very useful. For instance,

```
Val("1234 Main Street")
```

is the number 1234. Note, however, that *Val* does not recognize dollar signs or commas. Thus,

```
Val($12.00)
```

returns 0, not 12.00.

## Some Useful Control Statements

Let us now consider a few useful VBA control statements.

### The If ... Then statement

The *If...Then* statement is used for conditional control. The full syntax is:

```
If Condition Then
    …statements go here…
ElseIf AnotherCondition Then
    …more statements go here…
Else
    …more statements go here…
End If
```

Note that you may include as many *ElseIf* parts as desired and that both the *ElseIf* parts and the *Else* part are optional. Example 8-1 displays a student's letter grade, based on his or her average test score.

*Example 8-1. An Example of the If ... Then Statement*

```
Sub exaIfThen()

Dim intGrade As Integer
```

*Example 8-1. An Example of the If ... Then Statement (continued)*

```
intGrade = Val(InputBox("Enter student's average  _ test score: "))

If intGrade >= 90 Then
    MsgBox "You get an A"
ElseIf intGrade >= 80 Then
    MsgBox "You get a B"
ElseIf intGrade >= 70 Then
    MsgBox "You get a C"
ElseIf intGrade >= 60 Then
    MsgBox "You get a D"
Else
    MsgBox "Too bad"
End If

End Sub
```

### The For loop

This statement allows us to loop through some lines of code. Consider Example 8-2. (Note that an apostrophe at the beginning of a line signifies a *comment line*, which is not executed by VBA.)

*Example 8-2. A For Loop Example*

```
Sub exaForNext()

Dim intArray(10) As Integer
Dim i As Integer
Dim varIdx As Variant

' Demonstrate For...Next
For i = 0 To 10
    intArray(i) = i
Next i

' Demonstrate For Each
For Each varIdx In intArray
    Debug.Print Str(varIdx)
Next varIdx

End Sub
```

The lines

```
    For i = 0 To 10
        intArray(i) = i.
    Next i
```

use a *For loop* to assign values to each of the 11 integer variables *intArray(0)* through *intArray(10)*.

This example also illustrates the related *For Each* syntax, which uses a variable of type *variant* to cycle through the array *intArray*. This syntax also applies to collections, as we will see in Chapter 9.

Note that the line

```
Debug.Print Str(varIdx)
```

prints the value of *Str(varIdx)* to the debug window.

### The Do loop

The *Do* loop has several slight variations, summarized below. The statement

```
{While | Until}
```

means that you can use either the word *While* or the word *Until* (but not both). Here are the possible syntaxes for the *Do* loop:

```
Do {While | Until} 0condition

    ...statements go here...

Loop
```

or

```
Do

    ...statements go here...

Loop {While | Until} condition
```

Example 8-3 uses a *Do* loop to compute the sum of the first ten positive integers. The value of this sum is accumulated in the variable *intSum*.

*Example 8-3. A Do Loop Example*

```
Sub exaDoLoop()

Dim intCounter As Integer
Dim intSum As Integer

intSum = 0
Do While intCounter < 10
    intCounter = intCounter + 1
    intSum = intSum + intCounter
Loop

MsgBox Str(intSum)

End Sub
```

# 9

## *Programming DAO: Overview*

We have seen that Access SQL provides a way to create and manipulate database objects, such as tables and queries, through its DDL and DML components. In addition, users can enter SQL statements directly into the Access *SQL View* window.

On the other hand, Microsoft Access allows us to program the Jet database engine directly, through its programming interface, which is known as *Data Access Objects*, or *DAO*. This gives the user far more control over a database.

DAO is a complicated structure, and we will not discuss all of its aspects. Our focus in this book will be on gaining a general understanding of the following concepts and components:

- The organization of DAO, which is at least partly object-oriented

- The DDL component of DAO

- The DML component of DAO

We will certainly not cover all aspects of the DDL and DML components. Our main goal is to prepare you so that you can get whatever additional information you need from Microsoft Access's extensive on-line help for the DAO model, or from similar hardcopy reference manuals.

# *Objects*

Before discussing the various components of the DAO model, we must discuss the concept of an *object*. In the parlance of object-orientation, an object is something that is identified by its *properties* and its *methods* (or *actions*).

As we will see (and as the name implies) DAO is full of objects. For example, each saved table in an Access database is an object, called a *TableDef* object. (Actually, it is the *definition* of the table, rather than its data, that is an object of type *TableDef.*) Some of the properties of *TableDef* objects are *Name, Record- Count, DateCreated*, and *LastUpdated*.

An object's methods can be thought of as *procedures* or *functions* that act on the object. For instance, one of the methods of a *TableDef* object is *CreateField*, which, as the name implies, is used to create a new field for the *TableDef* object. Another method is *OpenRecordset,* which creates another object called a *Recordset object* that can be used to manipulate the data in the table. (A more object-oriented view of methods is that they are messages that are sent to the "object" saying, in effect, perform the following action.)

## *Object Variables*

In order to access the properties or invoke the methods of an object, we need to first define an *object variable* to reference that object.

VBA and DAO offer a wide variety of *object data types*. There is a slight difference in syntax when declaring and setting an object variable, as opposed to a standard variable. For instance, here is an example using the *Database* object type. Note that the full path name of the LIBRARY database on my PC is *d:\dbase\ library.mdb*.

```
Dim dbLibrary as Database
Set dbLibrary = "d:\dbase\library.mdb"
```

In general, the syntax is:

```
Dim objectVariable as ObjectDataType
Set objectVariable = ObjectName
```

Note that the only difference between setting object variables and setting standard variables is the keyword *Set*. However, this minor syntactic difference belies a much more significant difference between standard variables and object variables.

In particular, a standard variable can be thought of as a name for a location in the computer's memory that holds the data. For instance, in the code:

```
Dim intVar As Integer
intVar = 123
```

the variable *intVar* is a 4-byte memory location that holds the integer value 123. Figure 9-1 illustrates the variable *intVar*. (Actually, the 4-byte memory location holds the value 123 in *binary* format, but that is not relevant to our discussion.)

*Figure 9-1. An example of the intVar variable*

Of course, if we were to write:

```
Dim intVar As Integer
Dim intVar2 As Integer
intVar2 = intVar
intVar2 = 567
```

we would not expect the last line of code above to have any effect upon the value of the variable *intVar*, which should still be 123.

On the other hand, an object variable is not the name of a memory location that holds the object's "value," whatever that means. Rather, an object variable holds the *address* of the area of memory that holds the object. Put another way, the object variable holds a *reference* to, or *points* to, the object. It is therefore called a *pointer variable*. The idea is pictured in Figure 9-2, where *rsBooks* and *rsBooks2* are object variables, both pointing to an object of type *Recordset*.

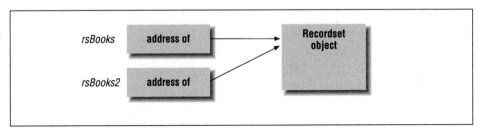

*Figure 9-2. An example of a pointer variable*

To illustrate this further, consider the code in Example 9-1.

*Example 9-1. An Object Variable Example*

```
Sub exaObjectVar()

'Declare some object variables
Dim dbLib As DATABASE
Dim rsBooks As Recordset
Dim rsBooks2 As Recordset

'Set dbLib to the current database (i.e. LIBRARY)
```

*Example 9-1. An Object Variable Example (continued)*

```
Set dbLib = CurrentDb

'Open a recordset object for the BOOKS table
Set rsBooks = dbLib.OpenRecordset("BOOKS")

'Two object variables will refer to the same object
Set rsBooks2 = rsBooks

'Use a property of this object
MsgBox "BOOKS record count: " & rsBooks.RecordCount

'Destroy the object using rsBooks2 reference
rsBooks2.Close

'Now rsBooks has nothing to refer to, so we get error
MsgBox "BOOKS record count: " & rsBooks.RecordCount
```

**End Sub**

First, we declare two object variables of type *Recordset* (we will discuss this type in detail later). The line:

```
Set rsBooks = dbLib.OpenRecordset("BOOKS")
```

sets *rsBooks* to point to (or refer to) a *Recordset* object created from the BOOKS table. Note again that, unlike standard variables, setting an object variable requires the use of the keyword *Set*. The line:

```
Set rsBooks2 = rsBooks
```

sets *rsBooks2* to point to the same *Recordset* object as *rsBooks*, as shown in Figure 9-2.

Next, the line:

```
MsgBox "BOOKS record count: " & rsBooks.RecordCount
```

displays the message box in Figure 9-3, showing that there are 14 books in the recordset.

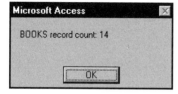

*Figure 9-3. The message box from the exaObjectVar() example*

To illustrate the fact that both variables point to the same object, the line:

```
rsBooks2.Close
```

uses the pointer *rsBooks2* to destroy (or close) the *Recordset* object. Then, when the line:

```
MsgBox "BOOKS record count: " & rsBooks.RecordCount
```

is executed, the *Recordset* object that both variables referred to is gone, and so the expression *rsBooks.RecordCount* causes an *Object is invalid or not set* error, as shown in Figure 9-4.

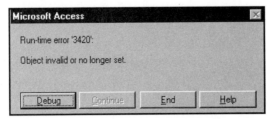

*Figure 9-4. Error message from the exaObjectvar() example*

The moral of this example is that it is important to remember that object variables *refer* to objects and that more than one variable can refer to the same object. Despite this, it is customary to use the misleading statement "the *objVar* object" when we really should be saying "the object referred to by *objVar*."

## Object Variable Naming Conventions

Tables 9-1 and 9-2 describe the naming convention for both standard and object variables that we will (try to) use in this book. (Table 9-1 is a repeat of Table 8-3.) We will explain the various object types as we proceed through this chapter.

*Table 9-1. Standard Variable Naming for VBA*

| Variable | Prefix |
| --- | --- |
| Boolean | bool, b, or f |
| Byte | byt |
| Currency | cur |
| Date | dte |
| Double | dbl |
| Integer | int |
| Long | lng |
| Single | sng |
| String | str |
| User-defined type | typ |
| Variant | var |

*Table 9-2. Object Variable Naming for VBA*

| Variable | Prefix |
|----------|--------|
| Container | con |
| Database | db or dbs |
| Document | doc |
| Dynaset | dyn |
| Error | err |
| Field | fld |
| Form | frm |
| Index | idx |
| Object | obj |
| Parameter | prm |
| Property | prp |
| QueryDef | qdf |
| Recordset | rs or rst |
| Relation | rel |
| Report | rpt |
| Snapshot | snp |
| Table | tbl |
| TableDef | tdf or tbl |
| User | usr |
| Workspace | ws or wrk |

# *Referencing the Properties and Methods of an Object*

The general syntax for referring to an object's properties and methods is very simple. Suppose that *objVar* is a variable that refers to an object. If *AProperty* is a property of this object, then we can access this property using the syntax:

```
objVar.AProperty
```

If *AMethod* is a method for this object, then we can invoke that method with the syntax:

```
objVar.AMethod(any required parameters)
```

To illustrate, consider the code in Example 9-2.

*Example 9-2. A Property and Method Example*

```
Sub exaPropertyMethod()

Dim dbLib As DATABASE
Dim qdfExpensive As QueryDef
```

*Example 9-2. A Property and Method Example (continued)*

```
' Get current database (LIBRARY)
Set dbLib = CurrentDb

' Show Name property
MsgBox dbLib.Name

' Invoke the CreateQueryDef method to create a query
Set qdfExpensive = dbLib.CreateQueryDef("Expensive",_
"SELECT * FROM BOOKS WHERE Price > 20")
```

**End Sub**

The line:

```
Set dbLib = CurrentDb
```

sets the object variable of type DATABASE to point to the current database, that is, the LIBRARY database. The line:

```
MsgBox dbLib.Name
```

displays the value of the *Name* property of *dbLib*. The line

```
Set qdfExpensive = dbLib.CreateQueryDef("Expensive",_
"SELECT * FROM BOOKS WHERE Price > 20")
```

invokes the method *CreateQueryDef* to create a new query named *Expensive* and defined by the SQL statement:

```
SELECT * FROM BOOKS WHERE Price > 20
```

Note that the code:

```
dbLib.CreateQueryDef("Expensive","SELECT * FROM BOOKS WHERE
Price > 20")
```

invokes the method, which returns the *QueryDef* object, which is then pointed to by the object variable *qdfExpensive*. If you run this program, you will notice a new entry in the *Query* tab of the *Database* window. (If the query *Expensive* is already in the database, delete it before running this program. Also, you may need to switch away from and then return to the *Query* tab to refresh the list.)

# *The DAO Object Model*

As the name *Data Access Objects* suggests, the DAO is, at least in part, an object-oriented environment. In particular, the DAO is implemented as a hierarchy of collections of objects. Figure 9-5 shows the DAO Object Model, describing the collections and their objects.

Each of the shaded boxes represents a collection of objects. (Thus *DBEngine* is the only noncollection.) The name of the objects contained within a given collec-

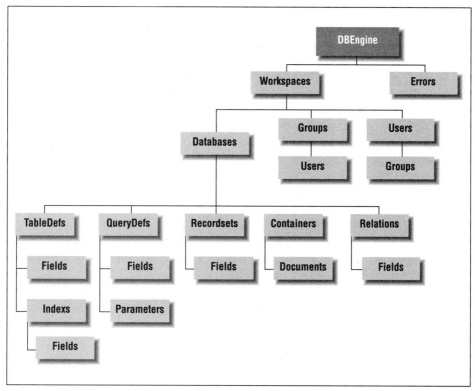

*Figure 9-5. The DAO Object Model*

tion is the just singular of the collection name. For instance, the *TableDefs* collection holds *TableDef* objects and the *Documents* collection holds *Document* objects. *DBEngine* is the only standalone object—not contained in any collection.

There is a potential point of confusion about the DAO object hierarchy in Figure 9-5 that we should address. Consider, for example, the relationship between the *Databases* and *Workspaces* collections. It would be incorrect to say, as one might infer from the diagram, that the *Databases* collection is contained in the *Workspaces* collection. Indeed, the line from *Workspaces* to *Databases* means that each *Workspace object* has (or as Microsoft would say, "contains") a *Databases* collection.

Perhaps the best way to view the situation is to say that each object in the DAO hierarchy has associated with it three things: collections, methods, and properties. For instance, a *Workspace* object has associated with it the following items:

*Collections*
 Databases
 Groups

Users
Properties (not shown in Figure 9-5)

*Methods*
BeginTrans
Close
CommitTrans
CreateDatabase
CreateGroup
CreateUser
OpenDatabase
Rollback

*Properties*
IsolateODBCTrans
Name
UserName

Let us pause for a brief aside. In an object-oriented environment such as C++, or even Visual Basic, a collection is also considered an object. Moreover, the value of a property of one object can be another object (these are so-called *object properties*). Hence, in such an object-oriented environment, we would probably think of the collections associated with an object as just additional properties of that object. However, Microsoft chose not to express this explicitly in the DAO.

Figure 9-6 shows a more detailed example of the object-collection relationship. The *Containers* collection in this case contains three *Container* objects, each of which has (the same) properties and methods. Each object also "contains" a *Documents* collection, which contains some *Document* objects.

Thus, according to this model, there may be more than one *Documents* collection. Indeed, there is one *Documents* collection for every *Container* object. Similarly, there is one *Databases* collection for each *Workspace* object and one *TableDefs* collection for each *Database* object.

## *The Microsoft Access Object Model*

You may notice that there are no collections in the DAO corresponding to Access forms or reports. The fact is that DAO is not the whole object story. Microsoft Access defines its own collections of objects, as shown in Figure 9-7.

Access defines the *Forms* collection to hold all *currently open* forms. (Note especially the words "currently open".) Similarly, the *Reports* collection holds all currently open reports. The objects *Application*, *DoCmd*, and *Screen* are not contained in a collection. The *Modules* collection, which is new for Access 8.0, holds all open code modules.

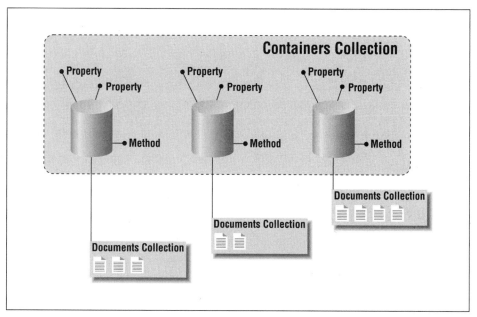

*Figure 9-6. A detailed example of the object-collection relationship*

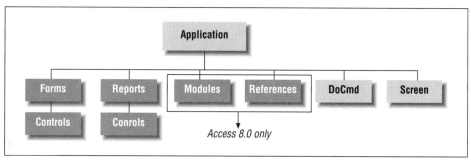

*Figure 9-7. The Microsoft Access object model*

The *References* collection, which is also new for Access 8.0, holds all *Reference* objects. A *Reference* object is a reference to another application's *type library*, which is a file containing information on the objects that the application exposes through Automation. It is through Automation objects that an application can share some of its features with other applications. However, we will not go further into this subject in this book. (Allow me to recommend the book entitled *Concepts of Object-Oriented Programming with Visual Basic*, by the present author, published by Springer-Verlag (ISBN 0-387-94889-9), for more information on OLE Automation, geared toward the Visual Basic programmer.)

We should also note that VBA itself has some very useful database-object manipulation instructions. For instance, the line:

```
Set dbLib = CurrentDb
```

sets the variable *dbLib* to point to the currently open database. The function *CurrentDb*, which we will discuss in more detail later, is not a DAO function—you will not find it in the DAO reference manual. It is a part of VBA. Thus, VBA, Access, and DAO all provide supporting objects and instructions for database management.

# *Referencing Objects*

The first step in understanding the objects in the DAO and Microsoft Access object hierarchies is to understand how to refer to an object in the hierarchy. In particular, we can refer to an object by the name of *ObjectName* that belongs to a collection named *CollectionName*, by any of the following syntaxes:

- CollectionName!ObjectName, or CollectionName![ObjectName] when Object-Name has illegal characters, such as spaces

- CollectionName("ObjectName")

- CollectionName(StringVar), where StringVar holds the string ObjectName

- CollectionName(Index), where Index is the index number of the object in the collection. Indices start with 0 and go up to one less than the number of objects in the collection. (As we will see, the number of elements in a collection is denoted by CollectionName.Count.)

For instance, the *TableDef* object named BOOKS in the *TableDefs* collection is denoted by:

```
TableDefs!BOOKS
```

or

```
TableDefs("BOOKS")
```

or

```
Dim strBooks as String
strBooks = "BOOKS"
TableDefs(strBooks)
```

or, if BOOKS happens to be the first *TableDef* object in the *TableDefs* collection,

```
TableDefs(0)
```

The exclamation point (!) used in the first syntax above is called the *bang operator*.

# *Fully Qualified Object Names*

There is a problem with these names. For instance, to which object does *Fields(0)* refer? There are several *Fields* collections in the DAO hierarchy, as can be seen from Figure 9-5. Let us refer to the names described in the previous syntax as *semiqualified names*. To avoid the problem that a semiqualified name may not be unique, we must use the *fully qualified object name*, which is formed by tracing the entire hierarchy from the top (*DBEngine*) to the desired object. For instance, the fully qualified name for BOOKS is

```
DBEngine.Workspaces(0).Databases![d:\dbase\library.mdb].TableDefs!BOOKS
```

Let us examine this name. It is composed of four separate semiqualified object names, separated by periods. These periods are referred to as the *dot operator*.

```
DBEngine.
Workspaces(0).
Databases![d:\dbase\library.mdb].
TableDefs!BOOKS
```

Perhaps the easiest way to make sense of this name is to start from the bottom. The semiqualified name of the object we are interested in is:

```
TableDefs!BOOKS
```

This object is contained in the *TableDefs* collection for the *Database* object named:

```
Databases![d:\dbase\library.mdb]
```

This object is, in turn, contained in the *Databases* collection of the default *Workspace* object (more on this later), which is:

```
Workspaces(0)
```

which, in turn, is contained in the *DBEngine* object. Separating each of these object names by the dot operator gives the fully qualified object name.

In general, the syntax for a semiqualified object name is:

```
Collection!Object
```

and for a fully qualified object name, it is:

```
DBEngine.Collection1!Object1. · · · .CollectionN!ObjectN
```

There seems to be much confusion over when to use the bang operator (!) and when to use the dot operator (.). Perhaps the following will help:

*   The bang operator is used to separate an object's name from the name of the collection of which it is a member. In other words, bang signifies a member of a collection. It thus appears in semiqualified object names.

- The dot operator is used to separate each semiqualified object name in a fully qualified object name. In other words, it signifies the next step in the hierarchy.

- The dot operator is also used to denote a property or method of an object.

This naming convention is really not as confusing as it may look at first, if you remember the previous three maxims. However, if you want confusing, stay tuned for default collections, coming soon.

## Using Object Variables to Advantage

As you can see, a fully qualified object name can be quite lengthy. This problem is compounded by the fact that it may be necessary to refer to the same object many times in a program. There are two common ways to deal with this issue.

One way is to use object variables. Consider the code in Example 9-3 to display the *RecordCount* property of the BOOKS table.

*Example 9-3. An Object Variable Example*

```
Sub exaObjVar()

Dim ws As Workspace
Dim dbLib As DATABASE
Dim tdfBooks As TableDef

Set ws = DBEngine.Workspaces(0)
Set dbLib = ws.Databases![d:\dbase\library.mdb]
Set tdfBooks = dbLib.TableDefs!BOOKS

MsgBox tdfBooks.RecordCount

End Sub
```

By defining three object variables, *ws*, *dbLib*, and *tdfBooks*, we were able to avoid writing the fully qualified name of BOOKS (on a single line, that is). Also, the line

```
    MsgBox tdfBooks.RecordCount
```

is much easier to read. (It reads: "Message me the record count of TableDef tdfBooks.")

The use of object variables in this way has several advantages, and is highly recommended. First, it tends to make the lines of code shorter and more readable. Second, we can refer to the object variable *tdfBooks* many times without having to write the fully qualified object name each time. As a result, the program will run somewhat faster, since VBA does not have to resolve the object name by climbing down the object hierarchy more than once.

## *Default Collections*

There is another method that can be used for shortening fully qualified object names. In particular, each object has a *default collection*, which can be used as follows. Consider a portion of a fully qualified name:

```
Collection1!Object1.Collection2!Object2
```

If *Collection2* is the default collection of *Object1*, then this name may be shortened to:

```
Collection1!Object1!Object2
```

where we have omitted the default collection name *Collection2*, as well as the preceding dot.

For instance, the default collection of *DBEngine* is *Workspaces*. Hence,

```
DBEngine.Workspaces!MyWorkspace
```

can be shortened to:

```
DBEngine!MyWorkspace
```

and the phrase

```
DBEngine.Workspaces(0)
```

can be shortened to:

```
DBEngine(0)
```

Also, since the default collection for a *Workspace* object is *Databases*, the phrase:

```
DBEngine.Workspaces(0).Databases(0)
```

can be shortened to:

```
DBEngine(0)(0)
```

Table 9-3 shows the default collections in the DAO and Access object model.

*Table 9-3. DAO and Access Object Default Collections*

| Object | Default Collection |
|---|---|
| DBEngine | Workspaces |
| Workspace | Databases |
| Database | TableDefs |
| TableDef | Fields |
| Recordset | Fields |
| QueryDef | Parameters |
| Index | Fields |
| Relation | Fields |

*Table 9-3. DAO and Access Object Default Collections (continued)*

| Object | Default Collection |
|--------|--------------------|
| Container | Documents |
| User | Groups |
| Group | Users |
| Forms | Controls |
| Reports | Controls |

The use of default collections can save space. However, it does very little for readability (to say the least) and is probably best left to programmers with so much experience that they hardly read the names anyway! To emphasize the point, each of the lines in Example 9-4 displays the *RecordCount* property of the BOOKS table. Note that the full name of the database library file on my computer is *d:\dbase\library.mdb*.

*Example 9-4. A Default Collections Example*

```
Sub exaDefaultCollections()

MsgBox DBEngine.Workspaces(0).Databases![d:\dbase\library.mdb]. _
TableDefs!BOOKS.RecordCount

MsgBox _
DBEngine(0).Databases![d:\dbase\library.mdb].TableDefs!BOOKS.RecordCount

MsgBox DBEngine(0)![d:\dbase\library.mdb].TableDefs!BOOKS.RecordCount

MsgBox DBEngine(0)![d:\dbase\library.mdb]!BOOKS.RecordCount

MsgBox DBEngine(0)(0)!BOOKS.RecordCount

End Sub
```

# *Collections Are Objects Too*

In a true object-centric environment, everything is an object. While Access, VBA and DAO may not go this far, it is true that collections are objects and so they have their own properties and methods.

In the Access environment, collections can be divided into three types:

- *Microsoft Access collections*, which are part of the Access object hierarchy
- *DAO collections*, which are part of the DAO hierarchy
- *User-defined collections*, which are VBA objects of type *Collection*

Note that only user-defined collections are of type *Collection*, which is a VBA data type, not a DAO data type. The properties and methods of collections are not very complicated, so let us list them here.

## *Properties and Methods of Access Collections*

The Access collections *Forms*, *Reports*, and *Controls* have no methods and only one property: *Count*, which reports the number of objects in the collection. Thus, the line:

```
Forms.Count
```

reports the number of *opened* forms in the current database. (We will see later, when we discuss *Container* objects, that there is a way to get the number of *saved* forms as well.)

## *Properties and Methods of DAO Collections*

DAO collections fall into two categories with respect to their properties and methods. All DAO collections have a single property: *Count*. All DAO collections also have the *Refresh* method, which we will discuss a bit later. In addition, some of the collections have the *Append* and corresponding *Delete* methods, while others do not.

*Collections that have Append and Delete methods:*

Workspaces
TableDefs
QueryDefs
Groups
Users
Relations
Fields
Indexes
Properties (explained later)

*Collections that do not have Append and Delete methods:*

Databases
Errors
Recordsets
Containers
Documents
Parameters

Evidently, some collections do not have *Append* or *Delete* methods because DAO does not want the user to append or delete objects from these collections. This is reasonable because DAO takes care of collection housekeeping automatically for these collections. For example, DAO automatically appends new databases to the *Databases* collection whenever they are created using the *CreateDatabase* method. However, it does not do so for new *TableDef* or *QueryDef* objects, for instance.

Note that Microsoft Access will do the housekeeping chores for you when objects are created and saved using the Access interface.

## *Properties and Methods of User-Defined Collections*

User-defined *Collection* objects have one property: *Count*. They have three methods: *Add, Remove*, and *Item*. *Add* and *Remove* perform as advertised by their names, and we will see an example shortly. The *Item* method is used to identify the items in the collection, since they may or may not have names.

A single user-defined collection can contain objects of various types, including other collections. Here is an example to illustrate the *Add* method.

In Example 9-5, we create two collections: *colParent* and *colChild*. We then place *colChild* inside *colParent*, along with the BOOKS *TableDef* object. Thus, the *colParent* collection contains two objects of very different types—one *Collection* object and one *TableDef* object. (While this example is not of much practical value, it does illustrate the point.)

*Example 9-5. A Collections Example*

```
Sub exaCollections()

' Declare two variables of type collection
Dim colParent As New Collection
Dim colChild As New Collection

Dim tdfBooks As TableDef
Dim objVar As Object

Set tdfBooks = DBEngine(0)(0).TableDefs!Books

' Use Add method of collection object
' to add objects to colParent collection
colParent.Add colChild
colParent.Add tdfBooks

' Display size of collection
MsgBox "Size of Parent collection " & colParent.Count

' Iterate through collection. Note use of
```

*Example 9-5. A Collections Example (continued)*

```
' TypeOf statement
For Each objVar In colParent
    If TypeOf objVar Is Collection Then
        MsgBox "Collection"
    ElseIf TypeOf objVar Is TableDef Then
        MsgBox objVar.Name
    End If
Next
```

**End Sub**

In Example 9-5, we used the *Add* method of the collection object to add items to the collection and the *Count* property of the collection object, which returns the size of the collection. Note also the use of the *TypeOf* statement to determine the type of each object in the collection.

Now let us consider the *Item* method, which returns a specific object from a collection. The general syntax is:

```
Collection.Item(index)
```

where *index* is an index into the collection. Note that DAO collections begin with index 0 and go to index *Collection.Count - 1*.

To illustrate the *Item* method, in place of the code:

```
For Each tbl In db.TableDefs
    strTbls = strTbls & vbCrLf & tbl.Name
Next tbl
```

of the previous example, we could have written:

```
For i = 0 To db.TableDefs.Count - 1

  strTbls = strTbls & vbCrLf & _
db.TableDefs.Item(i).Name

Next i
```

We should remark that an object's ordinal position in a collection is never guaranteed, and can sometimes change without warning. Thus, for example, it is unwise to rely on the fact that the object that is *Item(0)* at some time will always be *Item(0)*.

Incidentally, one of the drawbacks of collections that contain different types of objects, as in the previous example, is that we can seldom do the same thing to all of the objects in the collection. For this reason, creating collections containing different types of objects is not very useful in general.

## Say It Again

It is worth reemphasizing that the collections in the DAO hierarchy are not contained in their parent collections (as is the case for the user-defined collections in the previous example). For example, the *TableDefs* collection contains only *TableDef* objects (table definitions). It does not contain the *Fields* collection. Rather, each *TableDef object* contains a *Fields* collection. We can confirm this with the code in Example 9-6 which displays the size of the *TableDefs* collection for the LIBRARY database as 14, and then displays the names of each of its 14 objects, showing that there is nothing but *TableDef* objects in the *TableDefs* collection.

*Example 9-6. A TableDef Example*

```
Sub exaCheckTableDefs()

Dim db As DATABASE
Dim tbl As TableDef
Dim strTbls As String

Set db = CurrentDb

strTbls = ""
MsgBox db.TableDefs.Count
For Each tbl In db.TableDefs
    strTbls = strTbls & vbCrLf & tbl.Name & " - " & TypeName(tbl)
Next

MsgBox strTbls

End Sub
```

Running the code in Example 9-6 produces the message box shown in Figure 9-8, which also shows that most of the *TableDefs* in the database are system table definitions, created by Microsoft Access for its own use. (Just in case some additional tables get added to the LIBRARY database after this book goes to print, you may find a different list of tables when you run this example.) (It also illustrates the use of the function *TypeName.*)

## Refreshing Certain Collections

There are times when the Microsoft Jet engine does not have the latest information on the contents of a collection. For example, this can happen in a multi-user environment, when one user makes a change to a collection. Moreover, it can also happen when a host environment, such as Microsoft Access, makes a change to the environment. To see this, try the following simple experiment.

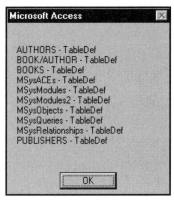

*Figure 9-8. A list of TableDefs generated by exaCheckTableDefs()*

Enter the following code:

```
Sub temp()

Dim db As DATABASE
Set db = DBEngine(0)(0)

' db.TableDefs.Refresh
MsgBox "Table count: " & db.TableDefs.Count

End Sub
```

Run the procedure. You should get a message that there are 13 tables in the *Table-Defs* collection. Now use Microsoft Access to create a new table and save the table. Then rerun the code above. It will still report that there are 13 tables! Now remove the comment mark on the line:

```
' db.TableDefs.Refresh
```

and rerun the code. You should now get an accurate table count.

The point here is that the Jet engine does not keep track of the machinations of its host application—Microsoft Access. Hence, to be certain that a collection is up to date, you may need to use the *Refresh* method.

# *The Properties Collection*

One item that has been left out of the diagram of the DAO object model which is shown earlier in Figure 9-5 (and is done so in most DAO diagrams) is the *Properties* collection. This is because every DAO object has a *Properties* collection, so it would clutter up the diagram considerably, without adding much information. Figure 9-9 shows a *Properties* collection.

*Figure 9-9. An Access properties collection diagram*

The purpose of the *Properties* collections is simple. Properties are objects too and so they are contained in collections, just like all other objects of the DAO (except *DBEngine*). Thus, the *Properties* collection of an object contains the *Property* objects (better known simply as properties) for the object.

The fact that the properties of an object are themselves objects, and thus reside in a collection, implies that we may access these properties in several different ways. For example, the *RecordCount* property of the *TableDef* object BOOKS can be referred to in any of the following ways (among others):

```
TableDefs!BOOKS.Properties!RecordCount
TableDefs("BOOKS").Properties("RecordCount")
```

or just:

```
TableDefs!BOOKS.RecordCount
```

Of course, the latter form is the simplest and most commonly used. Note that the *Properties* collection is never the default collection for any object. Hence, for example, the syntax

```
TableDefs!BOOKS!RecordCount
```

(which differs from the previous only by a bang) will cause VBA to look for the *RecordCount* object in the default *Fields* collection for the BOOKS *TableDef* object. Of course, it will not find such an object and so the error message *Item not found in this collection* will result.

## *The Virtues of Properties Collections*

There are several virtues to the existence of *Properties* collections. One is that it is possible to iterate through all of the properties of an object, using the *For Each* syntax discussed earlier, for instance, without even knowing the names of the properties.

For example, the following simple code:

```
Dim db As DATABASE
Dim prp As Property
Set db = CurrentDb
```

```
For Each prp In db.TableDefs!BOOKS.Properties
    Debug.Print prp.Name
Next prp
```

produces the following list of all properties of the BOOKS object:

```
Name
Updatable
DateCreated
LastUpdated
Connect
Attributes
SourceTableName
RecordCount
ValidationRule
ValidationText
ConflictTable
OrderByOn
OrderBy
```

Another virtue of *Properties* collections is that they allow for the creation (and storage) of new properties. We discuss this next.

## *Types of Properties*

In general, the properties of an object can be classified into three groups, depending upon their origin:

- Built-in properties

- Application-defined properties

- User-defined properties

The Jet database engine defines *built-in properties* for its objects. For instance, a *TableDef* object has a built-in *Name* property. In addition, Microsoft Access (and other applications that may be using the Jet engine) can create *application-defined properties*. For example, if you create a table in Microsoft Access and fill in the *Description* field in the *View ... Properties* dialog box, Access creates a *Description* property for the table and appends it to the *Properties* collection for that *TableDef* object. Finally, as we will see later, the user can create his or her own properties.

It is important to note that an application-defined property is created *only* if the user assigns a value to that property. For example, if you do not specifically type a description in the *Description* field, as discussed earlier, then Access will not create a *Description* property. In other words, Access does not create a blank *Description* property. If you then use to this property in your code, an error will result. Thus, when writing programs that refer to either application-defined or user-defined properties, it is important to check for errors, in case the referenced property does not exist.

Of course, each *Property* object, being an object, has its own properties, but you will be glad to hear that these properties do not have *Property* objects. (Where would this end?)

We should also mention that properties can be classified as *read/write, read-only,* or *write-only*. A read/write property can be both read and written to (i.e., changed), whereas a read-only property can be read but not changed, and a write-only property can be changed but not read. When an object is first created, its read/write properties can be set. However, in many cases, once the object is appended to a collection, some of these properties may become read-only, and can therefore no longer be changed.

The properties of a *Property* object are described below. A *Property* object has no methods.

### Property: Inherited

For the built-in *Property* objects, this value is always 0 (False). For user-defined properties, this value is true if the property exists because it was inherited from another object. For instance, any *Recordset* object that is created from a *QueryDef* object inherits the *QueryDef*'s properties.

### Property: Name

The usual *Name* property, which in this case is the name of the property represented by this property object.

### Property: Type

This value gives the data type of the object. Note that the *Type* property is read/write until the *Property* object is appended to a *Properties* collection, after which it becomes read-only. The value of the *Type* property is an integer. VBA provides built-in constants so that we do not need to remember integer values. Table 9-4 gives these values, along with their numerical values, which are returned in code such as *MsgBox Property.Type*.

*Table 9-4. Constants for the Type Property in VBA*

| Data Type | Constant | Numerical Value |
|-----------|----------|-----------------|
| Boolean | dbBoolean | 1 |
| Byte | dbByte | 2 |
| Integer | dbInteger | 3 |
| Long | dbLong | 4 |
| Currency | dbCurrency | 5 |
| Single | dbSingle | 6 |

*Table 9-4. Constants for the Type Property in VBA (continued)*

| Data Type | Constant | Numerical Value |
|-----------|----------|-----------------|
| Double | dbDouble | 7 |
| Date/Time | dbDate | 8 |
| Text | dbText | 10 |
| Long Binary (OLE Object) | dbLongBinary | 11 |
| Memo | dbMemo | 12 |
| GUID | dbGUID | 15 |

### Property: Value

Finally, we get to the main property of a *Property* object—its value, which can be any value commensurate with the assigned *Type* property of the *Property* object.

Let us consider another example of how to use the *Properties* collection.

The code in Example 9-7 will display the entire contents of the *Properties* collection for the BOOKS *TableDef* object in the LIBRARY database.

*Example 9-7. Properties Collection Example*

```
Sub exaProperties()

Dim db As DATABASE
Dim tbl As TableDef
Dim prp As Property
Dim str As String

Set db = CurrentDb
Set tbl = db!BOOKS

str = ""
For Each prp In tbl.Properties

    str = str & prp.Name
    str = str & " = " & prp.Value
    str = str & " (" & prp.Type & ") "
    str = str & prp.Inherited & vbCrLf

Next prp

MsgBox "BOOKS has " & tbl.Properties.Count _
& " properties: " & vbCrLf & str

End Sub
```

Running this procedure gives the window shown in Figure 9-10, where each line has the form *Name = Value (Type) Inherited*.

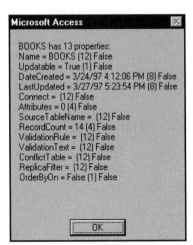

**Microsoft Access**

```
BOOKS has 13 properties:
Name = BOOKS (12) False
Updatable = True (1) False
DateCreated = 3/24/97 4:12:06 PM (8) False
LastUpdated = 3/27/97 5:23:54 PM (8) False
Connect = (12) False
Attributes = 0 (4) False
SourceTableName = (12) False
RecordCount = 14 (4) False
ValidationRule = (12) False
ValidationText = (12) False
ConflictTable = (12) False
ReplicaFilter = (12) False
OrderByOn = False (1) False
```

OK

*Figure 9-10. Window generated from executing exaProperties()*

## User-Defined Properties

We mentioned that a user can add user-defined properties to an object. Let us consider an example of adding a new property to the BOOKS *TableDef* object.

The code in Example 9-8 adds the user-defined property named *UserProperty* to the BOOKS table. It uses the *CreateProperty* method of the *TableDef* object.

*Example 9-8. A User-Defined Properties Example*

```
Sub exaUserDefinedProperty()

' Add user-defined property to BOOKS TableDef object

Dim db As DATABASE
Dim tbl As TableDef
Dim prp As Property

Dim str As String

Set db = CurrentDb
Set tbl = db!BOOKS

' Create new property using CreateProperty method
Set prp = tbl.CreateProperty("UserProperty", dbText,"Programming DAO is
fun.")

' Append it to Properties collection
tbl.Properties.Append prp

' List all properties
str = ""
For Each prp In tbl.Properties
```

*Example 9-8. A User-Defined Properties Example (continued)*

```
    str = str & prp.Name
    str = str & " = " & prp.Value
    str = str & " (" & prp.Type & ") "
    str = str & prp.Inherited & vbCrLf
Next prp

MsgBox "BOOKS has " & tbl.Properties.Count & " properties: " & vbCrLf & str

End Sub
```

This procedure produces the window shown in Figure 9-11. Note the last property on the list.

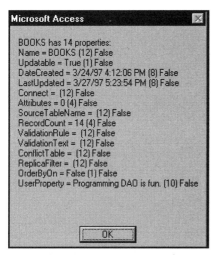

Figure 9-11. Window generated from executing exaUserDefinedProperty()

# Closing DAO Objects

We should make a few remarks about closing DAO objects that have been opened programmatically. The *Database, Recordset,* and *Workspace* objects each have a *Close* method. This method will remove these objects from their respective collections. This is appropriate for the three object types mentioned above for the following reasons:

- The *Databases* collection is defined to be the collection of all *open* database objects

- The *Recordset* objects are temporary objects, to be used only for data manipulation purposes

- Attempts to close the default *Workspace* object are ignored, but you can close other *Workspace* objects

Note that objects of types other than the three mentioned above are intended to be persistent members of their collections, stored on disk in the Access *mdb* file. However, they can be removed from their respective collections by using the *Delete* method.

Here are some caveats to keep in mind with respect to closing objects:

- As we will see in Chapter 11, *Programming DAO: Data Manipulation Language*, you should update (i.e., complete) all pending edits before closing an open *Recordset* object.

- When a procedure that declares a *Recordset* or *Database* object is exited, the recordset or database is closed and any unsaved changes or pending edits are lost.

- If you close a *Database* object while any *Recordset* objects are still open, or if you close a *Workspace* object while any of its *Database* objects are open, those *Recordset* objects will be automatically closed and any pending updates or edits will be lost.

# A Look at the DAO Objects

Now we can look briefly at each of the collections (and their objects) in the DAO Object Model. We will discuss each object and mention a few of the more commonly used properties and methods. A complete list of all collections, methods, and properties of each object is given in Appendix A, *DAO 3.0/3.5 Collections, Properties, and Methods*.

## DBEngine Object

The *DBEngine* object, of which there is only one, represents the Jet database engine. This is the only object in the DAO that is not contained in a collection. We have seen several examples of its use, along with the fact that the default collection for the *DBEngine* object is *Workspaces*, and so:

```
DBEngine.Workspaces(0)
```

is equivalent to:

```
DBEngine(0)
```

We have also seen that:

```
DBEngine(0)(0)
```

denotes the first database in the first (default) workspace.

The *DBEngine* object has methods to create a new workspace (*CreateWorkspace*), to compact a database (*CompactDatabase*), and to repair a database (*RepairDatabase*), among others.

## Errors

From time to time, an operation may cause one or more errors to occur (or so I am told). When this happens, the *Errors* collection is first emptied and then filled with one *Error* object for each error that the operation caused. (Some operations may cause more than one error.) Note that if no errors occur, the *Errors* collection remains as it was before the operation.

Example 9-9, which deliberately produces an error, illustrates the use of the *Errors* collection. It also demonstrates the use of three *Error* object properties: *Number* (the VBA error number), *Description* (a description in words of the error), and *Source* (the object or application that generated the error).

*Example 9-9. An Errors Collection Example*

```
Sub exaErrorsCollection()

' Note declaration of object variable of type Error
Dim dbsTest As DATABASE
Dim txtError As String
Dim errObj As Error

On Error GoTo ehTest

' A statement that produces an error
Set dbsTest = _
DBEngine.Workspaces(0).OpenDatabase("NoSuchDatabase")

Exit Sub

ehTest:

txtError = ""
' Loop through the Errors collection,
' to get the Number, Description and Source
' for each error object
For Each errObj In DBEngine.Errors
    txtError = txtError & Format$(errObj.Number)
    txtError = txtError & ": " & errObj.Description
    txtError = txtError & " (" & errObj.Source & ")"
    txtError = txtError & vbCrLf
Next

MsgBox txtError

Exit Sub

End Sub
```

Running this code produces the window in Figure 9-12.

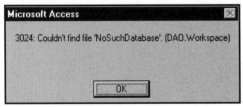

*Figure 9-12. Error message from executing exaErrorsCollection()*

## Workspaces

There is one *Workspace* object for each Access user session. In a single-user environment, there is generally only one session running. When a user starts Access with no security options enabled, Access automatically creates a *Workspace* called

```
DBEngine.Workspaces(0)
```

Since we are not concerned in this book with multiple users or with database security issues, we will not be creating multiple workspaces.

The values of the *Name* and *UserName* properties of the default *Workspace* object are easily determined by running the following code:

```
Sub Test()

MsgBox "Count: " & DBEngine.Workspaces.Count
MsgBox "Name: " & DBEngine.Workspaces(0).Name
MsgBox "UserName: " & DBEngine.Workspaces(0).UserName

End Sub
```

This code should produce three message boxes, indicating that there is only one open workspace, with name *#Default Workspace#* and username *admin*.

Among the methods of a *Workspace* object are *CreateDatabase* (for creating a new database) and *OpenDatabase* (for opening an existing database). Another interesting group of methods is *BeginTrans, CommitTrans,* and *Rollback,* which allow the programmer to group several operations into one *transaction*. At the end of the transaction, the programmer can commit the operations or *rollback* the database to its state prior to any of the operations in the transaction. One use for this is in updating related tables (as in transferring money from one table to another). If the entire group of operations is not completed successfully, then a rollback is probably desirable.

*Workspace* objects also have a *Close* method, for closing opened workspaces. However, the method is ignored when applied to the default *Workspace* under Microsoft Access.

## Users

The Jet engine provides security by assigning *access permissions* to users of the engine. A *User* object represents a user of the Jet engine. The *Users* collection contains all *User* objects. (Of course, female users are never to be considered objects.)

## Groups

A *Group* object represents a set of *User* objects (users) that have a common set of access permissions. By using *Group* objects, a new user can be given a set of access permissions simply by adding the corresponding *User* object to the appropriate *Group* object. The *Groups* collection holds all *Group* objects.

## Databases

A *Database* object represents a currently open database. In Microsoft Jet, you can have multiple databases open at one time (using the *OpenDatabase* function, discussed in Chapter 10). However, the Microsoft Access environment can display a graphical interface for only one database. In the Microsoft Access environment, when a database is opened it is assigned to *DBEngine.Workspaces(0).Databases(0)*.

*Database* objects have a variety of methods for creating new objects: *CreateProperty*, *CreateQueryDef*, *CreateTableDef*, and *OpenRecordset*. There is also an *Execute* method for running action queries or executing SQL statements on the database. As mentioned earlier, *Database* objects also have a *Close* method.

## TableDefs

A *TableDef* object represents a table definition for a saved table in the database. A *TableDef* object is more than a table scheme, in that it also has a *RecordCount* property that gives the number of rows in the table (and thus, in some sense, reflects the data in the table). However, it is less than a table, in that it does not describe the actual data in the table. The *TableDefs* collection contains all *TableDef* objects for a given database. *TableDef* objects have methods for creating fields (*CreateField*), indexes (*CreateIndex*), and opening recordsets (*Open-Recordset*).

## QueryDefs

A *QueryDef* object represents a saved query in the database. The *QueryDefs* collection contains all *QueryDef* objects for a given database. One of the most interesting properties of a *QueryDef* object is *SQL*, which can be used to set or read the SQL definition of the *QueryDef* object.

## Recordsets

A *Recordset* object represents data from one or more tables or queries, and is used to manipulate that data. Note that a *Recordset* object is temporary, in that it is not saved with the application. In fact, recordsets are created in code using the *OpenRecordset* function. The *Recordsets* collection contains all open *Recordset* objects in the current database.

*Recordset* objects are the workhorses of the DAO object model, with about 15 different methods and about 20 different properties. There are actually three types of *Recordset* objects—*Table-type, Dynaset,* and *Snapshot*—used for different purposes. We will discuss recordsets in Chapter 10.

## Relations

A *Relation* object represents a relationship between certain fields in tables or queries. The *Relation* object can be used to view or create relationships. The *Relations* collection contains all *Relation* objects for a given database. We will discuss how to create a relation in the next chapter.

## Containers

The Microsoft Jet engine provides the *Containers* collection as a location where a host application, such as Microsoft Access, can store its own objects. This is done through the use of *Container* objects, as shown in Figure 9-13.

The Jet engine itself creates three *Container* objects:

- A *Databases* container object, containing information about the database
- A *Tables* container object, containing information about each *saved* table and query
- A *Relations* container object, containing information about each *saved* relationship

It is important not to confuse these *Container* objects (which are *not* collections, despite their names) with the *Databases, TableDefs,* and *Relations* collections. Indeed, these objects are at entirely different locations in the DAO object hierarchy, and serve different purposes, as we will see.

In addition to the *Container* objects created by the Jet engine, Microsoft Access stores its forms, reports, macros, and modules in the *Containers* collection. Hence, the *Containers* collection also contains:

- A *Forms* container object, containing information about all *saved* forms
- A *Reports* container object, containing information about all *saved* reports

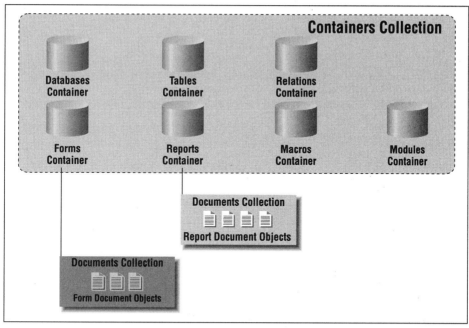

*Figure 9-13. Container objects diagram of the MS Jet engine*

- A *Macros* container object, containing information about all *saved* macros

- A *Modules* container object, containing information about all *saved* modules

The *Forms* and *Reports Container* objects should not be confused with the Microsoft Access collections of the same name (in the Access object model). In particular, the former contains information about all *saved* objects, whereas the latter contains information about all *open* objects.

To illustrate the aforementioned difference, create and save two forms in an Access session and make sure that only one form is open. Then run the code in Example 9-10, which should report that the open form count is 1 but the saved form count is 2.

*Example 9-10. A Container Collection Example*

```
Sub exaFormsContainer()

Dim db As DATABASE
Dim frm As Form
Dim doc As Document

Set db = CurrentDb

Debug.Print "Opened form count: " & Forms.Count
For Each frm In Forms
```

*Example 9-10. A Container Collection Example (continued)*

```
    Debug.Print frm.Name
Next
Debug.Print

Debug.Print "Saved form count: " & db.Containers!Forms.Documents.Count
For Each doc In db.Containers!Forms.Documents
    Debug.Print doc.Name
Next

End Sub
```

Note that a user cannot create new or delete existing *Container* objects—they are controlled by the Jet engine only. Put another way, there is no such thing as a user-defined *Container* object. The properties of a *Container* object generally reflect security related issues, such as permission and user/group names. *Container* objects have no methods.

## *Documents*

We have seen that applications (including Jet and Access) store objects through the use of *Container* objects. However, the *Forms Container* object, for example, is not of any real interest per se. It is the *Form* objects that reside within the *Forms* container that are of interest. Actually, these *Form* objects are referred to as *Document* objects and are contained in the *Documents* collection of the *Forms* container, also shown in Figure 9-6. (If you are getting a bit confused, Figure 9-6 should help—it always helps me.)

Thus, it is the *Document* objects (in a *Documents* collection) that are the *raison d'être* for the *Container* objects. The following example illustrates a few of the properties of a *Document* object: *Container, DateCreated, LastUpdated, Name,* and *Owner.*

Example 9-11 displays the value of various properties of the *Document* objects in the *Documents* collection of the *Tables Container* object.

*Example 9-11. Properties of the Document Object*

```
Sub exaTablesDocuments()
Dim db As DATABASE
Set db = CurrentDb
Dim docs As Documents
Dim doc As Document

Set docs = db.Containers!Tables.Documents
Debug.Print "Count: " & docs.Count

For Each doc In docs
```

*Example 9-11. Properties of the Document Object (continued)*

```
Debug.Print "Container: " & doc.Container
Debug.Print "DateCreated: " & doc.DateCreated
Debug.Print "LastUpdated: " & doc.LastUpdated
Debug.Print "Name: " & doc.Name
Debug.Print "Owner: " & doc.Owner
Debug.Print
```

```
Next doc
```

**End Sub**

Here is a portion of the output from executing Example 9-11:

```
Count: 16
Container: Tables
DateCreated: 10/22/96 3:16:44 PM
LastUpdated: 10/24/96 1:36:16 PM
Name: AUTHORS
Owner: admin

Container: Tables
DateCreated: 10/22/96 3:19:47 PM
LastUpdated: 10/24/96 1:36:16 PM
Name: BOOK/AUTHOR
Owner: admin

Container: Tables
DateCreated: 5/15/96 6:16:29 PM
LastUpdated: 5/15/96 6:16:29 PM
Name: MSysACEs
Owner: Engine

Container: Tables
DateCreated: 5/15/96 6:16:31 PM
LastUpdated: 5/15/96 6:16:31 PM
Name: MSysIMEXColumns
Owner: admin
```

# Fields

The *Fields* collection contains *Field* objects, which describe the various fields in a *TableDef, QueryDef, Index, Relation,* or *Recordset* object.

# Parameters

The parameters of a parameter query are represented by *Parameter* objects, contained in the *Parameters* collection for that *QueryDef* object. Note that *Parameter* objects cannot be added to or deleted from the *Parameters* collection— *Parameter* objects represent existing parameters. Let us consider an example.

The code in Example 9-12 creates a parameter query named *ParameterQuery* and demonstrates some of the properties of a *Parameter* object;—namely, *Name*, *Type,* and *Value.*

*Example 9-12. A Parameter Query Example*

```
Sub exaParameters()
Dim db As DATABASE
Dim qdf As QueryDef
Dim strSQL As String

Set db = CurrentDb

' Create an SQL statement with parameters
strSQL = "SELECT * FROM BOOKS WHERE _
Price > [Enter minimum price]"

' Create a new QueryDef object
Set qdf = db.CreateQueryDef("ParameterQuery", strSQL)

' Supply value for parameter
qdf.PARAMETERS![Enter minimum price] = 15

' Now query query
Debug.Print qdf.PARAMETERS![Enter minimum price].Name
Debug.Print qdf.PARAMETERS![Enter minimum price].Type
Debug.Print qdf.PARAMETERS![Enter minimum _
price].Value

End Sub
```

## Indexes

An *Indexes* collection contains all of the *saved Index* objects (i.e., indices) for a *TableDef* object. We will discuss how to create an index in the next chapter.

# *The CurrentDb Function*

We have seen that DAO refers to the current database as:

```
DBEngine.Workspaces(0).Databases(0)
```

or, through default collections, as:

```
DBEngine(0)(0)
```

However, within Microsoft Access, there is a preferred way to refer to this database, since, unlike *DBEngine(0)(0)*, it is always current with respect to changes made using the Access graphical interface. This preferred way is to use the Access function *CurrentDb*. Unfortunately, there is some confusion as to precisely what this function does.

Here is part of what the Access Help system (for both Access 7.0 and Access 8.0) says about this function:

> The CurrentDb function returns an object variable of type *Database* that represents the database currently open in the Microsoft Access window.
>
> The CurrentDb function provides a way to access the current database from Visual Basic code without having to know the name of the database. Once you have a variable that points to the current database, you can also access and manipulate other objects and collections in the data access object hierarchy.
>
> You can use the CurrentDb function to create multiple object variables that refer to the current database. In the following example, the variables *dbsA* and *dbsB* both refer to the current database:

```
Dim dbsA As Database, dbsB As Database
Set dbsA = CurrentDb
Set dbsB = CurrentDb
```

This certainly makes it appear as though the object variables *dbsA* and *dbsB* point to a *single Database* object, namely, the currently open database. In other words, executing the instruction:

```
Set db = CurrentDb
```

implies that *db* points to the *Database* object known to DAO as *DBEngine(0)(0)*. However, the Help system goes on to say:

> Note: In previous versions of Microsoft Access, you may have used the syntax *DBEngine.Workspaces(0).Databases(0)*, or *DBEngine(0)(0)* to return a pointer to the current database. In Microsoft Access for Windows 95, you should use the *CurrentDb* function instead. The *CurrentDb* function creates another instance of the current database, while the *DBEngine(0)(0)* syntax refers to the open copy of the current database. Using the *CurrentDb* function enables you to create more than one variable of type *Database* that refers to the current database. Microsoft Access still supports the *DBEngine(0)(0)* syntax, but you should consider making this modification to your code in order to avoid possible conflicts in a multiuser database.

This seems to contradict the previous statements, by indicating that each time *CurrentDb* is executed, it creates a new *Database* object. Actually, if the current database is considered an object, then the statement "... creates another instance of the current database..." makes no sense, since one cannot create an instance of an *object*. (In object-oriented terms, one can create an instance of a *class*, and such an instance is *called* an *object*.)

In any case, each call to *CurrentDb* does seem to create a new object, as we can see from the experiment in Example 9-13, which checks the *Count* property of the *Databases* collection both before and after calling *CurrentDb*, showing that the count goes up!

*Example 9-13. A CurrentDb Function Example*

```
Sub exaCurrentDB()

Dim db, dbExtra, dbOriginal As DATABASE
Dim str As String
Dim i As Integer

Set dbOriginal = DBEngine(0)(0)

' Check the database count
MsgBox "Initial db count: " & _
DBEngine.Workspaces(0).Databases.Count

' Invoke CurrentDB
Set dbExtra = CurrentDb()

' Check the database count again
MsgBox "Count after CurrentDb run: " & _
DBEngine.Workspaces(0).Databases.Count

' Display the two database names
str = ""
For Each db In DBEngine.Workspaces(0).Databases
    str = str & vbCrLf & db.Name
Next db
MsgBox "Db Names: " & vbCrLf & str

dbExtra.Close

End Sub
```

If each call to *CurrentDb* produces a pointer to a new object, then it is natural to wonder what happens if we change the object pointed to by one of these pointers. Does it affect the other objects? What about *DBEngine(0)(0)?* Consider the code in Example 9-14, which does the following:

- Creates two *Database* object variables *dbOne* and *dbTwo*, and sets both equal to *CurrentDb*

- Adds a new field *NewField1* to the BOOKS table using *dbOne*

- Adds a new field *NewField2* to the BOOKS table using *dbTwo*

- Displays the list of fields for BOOKS using *dbOne*

- Displays the list of fields for BOOKS using *dbTwo*

- Closes *dbOne* and *dbTwo;* that is, it removes their objects from the *Databases* collection

## Running exaCurrentDb2

To examine the behavior of the procedure shown in Example 9-14, do the following:

1. Run the program as is. Access displays the dialog in Figure 9-14.

2. Delete NewField1 and NewField2 from the BOOKS table. You can do this by opening the table in Design view, selecting each field separately, and choosing the Delete Row option from the Edit menu.

3. Comment out (using either the *Rem* statement or the ' character) the call to the *Refresh* method, then run the procedure. Access displays the dialog in Figure 9-15.

4. Once again, delete NewField1 and NewField2 from the BOOKS table.

5. Remove the comment from the call to the *Refresh* method, and change it to read `dbOne.TableDefs!Books.Fields.Refresh`. When you run the procedure, Access once again displays the dialog shown in Figure 9-15.

6. Once again, delete NewField1 and NewField2 from the BOOKS table.

It's necessary to delete both NewField1 and NewField2 each time you run some variation of this procedure, since otherwise Access will display a "Can't define field more than once" error message.

---

*Example 9-14. The dbOne and dbTwo Variable Example*

```
Sub exaCurrentDb2()

Dim dbOne As Database, dbTwo As DATABASE
Dim fldNew As Field
Dim str As String

Set dbOne = CurrentDb
Set dbTwo = CurrentDb

' Get field list in BOOKS
str = "Fields before: " & vbCrLf
''MsgBox dbOne.TableDefs!Books.Fields.Count
For Each fldNew In dbOne.TableDefs!Books.Fields
    str = str & fldNew.Name & vbCrLf
Next

' Use dbOne to add a new field to BOOKS
Set fldNew = dbOne.TableDefs!Books.CreateField("NewField1", dbInteger)
dbOne.TableDefs!Books.Fields.Append fldNew

' Use dbTwo to add a new field to BOOKS
Set fldNew = dbTwo.TableDefs!Books.CreateField("NewField2", dbInteger)
```

*Example 9-14. The dbOne and dbTwo Variable Example (continued)*

```
dbTwo.TableDefs!Books.Fields.Append fldNew

''Stop - (see the explanation in the text)

' Refresh Fields collection using dbOne!!!
dbOne.TableDefs!BOOKS.Fields.Refresh

' Get field list now using dbOne
str = str & vbCrLf & "Fields after using dbOne: " & vbCrLf
For Each fldNew In dbOne.TableDefs!Books.Fields
    str = str & fldNew.Name & vbCrLf
Next

' Get field list now using dbTwo
str = str & vbCrLf & "Fields after using dbTwo: " & vbCrLf
For Each fldNew In dbTwo.TableDefs!Books.Fields
    str = str & fldNew.Name & vbCrLf
Next

MsgBox str

dbOne.Close
dbTwo.Close

End Sub
```

Running this code produces the window shown in Figure 9-14.

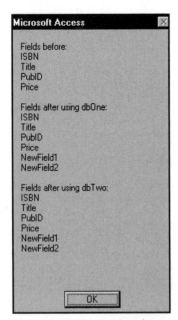

*Figure 9-14. Message box from executing exaCurrentDb2()*

Thus, it appears that changing the *Database* object pointed to by *dbTwo* does in fact also change the *Database* object pointed to by *dbOne*. However, if we do not refresh the *Fields* collection using the variable *dbOne*, or if we refresh using the variable *dbTwo* instead, we get the message box shown in Figure 9-15. Note that *NewField2* is missing from the second group.

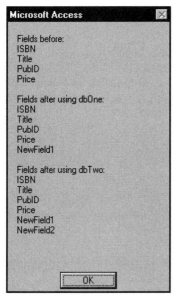

*Figure 9-15. Message box from executing exaCurrentDb2() when refreshing with dbTwo*

Note also that even before the two objects *dbOne* and *dbTwo* have been closed, the Access graphical interface has been updated to reflect the two new fields. In fact, if you uncomment the *Stop* line in the code above and check the design of the BOOKS table though Access, you will find that both new fields appear, even before the *Refresh* method is called.

All of this experimenting leaves us with a feeling that there are some mysteries associated with *CurrentDb* that Microsoft is not revealing (at least not readily). We can summarize as follows:

- Invoking *CurrentDb* creates another member of the *Databases* collection.

- On the other hand, each variable set through *CurrentDb* seems to affect the same database.

- Refreshing is required to keep objects created through multiple invocations of *CurrentDb* current, belying the purpose of *CurrentDb* to some extent.

- On the other hand, the Access interface does not require refreshing—it reflects the latest operations performed using any of the invocations of *CurrentDb*.

These issues notwithstanding, it makes sense to follow Microsoft's recommendation to use *CurrentDb*, since it does reflect the current state of the Access environment more accurately than *DBEngine(0)(0)*. Just be advised that some circumspection (refreshing) is needed when creating more than one variable through *CurrentDb*.

Finally, if you do use *CurrentDb*, then you should use it according to Microsoft's rules, found in the Access 7.0 readme file *acreadme.txt* (but missing from the Access 8.0 readme file *acread80.wri*). Its text is reproduced below. Note the use of the word "once."

Using the CurrentDb Function to Return a Reference to the Current Database

When you write code that includes a reference to the current database, you should declare a variable of type Database and use the CurrentDb function once to assign to it a pointer to the current database. You should avoid using CurrentDb to return the current database in a statement that also returns a reference to another object, such as a Set statement. It was possible to do this in some beta versions of Microsoft Access, but in Microsoft Access for Windows 95, your code may not run properly. For example, to determine the number of Document objects in the Documents collection, you should write code such as that shown in the following two examples:

```
Dim dbs As Database, con As Container
Set dbs = CurrentDb
Set con = dbs.Containers!Forms
Debug.Print con.Documents.Count
```

-or-

```
Debug.Print _
CurrentDb.Containers!Forms.Documents.Count
```

Code such as the following will not work:

```
Dim con As Container
Set con = CurrentDb.Containers!Forms
Debug.Print con.Documents.Count
```

# 10

# *Programming DAO: Data Definition Language*

In our overview of DAO, we noted that Data Access Objects consists of two conceptually distinct components: a data definition language (or DDL) which allows us to create or access some basic database system objects, like databases, table definitions, and indexes; and a data manipulation language (or DML) which allows us to perform the practical operations of adding data (records) to our tables, deleting unwanted data, and modifying existing data. In this chapter, we discuss the data definition language (DDL) aspects of DAO.

Let us begin by noting the following:

- To indicate variables of a certain type, we will write the type name followed by the suffix *Var*. For example, *DatabaseVar* denotes a variable of type *Database* and *TableDefVar* denotes a variable of type *TableDef*.

- In describing the syntax of certain methods, we will use square brackets ([ ]) to indicate optional items.

- We will generally give the full syntax of methods, but will only give details on the more common options. Of course, full details are available through the Access Help system.

## *Creating a Database*

Databases are created using the *CreateDatabase* method of a *Workspace* object. The general syntax of this method is:

```
Set DatabaseVar = [WorkspaceVar.]CreateDatabase _
(DatabaseName, locale [, options])
```

where:

- *DatabaseName* is a string expression representing the full path and name of the database file for the database being created. If you don't supply a file-name extension, then the extension *.mdb* is automatically appended.

- *locale* is a string expression used to specify collating order for creating the database. You must supply this argument or an error will occur. For the English language, use the built-in constant *dbLangGeneral.*

- *options* relates to specifying encryption or use of a specific version of the Jet database engine. For more information, please see Access Help.

*Notes:*

- The *CreateDatabase* method creates a new *Database* object, appends the database to the *Databases* collection, saves the database on disk, and then returns an opened *Database* object, but the database has no structure or content at this point.

- To duplicate a database, you can use the *CompactDatabase* method of a *Workspace* object, specifying a different name for the compacted database.

- A database cannot be deleted programmatically through DAO. To delete a database programatically, use the KILL statement in VBA.

Example 10-1 creates a new database named *MoreBks.mdb* on the directory *c:/temp*, and then lists the tables that are contained in the database.

*Example 10-1. A CreateDatabase Method Example*

```
Sub exaCreateDb()

Dim dbNew As DATABASE
Dim tbl As TableDef

Set dbNew = CreateDatabase _
("c:\temp\MoreBks", dbLangGeneral)

For Each tbl In dbNew.TableDefs
    Debug.Print tbl.Name
Next

dbNew.Close

End Sub
```

The program in Example 10-1 displays the following list of tables:

> *MSysACEs*
> *MSysObjects*

*MSysQueries*
*MSysRelationships*

These tables are created by Microsoft Access for its own use.

# Opening a Database

To open an existing database, use the *OpenDatabase* method of a *Workspace* object. The syntax is:

```
Set DatabaseVar = [WorkspaceVar.]OpenDatabase _
(DatabaseName[, exclusive[, read-only[, source]]])
```

where *DatabaseName* is the name of an existing database. (As indicated by the square brackets, the other parameters are optional.) For information about the optional parameters, see the Access Help system.

It is important to remember to close a database opened through the *OpenDatabase* method. This removes the database from the *Databases* collection.

# Creating a Table and Its Fields

Tables are created using the *CreateTableDef* method of a *Database* object. The full syntax of this method is:

```
Set TableDefVar = DatabaseVar.CreateTableDef _
([TableDefName[, attributes[, source[, connect]]]])
```

where:

- *TableDefName* is a string or string variable holding the name of the new *TableDef* object.

- For information about the optional parameters, see the Access Help system.

*Notes:*

- The new *TableDef* object must be appended to the *TableDefs* collection using the *Append* method. However, before appending, the table must have at least one field.

- *CreateTableDef* does not check for an already used *TableDefName*. If *TableDefName* does refer to an object already in the *TableDefs* collection, an error will occur when you use the *Append* method, but not before.

- To remove a *TableDef* object from a *TableDefs* collection, use the *Delete* method.

Fields are created for a table using the *CreateField* method of the *TableDef* object. The syntax is:

```
Set FieldVar =TableDefVar.CreateField _
([FieldName[, type [, size]]])
```

where:

- *FieldName* is a string or string variable that names the new *Field* object.

- *type* is an integer constant that determines the data type of the new *Field* object. (See Table 10-1.)

- *size* is an integer between 1 and 255 that indicates the maximum size, in bytes, for a text field. This argument is ignored for other types of fields.

*Note:*

To remove a field from a *TableDef* object, use the *Delete* method.

*Table 10-1. Constants for the Type Property*

| Data Type | Constant | Numerical Value |
|---|---|---|
| Boolean | dbBoolean | 1 |
| Byte | dbByte | 2 |
| Integer | dbInteger | 3 |
| Long | dbLong | 4 |
| Currency | dbCurrency | 5 |
| Single | dbSingle | 6 |
| Double | dbDouble | 7 |
| Date/Time | dbDate | 8 |
| Text | dbText | 10 |
| Long Binary (OLE Object) | dbLongBinary | 11 |
| Memo | dbMemo | 12 |
| GUID | dbGUID | 15 |

*Field* objects have a variety of properties, among which are:

- *AllowZeroLength*: **True** if a zero-length value is valid for a text or memo field. (Setting this property for a nontext field generates an error.)

- *DefaultValue*: Sets or returns the default value of a *Field* object.

- *Required*: **True** indicates that a null value is not allowed.

- *ValidationRule* and *ValidationText*: Used for validation of field values. (See the following example.)

The procedure in Example 10-2 creates a new table named *NewTable*, creates a new field named *NewField*, sets certain properties of the field and appends it to the *Fields* collection, and then appends the new table to the *TableDefs* collection.

*Example 10-2. A CreateTableDef Method Example*

```
Sub exaCreateTable()

Dim db As DATABASE
Dim tblNew As TableDef
Dim fld As Field

Set db = CurrentDb

Set tblNew = db.CreateTableDef("NewTable")
Set fld = tblNew.CreateField("NewField", dbText, 100)

' Set properties of field BEFORE appending

' zero length value is OK
fld.AllowZeroLength = True
' default value is 'Unknown'
fld.DefaultValue = "Unknown"
' Null value not allowed
fld.Required = True
' Validation
fld.ValidationRule = "Like 'A*' or Like 'Unknown'"
fld.ValidationText = "Known value must begin with A"

' Append field to Fields collection
tblNew.Fields.Append fld

' Append table to TableDef collection
db.TableDefs.Append tblNew

End Sub
```

Setting the validation properties of a field requires setting two properties. The *ValidationRule* property is a text string that describes the rule for validation and the *ValidationText* is a string that is displayed to the user when validation fails. After running the code from Example 10-2, a new table appears in the Access Database window. (You may need to move away from the *Tables* tab and then return to that tab to see the new table.) Opening this table in Design View shows the window in Figure 10-1. Note that the field properties setting reflects the properties set in our code.

Incidentally, *TableDef* objects also have *ValidationRule* and *ValidationText* properties, used to set validation rules that involve multiple fields in the table.

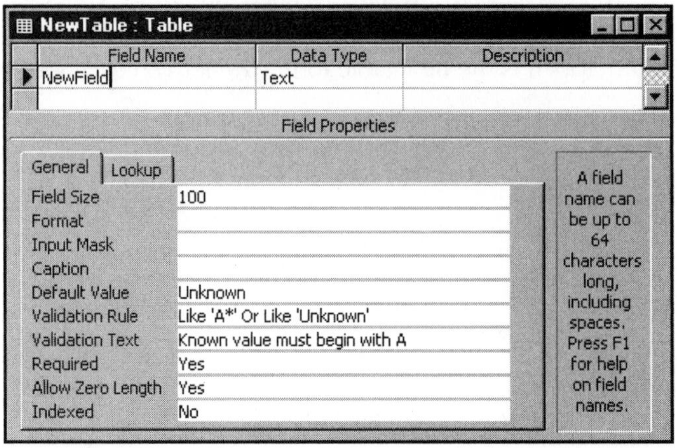

*Figure 10-1. Design view of table generated from running exaCreateTable()*

## Changing the Properties of an Existing Table or Field

We have remarked that some properties that are read/write before the object is appended to its collection become read-only after appending. One such example is the *Type* property of a field. On the other hand, the *Name* property of a field can be changed. This is an example of a change that can be made using DAO but not by using SQL.

# Creating an Index

Indexes are created using the *CreateIndex* method for a *TableDef* object. Here is the syntax:

```
Set IndexVar = TableDefVar.CreateIndex([IndexName])
```

Creating an index by itself does nothing. We must append one or more fields to the *Fields* collection of the index in order to actually index the table. Moreover, the order in which the fields are appended (when there is more than one field) has an effect on the index order. Here is an example.

Example 10-3 adds a new index called *PriceTitle* to the BOOKS table.

*Example 10-3. A CreateIndex Method Example*

```
Sub exaCreateIndex()

Dim db As DATABASE
Dim tdf As TableDef
Dim idx As INDEX
Dim fld As Field
```

*Example 10-3. A CreateIndex Method Example (continued)*

```
Set db = CurrentDb
Set tdf = db.TableDefs!BOOKS

' Create index by the name of PriceTitle
Set idx = tdf.CreateIndex("PriceTitle")

' Append the price and then the Title fields
' to the Fields collection of the index
Set fld = idx.CreateField("Price")
idx.Fields.Append fld
Set fld = idx.CreateField("Title")
idx.Fields.Append fld

' Append the index to the indexes collection
' for BOOKS
tdf.Indexes.Append idx
```

**End Sub**

Figure 10-2 shows the result of running the program from Example 10-3. (To view this dialog box, open the BOOKS table in design view and select the *Indexes* option from the *View* menu.) The figure shows clearly why we first create two fields—*Price* and *Title*—and append them, in that order, to the *Fields* collection of the index.

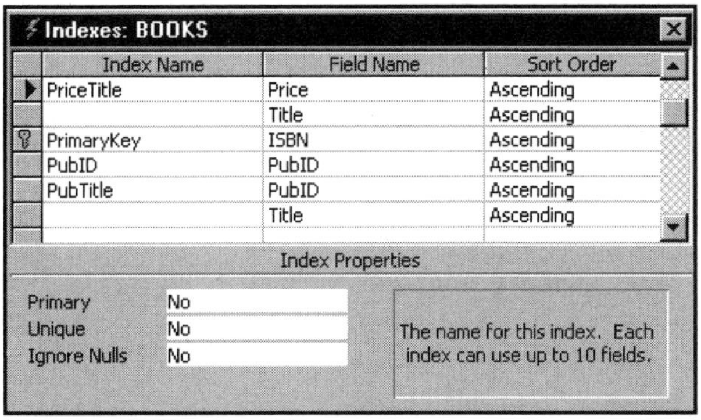

*Figure 10-2. Indexes view of BOOKS table from running exaCreateIndex()*

As we discussed in an earlier chapter, an index for a table is actually a file that contains the values of the fields that make up the index, along with a pointer to the corresponding records in the table. Microsoft tends to blur the distinction between an index (as a file) and the fields that contribute to the index. Thus, to say that an index is *primary* is to say that the fields (actually, the attributes) that make up the index constitute a primary key.

With this in mind, some of the important index properties are:

- *DistinctCount*: Gives the number of distinct values in the index.

- *IgnoreNulls*: Determines whether a record with a null value in the index field (or fields) should be included in the index.

- *Primary*: Indicates that the index fields constitute the primary key for the table.

- *Required*: Determines whether or not all of the fields in a multifield index must be filled in.

- *Unique*: Determines whether or not the values in a index must be unique, thus making the index fields a key for the table.

Note that the difference between a *primary* key index and a *unique* values index is that a primary key is not allowed to have NULL values.

## *Creating a Relation*

Relations are created in DAO using the *CreateRelation* method. The syntax is:

```
Set RelationVar = DatabaseVar.CreateRelation _
([RelName[, KeyTable[, ForeignTable[, Attributes]]]])
```

where:

- *RelName* is the name of the new relation

- *KeyTable* is the name of the *referenced* table in the relation (containing the key)

- *ForeignTable* is the name of the *referencing* table in the relation (containing the foreign key)

- *Attributes* is a constant, whose values are shown in Table 10-2

*Table 10-2. Attributes for a Relation Object*

| Constant | Description |
| --- | --- |
| dbRelationUnique | Relationship is one-to-one |
| dbRelationDontEnforce | No referential integrity |
| dbRelationInherited | Relationship exists in a noncurrent database that contains the two attached tables |
| dbRelationUpdateCascade | Cascading updates enabled |
| dbRelationDeleteCascade | Cascading deletions enabled |

*Notes:*

- All of the properties of a *Relation* object become read-only after the object is appended to a *Relations* collection.

- *Field* objects for the referenced and referencing tables must be appended to the *Fields* collection prior to appending the *Relation* object to the *Relations* collection.

- Duplicate or invalid names will cause an error when the *Append* method is invoked.

- To remove a *Relation* object from a collection, use the *Delete* method for that collection.

Example 10-4 illustrates the use of *Relation* objects. In this example, we will create a new relation in the LIBRARY database. The first step is to create a new table, using Microsoft Access. Call the table SALESREGIONS and add two text fields: *PubID* and *SalesRegions.* Then add a few rows shown in Table 10-3 to the table.

*Table 10-3. The SALESREGIONS Table*

| PubID | SalesRegions |
|-------|--------------|
| 1 | United States |
| 1 | Europe |
| 1 | Asia |
| 2 | United States |
| 2 | Latin America |

The code in Example 10-4 creates a relation between the PubID field of the PUBLISHERS table (the primary key) and the PubID field of the SALESREGIONS table (the foreign key).

*Example 10-4. A CreateRelation Method Example*

```
Sub exaRelations()

Dim db As DATABASE
Dim rel As Relation
Dim fld As Field

Set db = CurrentDb

' Create relation
Set rel = db.CreateRelation("PublisherRegions", _
"PUBLISHERS", "SALESREGIONS")

' Set referential integrity with cascading updates
```

*Example 10-4. A CreateRelation Method Example (continued)*

```
rel.Attributes = dbRelationUpdateCascade

' Specify the key field in referenced table
Set fld = rel.CreateField("PubID")

' Specify foreign key field in referencing table.
fld.ForeignName = "PubID"

'Append Field object to Fields collection of
' Relation object.
rel.Fields.Append fld

' Append Relation object to Relations collection.
db.Relations.Append rel

End Sub
```

After running this code, make sure the *Database* window is active and select *Tools … Relationships* from the Access menu bar. Then select *Relationships … Show All* and you should see a window similar to that in Figure 10-3, showing the new relationship!

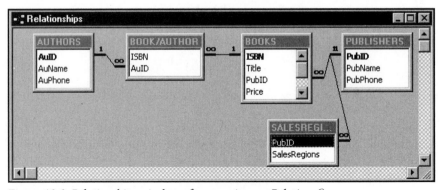

*Figure 10-3. Relationships window after running exaRelations()*

# *Creating a QueryDef*

Creating a *QueryDef* object is done using the *CreateQueryDef* method. The syntax is:

```
Set QueryDefVar = DatabaseVar.CreateQueryDef _
    ([QueryDefName][, SQLText])
```

where *QueryDefName* is the name of the new *QueryDef* object and *SQLText* is a string expression that constitutes a valid Access SQL statement.

*Notes:*

- If you include *QueryDefName* the *QueryDef* is automatically saved (appended to the appropriate *QueryDefs* collection) when it is created. The *Name* property and the *SQL* property of a *QueryDef* can be changed at any time.

- You can create a temporary *QueryDef*, which is not appended to a collection, by setting the *QueryDefName* property to a zero-length string (""). You cannot change the name of a temporary *QueryDef*.

- If you omit the *SQLText* argument, you can define the *QueryDef* by setting its SQL property before or after you append it to a collection.

- To remove a *QueryDef* object from a *QueryDefs* collection, use the *Delete* method.

## Running a Query

Recall from Chapter 6, *Access Structured Query Language (SQL)*, that Microsoft Access supports several types of queries. In particular, a *select query* returns a recordset, whereas an *action query* does not return a recordset, but rather takes action on existing data, such as making a new table, deleting rows from a table, appending rows to a table, or updating the values in a table.

If a *QueryDef* object represents an action query, then we can use its *Execute* statement to run the query. If the *QueryDef* object represents a select query, then we can open the corresponding result table (recordset) using the *OpenRecordset* method on the *QueryDef* object. Let us illustrate.

The code in Example 10-5 creates a new select query and displays the record count for the resulting recordset.

*Example 10-5. A CreateQueryDef Method Example*

```
Sub exaCreateSelect()

Dim db As DATABASE
Dim qdf As QueryDef
Dim strSQL As String
Dim rs As Recordset

Set db = CurrentDb

' Create an SQL SELECT statement
strSQL = "SELECT * FROM BOOKS WHERE Price > 20"

' Create a new QueryDef object
Set qdf = db.CreateQueryDef("NewQuery", strSQL)

' Open a recordset for this query
```

*Example 10-5. A CreateQueryDef Method Example  (continued)*

```
Set rs = qdf.OpenRecordset

' Move to end of recordset
rs.MoveLast

' Show record count
MsgBox "There  are " & rs.RecordCount & " books with price exceeding $20"
```

**End Sub**

The code in Example 10-6 creates a new action query and executes it. The effect is to raise the price of each book in the BOOKS table by 10%.

*Example 10-6. A New Action Query Example*

```
Sub exaCreateAction()

' Creates an action query and executes it

Dim db As DATABASE
Dim qdf As QueryDef
Dim strSQL As String

Set db = CurrentDb

' Create an SQL UPDATE statement
' to raise prices by 10%
strSQL = "UPDATE BOOKS SET Price = Price*1.1"

' Create a new QueryDef object
Set qdf = db.CreateQueryDef("PriceInc", strSQL)

qdf.Execute
```

**End Sub**

Note that once a *QueryDef* object exists, we may still use the *OpenRecordset* or *Execute* methods to run the query. Also, the *Execute* method can be used on a *Database* object to run an SQL statement. Here is an example that reduces the price of each book in the BOOKS table by 10%:

```
Dim db As DATABASE
Set db = CurrentDb
db.Execute "UPDATE BOOKS SET Price = Price*0.9"
```

## *Properties of a QueryDef Object*

When a *QueryDef* object is created or changed, Jet sets certain of its properties, such as *DateCreated*, *LastUpdated*, and *Type*. (Note that the *QueryDefs* collection may need refreshing before these properties can be read.) Some of the possible query types are listed in Table 10-4.

*Table 10-4. Possible Query Type Constants*

| Constant | Query Type | Value |
|---|---|---|
| dbQSelect | Select | 0 |
| dbQAction | Action | 240 |
| dbQCrosstab | Crosstab | 16 |
| dbQDelete | Delete | 32 |
| dbQUpdate | Update | 48 |
| dbQAppend | Append | 64 |
| dbQMakeTable | Make-table | 80 |

The *RecordsAffected* property returns the number of records affected by the last application of the *Execute* method. Let us illustrate.

Example 10-7 modifies the earlier action query example to perform the action (10% price increase) if and only if the increase will affect more than 15 books in the table. This is done using the *BeginTrans, Committrans,* and *Rollback* properties of the current *Workspace* object.

*Example 10-7. A RecordsAffected Property Example*

```
Sub exaCreateAction2()

Dim ws As Workspace
Dim db As DATABASE
Dim qdf As QueryDef
Dim strSQL As String

Set ws = DBEngine(0)
Set db = CurrentDb

' Create an SQL UPDATE statement
' to raise prices by 10%
strSQL = "UPDATE BOOKS SET Price = Price*1.1 WHERE Price > 20"

' Create a new QueryDef object
Set qdf = db.CreateQueryDef("PriceInc", strSQL)

' Begin a transaction
ws.BeginTrans

' Execute the query
qdf.Execute

' Check the number of records effected and either rollback transaction or
proceed
If qdf.RecordsAffected > 15 Then
    MsgBox qdf.RecordsAffected & " records affected _
by this query. Transaction cancelled."
    ws.Rollback
```

*Example 10-7. A RecordsAffected Property Example (continued)*

```
Else
    MsgBox qdf.RecordsAffected & " records affected _
by this query. Transaction completed."
    ws.CommitTrans
End If

End Sub
```

# 11

# *Programming DAO: Data Manipulation Language*

In Chapter 10, *Programming DAO: Data Definition Language*, we examined how to use DAO to create and access the major components of a database, like its tables, its indexes, or its query definitions. For the most part, though, the focus of a database application is on accessing and manipulating discrete items of data stored in one or more records. In this chapter, we'll continue our overview of Data Access Objects by examining its data manipulation component, which allows you to perform such practical maintenance operations as adding, deleting, and updating records and accessing the records that your application is to display.

## *Recordset Objects*

The main tool for manipulating data is the *Recordset* object. There are three types of *Recordset* objects:

- A *table-type Recordset* object is a representation of the records in a single table in the database. It is like a window into the table. Thus, operations on this type of recordset directly affect the table. We emphasize that a table-type recordset can be opened for a single table only. It cannot be opened for a join of more than one table, or for a query. A table-type recordset can be indexed using a table index. This provides for quick manuvering within the table, using the *Seek* method, which we will discuss later in the chapter.

- A *dynaset-type Recordset* object is a dynamic (changeable) set of records that can contain fields from one or more tables or queries. Dynaset-type recordsets are generally updatable in both directions. Thus, changes in the recordset are reflected in the underlying tables or queries and changes in the underlying tables or queries are reflected in the dynaset-type recordset. With a dynaset-type recordset, no data are brought into memory. Rather a unique key is brought into memory to reference each row of data. Searching through a dynaset-type recordset is done with the *Find* method, which is generally slower than the *Seek* method (which uses one of the table's indexes).

- A *snapshot-type Recordset* object is a *static* (nonchangeable) set of records that can contain fields from one or more tables or queries. These recordsets cannot be updated. For searching, a snapshot-type recordset can be faster than a dynaset-type recordset.

# *Opening a Recordset*

To create, or open, a recordset, Jet provides the *OpenRecordset* method. This method can be used on *Database, TableDef, QueryDef,* or existing *Recordset* objects. The syntax is:

```
Set RecSetVar = DatabaseVar.OpenRecordset _
(source[, type[, options]])
```

or

```
Set RecSetVar = ObjectVar.OpenRecordset _
([type[, options]])
```

where:

- *ObjectVar* points to an existing *TableDef, QueryDef,* or *Recordset* object

- When opening a recordset based upon a database (the first syntax above), *source* is a string specifying the source of the records for the new recordset. The source can be a table name, a query name, or an SQL statement that returns records. For table-type *Recordset* objects, the source can only be a table name.

- If you do not specify a type, then a table-type recordset is created if possible. Otherwise, the *Type* value can be one of the following integer constants:

  — *dbOpenTable* to open a table-type Recordset object

  — *dbOpenDynaset* to open a dynaset-type Recordset object

  — *dbOpenSnapshot* to open a snapshot-type Recordset object

- *Options* has several possible values related to multiuser situations. It also can take the value *dbForwardOnly*, which means that the recordset is a forward-only scrolling snapshot. This type of snapshot is useful for rapid searching.

*Note:*

A new *Recordset* object is automatically added to the *Recordsets* collection when you open the object, and is automatically removed when you close it, using the *Close* method.

The code in Example 11-1 opens (and then closes) a recordset of each type, based on the BOOKS table. It also displays (in the debug window) the value of the *RecordCount* property for these recordsets. For a dynaset and snapshot type recordset, the *RecordCount* property is the number of records *accessed*. Accordingly, to determine the total number of records in such a recordset, we need to invoke the *MoveLast* method, thereby accessing all records. For a table-type recordset, the *RecordCount* property gives the total number of records. (We will discuss the *MoveLast* method later.)

*Example 11-1. An OpenRecordset Method Example*

```
Sub exaRecordsets()

Dim db As DATABASE
Dim rsTable As Recordset
Dim rsDyna As Recordset
Dim rsSnap As Recordset

Set db = CurrentDb

' Open table-type recordset
Set rsTable = db.OpenRecordset("Books")
Debug.Print "TableCount: " & rsTable.RecordCount

' Open dynaset-type recordset
Set rsDyna = db.OpenRecordset("Books", dbOpenDynaset)
Debug.Print "DynaCount: " & rsDyna.RecordCount
rsDyna.MoveLast
Debug.Print "DynaCount: " & rsDyna.RecordCount

' Open snapshot-type recordset
Set rsSnap = db.OpenRecordset("Books", dbOpenSnapshot)
Debug.Print "SnapCount: " & rsSnap.RecordCount
rsSnap.MoveLast
Debug.Print "SnapCount: " & rsSnap.RecordCount

' Close all
rsTable.Close
rsDyna.Close
rsSnap.Close

End Sub
```

## Default Recordset Types

If you do not specify a type in the *OpenRecordset* method, Jet will choose one for you according to the following rules:

- The default *Type* when opening a recordset on a *Database* object (first syntax above) or a *TableDef* object (second syntax) is a table-type *Recordset* object.

- The default *Type* when opening a recordset on a *QueryDef* object is a dynaset-type *Recordset* object. (Table-type recordsets are not available.)

- The default *Type* when opening a recordset on an existing table-type *Recordset* object is a dynaset-type recordset. If the recordset is not table-type, then the new recordset has the same type as the original.

# Moving Through a Recordset

All recordsets have a *current position* (pointed to by the *current record pointer*) and a *current record*. Normally, the current record is the record at the current position. However, there are two exceptions. The current position can be:

- *Before* the first record
- *After* the last record

in which cases there is no current record.

To change the current position (and hence the current record), Jet provides several *Move* methods:

- *MoveFirst*: moves to the first record
- *MoveLast*: moves to the last record
- *MoveNext*: moves to the next record
- *MovePrevious*: moves to the previous record
- *Move[n]*: moves forward or backward *n* positions

In each case the syntax has the form:

```
RecordSetVar.MoveCommand
```

## BOF and EOF

The properties BOF (Beginning of File) and EOF (End of File) are set by Jet after each move command. The concepts of BOF, EOF, current record, and current position can be confusing. Perhaps the following notes will help.

*Notes on the BOF and EOF properties:*

- BOF is *True* when the current position is *before* the first record in the recordset, not *at* the first record.

- EOF is *True* when the current position is *past* the last record in the recordset, not *at* the last record.

- If either of BOF or EOF is *True*, then there is no current record.

- If you open a recordset containing no records, then BOF and EOF are set to *True*. If the recordset has some records, then Jet does a tacit *MoveFirst*, so the first record becomes the current record and both BOF and EOF are set to *False*.

- If you delete the last remaining record in a recordset, then BOF and EOF remain *False* until you attempt to change the current position.

*Notes on the Move methods:*

- If you use *MovePrevious* when the first record is current, the BOF property is set to *True*, and there is no current record. A further *MovePrevious* will produce an error and BOF remains *True*.

- If you use *MoveNext* when the last record is current, the EOF property is set to *True*, and there is no current record. A further *MoveNext* will produce an error and EOF remains *True*.

- If the recordset is a table-type recordset, then movement follows the current index, which is set using the *Index* property of the *Recordset* object. If no index is set (or if the recordset is not table-type), the order of returned records is not predictable.

The most common use of the *Move* methods is to cycle through each record in a recordset. Example 11-2 illustrates this. It creates both a table-type and a dynaset-type recordset on BOOKS and prints (in the debug window) a list of PubIDs and Titles. Note the use of the:

```
Do while not rs.EOF
```

statement, which is typical of this type of procedure. Also, note the presence of this line:

```
rsTable.MoveNext
```

within the *Do* loop. It is a common error to forget to advance the current record pointer, in which case the PC will enter an endless loop, in this case printing the same line over and over again!

*Example 11-2. Moving Through a Recordset*

```
Sub exaRecordsetMove()

Dim db As DATABASE
Dim rsTable As Recordset
Dim rsDyna As Recordset

Set db = CurrentDb

Set rsTable = db.OpenRecordset("Books")
Debug.Print "Books indexed by PubID/Title:"

' Move through table-type recordset using PubTitle index
rsTable.INDEX = "PubTitle"
rsTable.MoveFirst
Do While Not rsTable.EOF
    Debug.Print rsTable!PubID & " / " & rsTable!Title
    rsTable.MoveNext
Loop

Debug.Print

' Move through dynaset-type recordset
Debug.Print "Dynaset-type recordset order:"
Set rsDyna = db.OpenRecordset("Books", dbOpenDynaset)
rsDyna.MoveFirst
Do While Not rsDyna.EOF
    Debug.Print rsDyna!PubID & " / " & rsDyna!Title
    rsDyna.MoveNext
Loop

rsTable.Close
rsDyna.Close

End Sub
```

It is worth remarking that, for a dynaset-type or snapshot-type recordset, or for a table-type recordset for which the *Index* property has not been set, you cannot predict or rely on the order of records in the recordset.

In this connection, two *Recordset* properties of particular use are *AbsolutePosition* and *PercentPosition*, which give the ordinal position of the current record in a dynaset-type or snapshot-type recordset and the percent position, respectively. Let us illustrate by modifying Example 11-2, as shown in Example 11-3.

*Example 11-3. The Modified Recordset Position Example*

```
Sub exaRecordsetPosition()

Dim db As DATABASE
Dim rsDyna As Recordset
Dim strMsg As String
```

*Example 11-3. The Modified Recordset Position Example (continued)*

```
Set db = CurrentDb

Set rsDyna = db.OpenRecordset("Books", dbOpenDynaset)

' Move through recordset and display position
rsDyna.MoveFirst
Do While Not rsDyna.EOF

    strMsg = rsDyna!PubID & " / " & rsDyna!Title
    strMsg = strMsg & " / " & _
str$(rsDyna.AbsolutePosition)
    strMsg = strMsg & " / " & _
Format$(rsDyna.PercentPosition, "##")
    Debug.Print strMsg

    rsDyna.MoveNext
Loop

rsDyna.Close
```

**End Sub**

# Finding Records in a Recordset

The method used to search for a record in a recordset is different for indexed table-type recordsets than for other recordsets.

## Finding Records in a Table-Type Recordset

To locate a record in an indexed table-type recordset, you use the *Seek* method. Note that the recordset's *Index* property must be set before the *Seek* method can be used. The syntax of the *Seek* method is:

```
TableTypeRecSetVar.Seek comparison, key1, key2,...
```

where *comparison* is one of the following strings:

```
"<"
"<="
"="
">="
">"
```

and *key1, key2,...* are values corresponding to each field in the current index.

*Notes:*

- The *Seek* method searches through the specified key fields and locates the first matching record. Once found, it makes that record current and the *NoMatch* property of the recordset is set to *False*. If the *Seek* method fails to locate a match, the *NoMatch* property is set to *True*, and the current record is undefined.

- If *comparison* is equal (=), greater than or equal to (>=), or greater than (>), *Seek* starts its search at the beginning of the index. If *comparison* is less than (<) or less than or equal to (<=), *Seek* starts its search at the end of the index and searches backward unless there are duplicate index entries at the end. In this case, *Seek* starts at an arbitrary entry among the duplicate index entries at the end of the index.

The code in Example 11-4 uses the *Seek* method on the *Title* index of BOOKS to find the first title that begins with the word "On".

*Example 11-4. The Seek Method Example*

```
Sub exaRecordsetSeek()

Dim db As DATABASE
Dim rsTable As Recordset

Set db = CurrentDb

Set rsTable = db.OpenRecordset("Books")

' Find first book (if any) with title beginning
' with the word "On".
rsTable.INDEX = "Title"
rsTable.Seek ">=", "On"
If Not rsTable.NoMatch Then
    MsgBox rsTable!Title
Else
    MsgBox "No title beginning with word 'On'."
End If

rsTable.Close

End Sub
```

## *Finding Records in a Dynaset-Type or Shapshot-Type Recordset*

To search for a record in a dynaset-type or snapshot-type recordset, Jet provides various *Find* methods:

- *FindFirst*: finds the first matching record in the recordset
- *FindNext*: finds the next matching record, starting at the current record
- *FindPrevious*: finds the previous matching record, starting at the current record
- *FindLast*: finds the last matching record in the recordset

The syntax of these methods is:

```
RecordsetVar.FindMethod criteria
```

where:

- *RecordsetVar* represents an existing dynaset-type or snapshot-type *Recordset* object

- *criteria* is a string expression, using the same syntax as a WHERE SQL clause (but without the word WHERE)

It is important to note that, if a record matching the criteria is not located, the *NoMatch* property is set to *True*, the current position is undetermined and so there is no current record. It is thus important to position the current record pointer. This is usually done by setting a *bookmark* at the current record before starting the search. Then, if the search fails, the original position can be restored using the bookmark. In fact, a bookmark is a system-generated string that Jet can use to identify a record. Thus, by setting a bookmark on the current record and then moving to another record, we can return to the bookmarked record. Let us illustrate.

The following code displays all book titles starting with "M" and then returns to the current record before the search.

*Example 11-5. A Find Method Example*

```
Sub exaRecordsetFind()

Dim db As DATABASE
Dim rs As Recordset
Dim bmkReturnHere As Variant

Set db = CurrentDb

Set rs = db.OpenRecordset("Books", dbOpenDynaset)

' Display current title
Debug.Print "Current title: " & rs!Title

' Set bookmark at current record
bmkReturnHere = rs.Bookmark

' Find books (if any) with first letter of title
' equal to 'M'.
rs.FindFirst "Left$(Title,1) = 'M'"
Do While Not rs.NoMatch
    Debug.Print rs!Title
    rs.FindNext "Left$(Title,1) = 'M'"
Loop

' Return to original location
```

*Example 11-5. A Find Method Example  (continued)*

```
rs.Bookmark = bmkReturnHere
Debug.Print "Returned to: " & rs!Title

rs.Close

End Sub
```

# Editing Data Using a Recordset

Let us now discuss the methods used to edit, add, or delete data from a table-type or dynaset-type recordset. Snapshot-type recordsets are static, so data in such a recordset cannot be changed. Thus, in this section, the term *recordset* will refer to table-type or dynaset-type recordsets. Recall that any changes made to a recordset are reflected in the underlying tables or queries.

## Editing an Existing Record

Editing an existing record is done in four steps:

1. Make the record the current record.

2. Invoke the *Edit* method for the recordset.

3. Make the desired changes to the record.

4. Invoke the *Update* method for the recordset.

It is important to note that if you move the current record pointer before invoking the *Update* method, any changes to the record will be lost.

The code in Example 11-6 changes all of the titles in a copy of the BOOKS table to uppercase. Before running this code you should use the Copy and Paste menu options (under the Edit menu) to make a copy of BOOKS, called *Books Copy*. (Select BOOKS in the Database window, choose Edit, Copy, then choose Edit, Paste.)

*Example 11-6. Editing Data With Recordset*

```
Sub exaRecordsetEdit()

Dim db As DATABASE
Dim rs As Recordset

Set db = CurrentDb

Set rs = db.OpenRecordset("Books Copy")

rs.MoveFirst
Do While Not rs.EOF
```

*Example 11-6. Editing Data With Recordset (continued)*

```
    rs.Edit
    rs!Title = UCase$(rs!Title)
    rs.UPDATE
    rs.MoveNext
Loop

rs.Close

End Sub
```

To emphasize an earlier point, you might want to start over with a fresh *Books Copy* table and run the previous code without the line:

```
    rs.Update
```

to see that no changes are made to the table.

## Deleting an Existing Record

Deleting the current record is done with the *Delete* method of the *Recordset* object. The syntax is simply:

```
    RecordSetVar.Delete
```

*Notes:*

- Deletions are made without any warning or confirmation. If you want confirmation, you must write appropriate code to do so.

- Note that, immediately after a record is deleted, there is no current record. The current record pointer must be moved to an existing record (usually by invoking *MoveNext*).

The procedure in Example 11-7 deletes all books that have a price greater than $20.00 in a copy of the BOOKS table, after asking for confirmation. Before running this code, you should use the *Copy*, *Paste* commands to make a copy of BOOKS, called *Books Copy*.

*Example 11-7. Using the Delete Method with Recordset*

```
Sub exaRecordsetDelete()

' Demonstrates deleting records
' Deletes all books that have a price greater than
' $20.00 in a copy of the BOOKS table.
' Before running this, use Copy, Paste to make a
' copy of the BOOKS table

Dim db As DATABASE
Dim rs As Recordset
Dim DeleteCt As Integer
```

*Example 11-7. Using the Delete Method with Recordset (continued)*

```
Set db = CurrentDb

Set rs = db.OpenRecordset("Books Copy")
DeleteCt = 0

rs.MoveFirst
Do While Not rs.EOF
    If rs!Price > 20 Then
        If MsgBox("Delete " & rs!Title & "(" & _
Format(rs!Price, Currency) & ")?", vbYesNo) = _
vbYes Then
            rs.Delete
            DeleteCt = DeleteCt + 1
        End If
    End If
    rs.MoveNext
Loop

rs.Close

MsgBox Format$(DeleteCt) & " records deleted."

End Sub
```

## Adding a New Record

Adding a new record to a recordset is done in three steps:

1. Invoke the *AddNew* method to create a blank record, which Jet makes the current record.

2. Fill in the fields of the record.

3. Invoke the *Update* method to save the record.

The syntax of the *AddNew* method is simply:

```
RecordsetVar.AddNew
```

*Notes:*

- Once the *Update* method is invoked, the record that was the current record *prior* to invoking the *AddNew* method again becomes the current record. To make the new record current, use a bookmark together with the *LastModified* property, as shown in Example 11-8.

- In a table-type recordset, the new record is placed in its proper order with respect to the current index. In a dynaset-type recordset, the new record is placed at the end of the recordset. If the recordset has a sort order (such as might be inherited from an underlying query), the new record can be repositioned using the *Requery* method.

Example 11-8 adds a new book to the BOOKS table, and makes it the current record. It also demonstrates the *With...End With* construct.

*Example 11-8. Adding a Record with Recordset*

```
Sub exaRecordsetAddNew()

Dim db As DATABASE
Dim rs As Recordset

Set db = CurrentDb

' Open recordset
Set rs = db.OpenRecordset("Books")

Debug.Print "Current title: " & rs!Title

' Use With...End With construct
With rs
    .AddNew                ' Add new record
    !ISBN = "0-000"        ' Set fields
    !Title = "New Book"
    !PubID = 1
    !Price = 100
    .UPDATE                ' Save changes.
    .Bookmark = rs.LastModified   ' Go to new record
    Debug.Print "Current title: " & rs!Title
End With

rs.Close

End Sub
```

# A

# *DAO 3.0/3.5 Collections, Properties, and Methods*

Microsoft Access 97 comes with a utility known as the *Object Browser*, which can be used to explore the DAO object hierarchy. Figure A-1 shows the Object Browser, which can be invoked from an Access code module by striking the F2 function key (or from the *View* menu).

*Figure A-1. The Object Browser*

The Object Browser can be a very useful tool, but there are times when a hard-copy reference is also useful. Accordingly, this appendix contains information on the collections, properties, and methods of each of the objects in the DAO 3.0 object hierarchy (which underlies Access 95) and the DAO 3.5 (which underlies Access 97). If nothing else, this information should help point you to the right spot in the Access On-Line Help System.

In presenting this DAO reference, a table listing the classes and collections available in DAO is followed by tables listing the properties and methods exposed by each class, as well as the collections that are accessible from each object. The tables also indicate whether each item applies to DAO 3.0, DAO 3.5, or both. Finally, there is a summary description of each item.

# DAO Classes

| Class Name | Version | Description |
|---|---|---|
| Connection | 3.5 | An open ODBCDirect connection |
| Connections | 3.5 | A collection of Connection objects |
| Container | 3.0/3.5 | Storage for information about a predefined object type |
| Containers | 3.0/3.5 | A collection of Container objects |
| Database | 3.0/3.5 | An open database |
| Databases | 3.0/3.5 | A collection of Database objects |
| DBEngine | 3.0/3.5 | The Jet database engine |
| Document | 3.0/3.5 | Information about a saved, predefined object |
| Documents | 3.0/3.5 | A collection of Document objects |
| Error | 3.0/3.5 | Information about any error that occurred with a DAO object |
| Errors | 3.0/3.5 | A collection of Error objects |
| Field | 3.0/3.5 | A column that is part of a table, query, index, relation, or recordset |
| Fields | 3.0/3.5 | A collection of Field objects |
| Group | 3.0/3.5 | A group of user accounts |
| Groups | 3.0/3.5 | A collection of Group objects |
| Index | 3.0/3.5 | Object used to order values and provide efficient access to a recordset |
| Indexes | 3.0/3.5 | A collection of Index objects |
| Parameter | 3.0/3.5 | Parameter for a parameter query |
| Parameters | 3.0/3.5 | A collection of Parameter objects |
| Properties | 3.0/3.5 | A collection of Property objects |
| Property | 3.0/3.5 | A built-in or user-defined property |
| QueryDef | 3.0/3.5 | A saved query definition |

| Class Name | Version | Description |
|---|---|---|
| QueryDefs | 3.0/3.5 | A collection of Querydef objects |
| Recordset | 3.0/3.5 | The representation of the records in a table or that result from a query |
| Recordsets | 3.0/3.5 | A collection of Recordset objects |
| Relation | 3.0/3.5 | A relationship between fields in tables and queries |
| Relations | 3.0/3.5 | A collection of Relation objects |
| TableDef | 3.0/3.5 | A saved table definition |
| TableDefs | 3.0/3.5 | A collection of Tabledef objects |
| User | 3.0/3.5 | A user account |
| Users | 3.0/3.5 | A collection of User objects |
| Workspace | 3.0/3.5 | A session of the Jet database engine |
| Workspaces | 3.0/3.5 | A collection of Workspace objects |

# *A Collection Object*

Each of the Collection objects listed earlier in "DAO Classes" supports a single method and a single property.

## *Methods*

| Method | Type | Version | Description |
|---|---|---|---|
| Refresh | Sub | 3.0/3.5 | Updates the collection to reflect recent changes |

## *Properties*

| Property | Type | Version | Description |
|---|---|---|---|
| Count | Integer | 3.0/3.5 | Number of objects in the collection (read-only) |

In addition, DynaCollection objects—that is, Collection objects whose members can be dynamically added and removed—have the two additional methods:

## *Methods*

| Method | Parameters | Returns | Version | Description |
|---|---|---|---|---|
| Append | Object As Object | Sub | 3.0/3.5 | Appends an object to the collection |
| Delete | Name As String | Sub | 3.0/3.5 | Deletes an object from the collection |

# Connection Object (DAO 3.5 Only)

## Collections

| Property | Type | Version | Description |
|----------|------|---------|-------------|
| Database | Database | 3.5 | Returns a Database reference to this Connection object |
| QueryDefs | QueryDefs | 3.5 | A collection of QueryDef objects |
| Recordsets | RecordSets | 3.5 | A collection of Recordset objects open in this connection |

## Methods

| Method | Parameters | Returns | Version | Description |
|--------|-----------|---------|---------|-------------|
| Cancel | | Sub | 3.5 | Cancels execution of an asynchronous Execute or OpenRecordset method |
| Close | | Sub | 3.5 | Closes the Connection object and everything it contains |
| CreateQueryDef | [Name], [SQLText]) | QueryDef | 3.5 | Creates a new QueryDef object |
| Execute | Query As String, [Options] | Sub | 3.5 | Executes an SQL statement |
| OpenRecordSet | Name As String, [Type], [Options], [LockEdit] | Recordset | 3.5 | Creates a new Recordset object |

## Properties

| Property | Type | Version | Description |
|----------|------|---------|-------------|
| Connect | String | 3.5 | Information saved from the Connect argument of the *OpenDatabase* method |
| Name | String | 3.5 | Name of the Connection object |
| QueryTimeout | Integer | 3.5 | Number of seconds before timeout occurs when executing an ODBC query |
| RecordsAffected | Long | 3.5 | Number of records affected by the last Execute method |
| StillExecuting | Boolean | 3.5 | Indicates whether an asynchronous method call is still executing |

| Property | Type | Version | Description |
|---|---|---|---|
| Transactions | Boolean | 3.5 | Indicates whether the DAO object supports transactions |
| Updatable | Boolean | 3.5 | Indicates whether the connection allows data to be updated |

# Container Object

## Collections

| Property | Type | Version | Description |
|---|---|---|---|
| Documents | Documents | 3.0/3.5 | Collection of Document objects in the container |

## Properties

| Property | Type | Version | Description |
|---|---|---|---|
| AllPermissions | Long | 3.0/3.5 | All permissions that apply to the current user-name |
| Inherit | Boolean | 3.0/3.5 | Indicates whether new Document objects inherit a default permissions property |
| Name | String | 3.0/3.5 | The name of this object |
| Owner | String | 3.0/3.5 | Sets or returns the owner of the object |
| Permissions | Long | 3.0/3.5 | Sets or returns permissions for the user or group indicated by the UserName property when accessing the object |
| UserName | String | 3.0/3.5 | User or group to which the Permissions property applies |

# Database Object

## Collections

| Property | Type | Version | Description |
|---|---|---|---|
| Connection | Connection | 3.5 | An open ODBCDirect connection |
| Containers | Containers | 3.0/3.5 | Collection of Container objects in the Database object |
| QueryDefs | QueryDefs | 3.0/3.5 | Collection of QueryDef objects in the Database object |
| Recordsets | Recordsets | 3.0/3.5 | Collection of Recordset objects open in Database object |

| Property | Type | Version | Description |
|---|---|---|---|
| Relations | Relations | 3.0/3.5 | Collection of Relation objects in the Database object |
| TableDefs | TableDefs | 3.0/3.5 | Collection of TableDef objects in the Database object |

## Methods

| Method | Parameters | Returns | Version | Description |
|---|---|---|---|---|
| Close | | Sub | 3.0/3.5 | Closes the Database object and everything it contains |
| CreateProperty | [Name], [Type], [Value], [DDL] | Property | 3.0/3.5 | Creates a new user-defined Property object |
| CreateQueryDef | [Name], [SQLText] | QueryDef | 3.0/3.5 | Creates a new QueryDef object |
| CreateRelation | [Name], [Table], [ForeignTable], [Attributes] | Relation | 3.0/3.5 | Creates a new Relation object |
| CreateTableDef | [Name], [Attributes], [SourceTableName], [Connect] | TableDef | 3.0/3.5 | Creates a new Tabledef object |
| Execute | Query As String, [Options] | Sub | 3.0/3.5 | Executes a query |
| MakeReplica | PathName As String, Description As String, [Options] | Sub | 3.0/3.5 | Makes a new replica based on the current replicable database |
| NewPassword | bstrOld As String, bstrNew As String | Sub | 3.0/3.5 | Changes the password of an existing database |
| OpenRecordset | Name As String, [Type], [Options] | Recordset | 3.0/3.5 | Creates a new Recordset object |
| PopulatePartial | DbPathName As String | Sub | 3.5 | Synchronizes a partial replica |
| Synchronize | DbPathName As String, [Exchange-Type] | Sub | 3.0/3.5 | Synchronizes the database object |

## Properties

| Property | Type | Version | Description |
|---|---|---|---|
| CollatingOrder | Long | 3.0/3.5 | Defines the order used for sorting and comparisons |
| Connect | String | | Information saved from the Connect argument of the OpenDatabase method |
| DesignMasterID | String | 3.0/3.5 | Unique identifier for a replica design master |
| Name | String | 3.0/3.5 | The name of this Database object |
| QueryTimeout | Integer | 3.0/3.5 | Number of seconds before timeout occurs when executing an ODBC query |
| RecordsAffected | Long | 3.0/3.5 | Number of records affected by the last Execute method |
| ReplicaID | String | 3.0/3.5 | Unique identifier for a replica |
| Transactions | Boolean | 3.0/3.5 | Indicates whether the Database object supports transactions |
| Updatable | Boolean | 3.0/3.5 | Indicates whether the Database object can be modified |
| Version | String | 3.0/3.5 | Version number of the Database object format |

# DBEngine Object

## Collections

| Property | Type | Version | Description |
|---|---|---|---|
| Errors | Errors | 3.0./3.5 | Collection of errors from the most recently failed DAO operation |
| Properties | Properties | 3.0/3.5 | Collection of Property objects |
| Workspaces | Workspaces | 3.0/3.5 | Collection of open Workspace objects |

## Methods

| Method | Parameters | Returns | Version | Description |
|---|---|---|---|---|
| BeginTrans | | Sub | 3.0/3.5 | Begins a new transaction |
| CommitTrans | | Sub | 3.0 | Ends the transaction and saves any changes |
| CommitTrans | [Option as Long] | Sub | 3.5 | Ends the transaction and saves any changes |

| Method | Parameters | Returns | Version | Description |
|---|---|---|---|---|
| CompactDatabase | SrcName As String, DstName As String, [DstConnect], [Options], [SrcConnect] | Sub | 3.0 | Compacts a closed database |
| CompactDatabase | SrcName As String, DstName As String, [DstLocale], [Options], [SrcLocale] | Sub | 3.5 | Compacts a closed database |
| CreateDatabase | Name As String, Connect As String, [Option] | Database | 3.0 | Creates a new database |
| CreateDatabase | Name As String, Locale As String, [Option] | Database | 3.5 | Creates a new .MDB database |
| CreateWorkspace | Name As String, UserName As String, Password As String | Workspace | 3.0 | Creates a new Workspace object |
| CreateWorkspace | Name As String, UserName As String, Password As String, [UseType] | Workspace | 3.5 | Creates a new Workspace object |
| Idle | [Action] | Sub | 3.0/3.5 | Completes pending engine tasks such as lock removal |
| OpenConnection | Name As String, [Options], [ReadOnly], [Connect] | Connection | 3.5 | Opens a connection to a database |
| OpenDatabase | Name As String, [Exclusive], [ReadOnly], [Connect] | Database | 3.0 | Opens a specified database |
| OpenDatabase | Name As String, [Options], [ReadOnly], [Connect] | Database | 3.5 | Opens a specified database |
| RegisterDatabase | Dsn As String, Driver As String, Silent As Boolean, Attributes As String | Sub | 3.0/3.5 | Enters connection information for an ODBC data source |
| RepairDatabase | Name As String | Sub | 3.0/3.5 | Repairs a corrupted database |

| Method | Parameters | Returns | Version | Description |
|---|---|---|---|---|
| Rollback | | Sub | 3.0/3.5 | Rolls back any changes since the last BeginTrans |
| SetOption | Option As Long, Value | Sub | 3.5 | Overrides Jet registry settings |

## Properties

| Property | Type | Version | Description |
|---|---|---|---|
| DefaultPassword | String | 3.0/3.5 | Password if a Workspace object is created without a password |
| DefaultType | Long | 3.5 | Sets the default Workspace type |
| DefaultUser | String | 3.0/3.5 | User name if a Workspace object is created without a user name |
| IniPath | String | 3.0/3.5 | Path and filename of the initialization file (in Jet 3.0) or the complete Registry path (Jet 3.5) containing Jet engine settings |
| LoginTimeout | Integer | 3.0/3.5 | Number of seconds allowed for logging in to an ODBC database |
| SystemDB | String | 3.0/3.5 | Path to the system database |
| Version | String | 3.0/3.5 | Version number of the Jet database engine |

# Document Object

## Methods

| Method | Parameters | Returns | Version | Description |
|---|---|---|---|---|
| CreateProperty | [Name], [Type], [Value], [DDL] | Property | 3.0/3.5 | Creates a new user-defined Property object |

## Properties

| Property | Type | Version | Description |
|---|---|---|---|
| AllPermissions | Long | 3.0/3.5 | All permissions that apply to the current username |
| Container | String | 3.0/3.5 | Name of the Container object this Document object belongs to |
| DateCreated | Variant | 3.0/3.5 | Date and time when the Document object was created |
| LastUpdated | Variant | 3.0/3.5 | Date and time of the most recent change to the Document object |
| Name | String | 3.0/3.5 | Name of this Document object |

| Property | Type | Version | Description |
|---|---|---|---|
| Owner | String | 3.0/3.5 | The owner of the object |
| Permissions | Long | 3.0/3.5 | Permissions for user or group accessing the Document object |
| UserName | String | 3.0/3.5 | User or group for which the Permissions property applies |

# Error Object

## Properties

| Property | Type | Version | Description |
|---|---|---|---|
| Description | String | 3.0/3.5 | Description of the error |
| HelpContext | Long | 3.0/3.5 | Help context ID for a topic describing the error |
| HelpFile | String | 3.0/3.5 | Path to Help file describing the error |
| Number | Long | 3.0/3.5 | Error code of the most recent error |
| Source | String | 3.0/3.5 | Name of the object class that generated the error |

# Field Object

## Collections

| Property | Type | Version | Description |
|---|---|---|---|
| Properties | Properties | 3.0/3.5 | Collection of Property objects |

## Methods

| Method | Parameters | Returns | Version | Description |
|---|---|---|---|---|
| AppendChunk | Val | Sub | 3.0/3.5 | Writes long binary data to a field |
| CreateProperty | [Name], [Type], [Value], [DDL] | Property | 3.0/3.5 | Creates a new user-defined Property object |
| FieldSize | | Long | 3.0 | Returns the field size field |
| GetChunk | Offset As Long, Bytes As Long | Byte | 3.0/3.5 | Reads binary data from a field |

## Properties

| Property | Type | Version | Description |
|---|---|---|---|
| AllowZeroLength | Boolean | 3.0/3.5 | Indicates whether a zero-length string is valid for this field |
| Attributes | Long | 3.0/3.5 | Value indicating characteristics of this Field object |
| CollatingOrder | Long | 3.0/3.5 | Language used for sorting and comparisons |
| DataUpdatable | Boolean | 3.0/3.5 | Indicates whether the data in the field are updatable |
| DefaultValue | String | 3.0/3.5 | Default value of the field for a new record |
| FieldSize | Long | 3.5 | The size of a memo field or a long binary field |
| ForeignName | String | 3.0/3.5 | The name of the foreign field |
| Name | String | 3.0/3.5 | The name of this Field object |
| OrdinalPosition | Integer | 3.0/3.5 | The relative position of this field object |
| OriginalValue | Variant | 3.5 | Value stored in the database server at the start of a batch update |
| Required | Boolean | 3.0/3.5 | Indicates whether the Field requires a non-Null value |
| Size | Long | 3.0/3.5 | Maximum size of the field |
| SourceField | String | 3.0/3.5 | Name of the original source of data for a Field object |
| SourceTable | String | 3.0/3.5 | Name of the original source table |
| Type | Integer | 3.0/3.5 | Data type of the field |
| ValidateOnSet | Boolean | 3.0/3.5 | Determines whether validation occurs immediately (a True value) or is delayed until an update (a False value) |
| ValidationRule | String | 3.0/3.5 | Expression that must evaluate to True for a successful update |
| ValidationText | String | 3.0/3.5 | Message to display if validation with ValidationRule fails |
| Value | Variant | 3.0/3.5 | The Field object's data |
| VisibleValue | Variant | 3.5 | Data currently stored in the database server |

# Group Object

## Collections

| Property | Type | Version | Description |
|---|---|---|---|
| Properties | Properties | 3.0/3.5 | A collection of Property objects |
| Users | Users | 3.0/3.5 | A collection of User objects |

## *Methods*

| Method | Parameters | Returns | Version | Description |
|---|---|---|---|---|
| CreateUser | [Name], [PID], [Password] | User | 3.0/3.5 | Creates a new User object |

## *Properties*

| Property | Type | Version | Description |
|---|---|---|---|
| Name | String | 3.0/3.5 | Name of the Group object |
| PID | String | 3.0/3.5 | Personal identifier (PID) for the group or user account |

# *Index Object*

## *Collections*

| Property | Type | Version | Description |
|---|---|---|---|
| Fields | Fields | 3.0/3.5 | Collection of fields in the Index object |
| Properties | Properties | 3.0/3.5 | Collection of Property objects |

## *Methods*

| Method | Parameters | Returns | Version | Description |
|---|---|---|---|---|
| CreateField | [Name], [Type], [Size] | Field | 3.0/3.5 | Creates a new Field object |
| CreateProperty | [Name], [Type], [Value], [DDL] | Property | 3.0/3.5 | Creates a new user-defined Property object |

## *Properties*

| Property | Type | Version | Description |
|---|---|---|---|
| Clustered | Boolean | 3.0/3.5 | Indicates whether the index is clustered |
| DistinctCount | Long | 3.0/3.5 | Number of unique values in this Index object |
| Foreign | Boolean | 3.0/3.5 | Indicates whether an Index object represents a foreign key |
| IgnoreNulls | Boolean | 3.0/3.5 | Indicates whether Null values are stored in the index |
| Name | String | 3.0/3.5 | Name of this Index object |
| Primary | Boolean | 3.0/3.5 | Indicates whether this is a primary index |

| Property | Type | Version | Description |
|----------|------|---------|-------------|
| Required | Boolean | 3.0/3.5 | Indicates whether the index requires a non-Null value |
| Unique | Boolean | 3.0/3.5 | Indicates whether this is a unique index for a table |

# Parameter Object

## Properties

| Property | Type | Version | Description |
|----------|------|---------|-------------|
| Direction | Integer | 3.5 | Indicates whether a Parameter is for input, output, or returned values |
| Name | String | 3.0/3.5 | Name of this Parameter object. |
| Type | Integer | 3.0/3.5 | Data type of the object |
| Value | Variant | 3.0/3.5 | The object's value |

# Property Object

## Properties

| Property | Type | Version | Description |
|----------|------|---------|-------------|
| Inherited | Boolean | 3.0/3.5 | Indicates whether a property is inherited from an underlying object |
| Name | String | 3.0/3.5 | Name of the Property object |
| Type | Integer | 3.0/3.5 | The Property object's data type |
| Value | Variant | 3.0/3.5 | The property value |

# QueryDef Object

## Collections

| Property | Type | Version | Description |
|----------|------|---------|-------------|
| Fields | Fields | 3.0/3.5 | Collection of fields in the QueryDef object |
| Parameters | Parameters | 3.0/3.5 | Collection of Parameter objects in the QueryDef object |
| Properties | Properties | 3.0/3.5 | Collection of Property objects in the QueryDef object |

# *Methods*

| Method | Parameters | Returns | Version | Description |
|---|---|---|---|---|
| Cancel | | Sub | 3.5 | Cancels execution of an asynchronous OpenRecordset method |
| Close | | Sub | 3.0/3.5 | Closes the open QueryDef object |
| CreateProperty | [Name], [Type], [Value], [DDL] | Property | 3.0/3.5 | Creates a new user-defined Property object |
| Execute | [Options] | Sub | 3.0/3.5 | Execute the Querydef |
| OpenRecordset | [Type], [Options] | Recordset | 3.0 | Creates a new Recordset object |
| OpenRecordset | [Type], [Options], [LockEdit] | Recordset | 3.5 | Creates a new Recordset object |

# *Properties*

| Property | Type | Version | Description |
|---|---|---|---|
| CacheSize | Long | 3.5 | Number of records to be locally cached from an ODBC data source |
| Connect | String | 3.0/3.5 | Value providing information about a data source for a QueryDef |
| DateCreated | Variant | 3.0/3.5 | Date and time the QueryDef was created |
| LastUpdated | Variant | 3.0/3.5 | Date and time of the most recent change to the QueryDef |
| MaxRecords | Long | 3.5 | Maximum number of records to return from the query |
| Name | String | 3.0/3.5 | Name of this QueryDef object |
| ODBCTimeout | Integer | 3.0/3.5 | Number of seconds to wait before a timeout occurs when querying an ODBC database |
| Prepare | Variant | 3.5 | Indicates whether to prepare a temporary stored procedure from the query |
| RecordsAffected | Long | 3.0/3.5 | Number of records affected by the last Execute method |
| ReturnsRecords | Boolean | 3.0/3.5 | Indicates whether a SQL pass-through query returns records |
| SQL | String | 3.0/3.5 | SQL statement that defines the query |
| StillExecuting | Boolean | 3.5 | Indicates whether an asynchronous method call is still executing |

| Property | Type | Version | Description |
|---|---|---|---|
| Type | Integer | 3.0/3.5 | The data type of the object |
| Updatable | Boolean | 3.0/3.5 | Indicates whether the query definition can be changed |

# Recordset Object

## Collections

| Property | Type | Version | Description |
|---|---|---|---|
| Connection | Connection | 3.5 | Indicates which Connection owns the Recordset |
| Fields | Fields | 3.0/3.5 | Collection of fields in the Recordset object |

## Methods

| Method | Parameters | Returns | Version | Description |
|---|---|---|---|---|
| AddNew | | Sub | 3.0/3.5 | Adds a new record to the Recordset |
| Cancel | | Sub | 3.5 | Cancels execution of an asynchronous Execute, OpenRecordset, or OpenConnection method |
| CancelUpdate | | Sub | 3.0/3.5 | Cancels any pending *AddNew* or *Update* statements |
| Clone | | Recordset | 3.0/3.5 | Creates a duplicate Recordset |
| Close | | Sub | 3.0/3.5 | Closes an open Recordset object |
| CopyQueryDef | | QueryDef | 3.0/3.5 | Returns a copy of the QueryDef that created the Recordset |
| Delete | | Sub | 3.0/3.5 | Deletes a record from the Recordset |
| Edit | | Sub | 3.0/3.5 | Prepares a row of the Recordset for editing |
| FillCache | [Rows], [Start-Bookmark] | Sub | 3.0/3.5 | Fills the cache for an ODBC-derived Recordset |
| FindFirst | Criteria As String | Sub | 3.0/3.5 | Locates the first record that satisfies the criteria |
| FindLast | Criteria As String | Sub | 3.0/3.5 | Locates the last record that satisfies the criteria |

| Method | Parameters | Returns | Version | Description |
|--------|-----------|---------|---------|-------------|
| FindNext | Criteria As String | Sub | 3.0/3.5 | Locates the next record that satisfies the criteria |
| FindPrevious | Criteria As String | Sub | 3.0/3.5 | Locates the previous record that satisfies the criteria |
| GetRows | [cRows] | Variant | 3.0/3.5 | Writes multiple records into an array |
| Move | Rows As Long, [StartBook-mark] | Sub | 3.0/3.5 | Reposition the record pointer relative to the current position or to a bookmark |
| MoveFirst | | Sub | 3.0/3.5 | Moves to the first record in the Recordset |
| MoveLast | | Sub | 3.0 | Moves to the last record in the Recordset |
| MoveLast | [Options As Long] | Sub | 3.5 | Moves to the last record in the Recordset |
| MoveNext | | Sub | 3.0/3.5 | Moves to the next record in the Recordset |
| MovePrevious | | Sub | 3.0/3.5 | Moves to the previous record in the Recordset |
| NextRecordset | | Boolean | 3.5 | Retrieves the next recordset in a multiquery Recordset |
| OpenRecordset | [Type], [Options] | Recordset | 3.0/3.5 | Creates a new Recordset object |
| Requery | [NewQue-ryDef] | Sub | 3.0/3.5 | Reexecutes the query on which the Recordset is based |
| Seek | Comparison As String, Key1... | Sub | 3.0/3.5 | Locates a record in a table-type Recordset |
| Update | | Sub | 3.0/3.5 | Saves changes initiated by the Edit or AddNew methods |

## *Properties*

| Property | Type | Version | Description |
|----------|------|---------|-------------|
| AbsolutePosition | Long | 3.0/3.5 | Returns or sets the relative record number of the current record |
| BatchCollisionCount | Long | 3.5 | Number of rows having collisions in the last batch update |
| BatchCollisions | Variant | 3.5 | Indicates which rows had collisions in the last batch update |
| BatchSize | Long | 3.5 | Determines how many updates to include in a batch |
| BOF | Boolean | 3.0/3.5 | Indicates whether the current record position is before the first record |

| Property | Type | Version | Description |
|---|---|---|---|
| Bookmark As | Byte | 3.0/3.5 | Uniquely identifies a particular record in a Recordset |
| Bookmarkable | Boolean | 3.0/3.5 | Indicates whether a Recordset supports bookmarks |
| CacheSize | Long | 3.0/3.5 | Number of records from an ODBC data source to be cached locally |
| CacheStart As | Byte | 3.0/3.5 | Bookmark of the first record to be cached from an ODBC data source |
| DateCreated | Variant | 3.0/3.5 | Date and time when the underlying base table was created |
| EditMode | Integer | 3.0/3.5 | Indicates the state of editing for the current record |
| EOF | Boolean | 3.0/3.5 | Indicates whether the current record position is after the last record |
| Filter | String | 3.0/3.5 | Defines a filter to apply to a Recordset |
| Index | String | 3.0/3.5 | Name of the current Index object (table-type Recordset only) |
| LastModified As | Byte | 3.0/3.5 | Bookmark indicating the most recently added or changed record |
| LastUpdated | Variant | 3.0/3.5 | Date and time of the most recent change to the underlying base table |
| LockEdits | Boolean | 3.0/3.5 | Indicates the type of locking (optimistic or pessimistic) in effect during editing |
| Name | String | 3.0/3.5 | Name of the Recordset object |
| NoMatch | Boolean | 3.0/3.5 | Indicates whether the Seek or Find methods succeeded in finding a record |
| PercentPosition | Single | 3.0/3.5 | Indicates or changes the approximate location of the current record |
| RecordCount | Long | 3.0/3.5 | Number of records in the Recordset object |
| RecordStatus | Integer | 3.5 | Indicates the batch update status of the current record |
| Restartable | Boolean | 3.0/3.5 | Indicates whether the Recordset supports the Requery method |
| Sort | String | 3.0/3.5 | Defines the sort order for records in a Recordset |
| StillExecuting | Boolean | 3.5 | Indicates whether an asynchronous method call is still executing |
| Transactions | Boolean | 3.0/3.5 | Indicates whether the Recordset supports transactions |
| Type | Integer | 3.0/3.5 | Indicates the object's data type |
| Updatable | Boolean | 3.0/3.5 | Indicates whether records in the Recordset can be updated |
| UpdateOptions | Long | 3.5 | Determines how a batch update query will be constructed |

| Property | Type | Version | Description |
|---|---|---|---|
| ValidationRule | String | 3.0/3.5 | Contains an expression that must evaluate True for a successful update |
| ValidationText | String | 3.0/3.5 | Message to appear if ValidationRule fails |

# Relation Object

## Collections

| Property | Type | Version | Description |
|---|---|---|---|
| Fields | Fields | 3.0/3.5 | Collection of fields in this Relation object |
| Properties | Properties | 3.0/3.5 | Collection of Property objects |

## Methods

| Method | Parameters | Returns | Version | Description |
|---|---|---|---|---|
| CreateField | [Name], [Type], [Size] | Field | 3.0/3.5 | Creates a new Field object |

## Properties

| Property | Type | Version | Description |
|---|---|---|---|
| Attributes | Long | 3.0/3.5 | Miscellaneous characteristics of the Relation object |
| ForeignTable | String | 3.0/3.5 | Specifies the name of the foreign (referencing) table in a relationship |
| Name | String | 3.0/3.5 | Name of this Relation object |
| PartialReplica | Boolean | 3.5 | Indicates whether the relation provides a partial replica's synchronizing rules |
| Table | String | 3.0/3.5 | Specifies the primary (referenced) TableDef or Querydef |

# TableDef Object

## Collections

| Property | Type | Version | Description |
|---|---|---|---|
| Fields | Fields | 3.0/3.5 | Collection of fields in this TableDef object |
| Indexes | Indexes | 3.0/3.5 | Collection of indexes associated with this TableDef object |
| Properties | Properties | 3.0/3.5 | Collection of Property objects |

# *Methods*

| Method | Parameters | Returns | Version | Description |
|---|---|---|---|---|
| CreateField | [Name], [Type], [Size] | Field | 3.0/3.5 | Creates a new Field object |
| CreateIndex | [Name] | Index | 3.0/3.5 | Creates a new Index object |
| CreateProperty | [Name], [Type], [Value], [DDL] | Property | 3.0/3.5 | Creates a new user-defined Property object |
| OpenRecordset | [Type], [Options] | Recordset | 3.0/3.5 | Creates a new Recordset object |
| RefreshLink | | Sub | 3.0/3.5 | Updates connection information for an attached table |

# *Properties*

| Property | Type | Version | Description |
|---|---|---|---|
| Attributes | Long | 3.0/3.5 | Miscellaneous characteristics of the TableDef object |
| ConflictTable | String | 3.0/3.5 | Name of table containing records that conflicted during replica synchronization |
| Connect | String | 3.0/3.5 | Data source for the TableDef |
| DateCreated | Variant | 3.0/3.5 | Date and time when the table was created |
| LastUpdated | Variant | 3.0/3.5 | Date and time when the TableDef was last changed |
| Name | String | 3.0/3.5 | Name of the TableDef |
| RecordCount | Long | 3.0/3.5 | Number of records |
| ReplicaFilter | Variant | 3.5 | Indicates which records to include in a partial replica |
| SourceTableName | String | 3.0/3.5 | Name of a linked table's original source table. |
| Updatable | Boolean | 3.0/3.5 | Indicates whether the TableDef definition can be changed |
| ValidationRule | String | 3.0/3.5 | Expression that must evaluate to True for a successful update |
| ValidationText | String | 3.0/3.5 | Message to display if ValidationRule fails |

# User Object

## Collections

| Property | Type | Version | Description |
|---|---|---|---|
| Groups | Groups | 3.0/3.5 | Collection of Group objects in a User object |
| Properties | Properties | 3.0/3.5 | Collection of Property objects |

## Methods

| Method | Parameters | Returns | Version | Description |
|---|---|---|---|---|
| CreateGroup | [Name], [PID] | Group | 3.0/3.5 | Creates a new Group object |
| NewPassword | bstrOld As String, bstrNew As String | Sub | 3.0/3.5 | Changes the password of an existing user account |

## Properties

| Property | Type | Version | Description |
|---|---|---|---|
| Name | String | 3.0/3.5 | The name of the User object |
| Password | String | 3.0/3.5 | Password for the user account |
| PID | String | 3.0/3.5 | Personal identifier (PID) for a group or user account |

# Workspace Object

## Collections

| Property | Type | Version | Description |
|---|---|---|---|
| Connections | Connections | 3.5 | Collection of Connection objects |
| Databases | Databases | 3.0/3.5 | Collection of open Database objects |
| Groups | Groups | | Collection of Group objects in a Workspace object |
| Users | Users | 3.0/3.5 | Collection of User objects for a Workspace object |

## *Methods*

| Method | Parameters | Returns | Version | Description |
|---|---|---|---|---|
| BeginTrans | | Sub | 3.0/3.5 | Begins a new transaction |
| Close | | Sub | 3.0/3.5 | Close the Workspace object |
| CommitTrans | | Sub | 3.0/3.5 | Ends the transaction and saves any changes |
| CreateDatabase | Name As String, Connect As String, [Option] | Database | 3.0/3.5 | Creates a new Microsoft Jet database (.mdb) |
| CreateGroup | [Name], [PID] | Group | 3.0/3.5 | Creates a new Group object |
| CreateUser | [Name], [PID], [Password] | User | 3.0/3.5 | Creates a new User object |
| OpenConnection | Name As String, [Options], [ReadOnly], [Connect] | Connection | 3.5 | Opens a connection to a database |
| OpenDatabase | Name As String, [Exclusive], [ReadOnly], [Connect] | Database | 3.0/3.5 | Opens a database |
| Rollback | | Sub | 3.0/3.5 | Undoes any changes since the last BeginTrans |

## *Properties*

| Property | Type | Version | Description |
|---|---|---|---|
| DefaultCursorDriver | Long | 3.5 | Selects the ODBC cursor library |
| IsolateODBCTrans | Integer | 3.0/3.5 | Indicates whether multiple transactions are isolated (ODBC only) |
| LoginTimeout | Long | 3.5 | Number of seconds allowed for logging in to an ODBC database |
| Name | String | 3.0/3.5 | Name of this Workspace object |
| UserName | String | 3.0/3.5 | User that created the Workspace object |

# B

## *The Quotient: An Additional Operation of the Relational Algebra*

The quotient of two tables is not used often, but has a very specific use. It arises when we wish to select those rows of a table that provide all possible values in certain columns. As an example, imagine a business that makes furniture. The database for this business has a table on the types of wood that they use and on suppliers of wood and which types they supply. Here is an example (of course, these tables would include more columns, but this is just to illustrate the point):

*Table B-1. WOOD*

| Type |
| --- |
| Mahogany |
| Red oak |
| Poplar |
| Walnut |

*Table B-2. SUPPLIER/TYPE*

| Sname | Type |
| --- | --- |
| Jones Wood Supply | mahogany |
| Austin Hardwoods | red oak |
| Orange Coast | mahogany |
| Jones Wood Supply | poplar |
| West Lumber | poplar |
| Jones Wood Supply | walnut |
| Austin Hardwoods | walnut |
| Jones Wood Supply | red oak |

*Table B-2. SUPPLIER/TYPE (continued)*

| Sname | Type |
|-------|------|
| Orange Coast | walnut |
| West Lumber | red oak |
| Orange Coast | poplar |
| Orange Coast | red oak |
| Fred's Woods | walnut |

Note that there are four types of wood. Suppose we want to know which suppliers supply all four types—a reasonable question. The answer in this case is:

*Table B-3. SUPPLIER/TYPE ÷ WOOD*

| Sname |
|-------|
| Jones Wood Supply |
| Orange Coast |

and is called the *quotient* of the table SUPPLIERS/TYPE by WOOD, written SUPPLIER/TYPE ÷ WOOD.

As you can see, the quotient can certainly come up in real-life situations. The reason for defining a specific operation for this purpose is that expressing the quotient in terms of the other relations is a bit complex. Let's do it to illustrate the virtue of the quotient.

The idea is actually relatively simple. We first get a table, call it T, containing all rows that are not in the SUPPLIER/TYPE table. This new table will involve only those suppliers who have not supplied all types of wood. (If a supplier supplies all four types of wood, then there will be four rows in the SUPPLIER/TYPE table and therefore no rows in T.) Then we subtract this from a table containing all (participating) suppliers. Here is the step-by-step procedure:

**Step 1**: Form the table

```
R = [projSName(SUPPLIER/TYPE) ↔ WOOD] - SUPPLIER/TYPE
```

This is the table containing all rows of the form (SName,Type) that are not in the SUPPLIER/TYPE table. Put another way, it is the set of "missing possibilities" in the Cartesian product (which is the set of all possibilities). Here is the table R:

*Table B-4. R*

| Sname | Type |
|-------|------|
| Austin Hardwoods | poplar |
| West Lumber | walnut |

*Table B-4. R (continued)*

| Sname | Type |
|---|---|
| Austin Hardwoods | mahogany |
| West Lumber | mahogany |
| Fred's Woods | walnut |

**Step 2**: Form the table

$$proj\text{SName}(R)$$

That is, project the table R onto the SName column, giving the SUPPLIERS that do not supply all types of wood.

*Table B-5. projSName(R)*

| SName |
|---|
| Austin Hardwoods |
| West Lumber |
| Fred's Woods |

**Step 3**: Finally, form the table

$$proj\text{SName}(\text{SUPPLIERS/TYPE}) - proj\text{SName}(R)$$

That is, subtract the table in Step 2 from the first column of the SUPPLIERS/TYPE table. This gives the suppliers that supply all four types of wood.

*Table B-6. SUPPLIER/TYPE ÷ WOOD*

| SName |
|---|
| Jones Wood Supply |
| Orange Coast |

# C

# *Obtaining or Creating the Sample Database*

The sample flat file "database," as well as the Access database and the sample programs, are all available for free download from the O'Reilly Internet site. You can choose from any of the three following methods to download the data that accompanies the book:

- **Via the World Wide Web**. The sample files are available from *ftp://ftp.ora.com/published/oreilly/windows/access.design/example.zip*.

- **Via an ftp client program**. You can use an ftp client such as WS_PTP32 to ftp to *ftp.ora.com*, change to the directory *published/oreilly/windows/access.design*, and get the file *example.zip*.

- **Via email (ftpmail)**. *ftpmail* is a mail server available to anyone who can send electronic mail to, and receive it from, Internet sites. This includes any company or service provider that allows email connections to the Internet. To receive the sample files via ftpmail, send mail to *ftpmail@online.ora.com*. In the message body, include the FTP commands you would otherwise enter during a command-line FTP session. (Or, to get a complete help file, you can send a message with no subject and the single word "help" in the body.) Figure C-1 shows a request for the file created with Microsoft Internet Mail.

In each case, the sample files are stored in a single file compressed using the PKZip file format. If you don't own a utility program capable of decompressing the software (or if you're still doing these things from the command line), we highly recommend that you download an evaluation copy of the shareware utility WinZip, from Nico Mak Computing, Inc.; it is available at *http://www.winzip.com/*.

*EXAMPLE.ZIP* contains *LIBRARY_FLAT.DOC*, the flat database created with Microsoft Word, as well as *LIBRARY95.MDB*, the sample Access database for Access for Office 95, and *LIBRARY97.MBD*, the sample Access database for Access

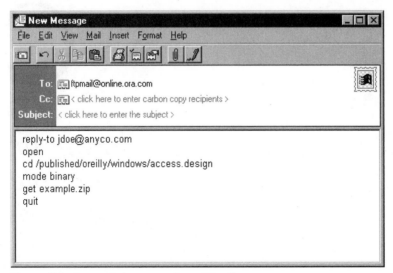

*Figure C-1. An email message to ftpmail@online.ora.com*

for Office 97. (The two versions perform optimally when using different file formats.) The *.MDB* file itself contains the following:

- The four tables (BOOKS, AUTHORS, PUBLISHERS, and BOOK/AUTHOR) and their primary indexes

- A code module, Examples, that contains all of the example programs from the book

It does not, however, contain definitions of relationships, nor does it include any query definitions. The book assumes that you'll be creating these from scratch.

If you don't have access to the Internet or to an email account from a service provider with a gateway to the Internet, it is quite easy to create the sample files yourself. In the remainder of this section, we'll guide you through the steps required to create each of the tables in the Library database, *LIBRARY.MDB*.

## Creating the Database

The first step is to create the database itself by doing the following:

1. Start Microsoft Access.

2. When the Microsoft Access dialog appears over the main Microsoft Access window, as shown in Figure C-2, select the Blank Database button and Click *OK*. Access opens the File New Database dialog.

3. Navigate to the directory in which you'd like to save the database file. If the directory doesn't exist, you can create it by clicking on the Create New Folder

*Figure C-2. The Microsoft Access dialog*

button (the third button from the left on the toolbar); you should then navigate to the newly created directory. In the File name text box, type in `library.mdb`. Then click the *Create* button.

Access creates the new database and opens the Library Database window, which should resemble Figure C-3. This is a completely empty database; it doesn't even contain any tables that are capable of holding data. Our next step is to define each of those tables and enter some data into them.

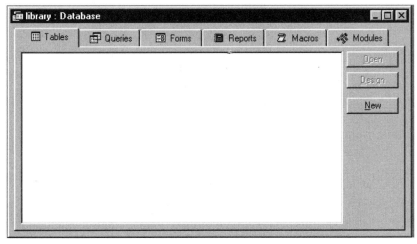

*Figure C-3. The Library Database window*

## *Creating the BOOKS Table*

To define the design of the Books table, perform the following steps:

1. Click the *New* button in the Library Database window. Access opens the New Table dialog, which contains a list box with a variety of options. Select Design View and click *OK*. Access opens the Table1 Table window, as shown in Figure C-4, which allows you to define the fields in a new database table.

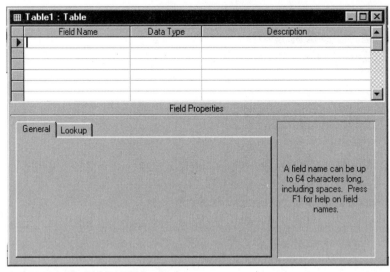

*Figure C-4. The Table1 Table window*

2. Enter the information shown in Table C-1 into the Field Name and Data Type columns of the Table1 Table window. Note that you can select the data type from a drop-down list box.

*Table C-1. Fields of the BOOKS table*

| Field Name | Data Type |
| --- | --- |
| ISBN | Text |
| Title | Text |
| PubID | Text |
| Price | Currency |

3. When you select a field, its properties are displayed in the lower portion of the dialog. Next, enter the individual field properties shown in Table C-2 in the Field Properties portion of the dialog. Note that you don't have to add or modify any properties of the Price field.

*Table C-2. Non-default properties of the BOOKS table*

| Field Name | Property | Value |
|---|---|---|
| ISBN | Indexed | Yes (No Duplicates) |
| Title | Field Size | 200 |
| | Indexed | Yes (Duplicates OK) |
| PubID | Indexed | Yes (Duplicates OK) |
| Price | Format | Currency |

4. Designate ISBN as the table's primary key. To do this, either click on the *Primary Key* button on the toolbar (the 11th button from the left of the toolbar, and immediately to the left of the *Undo* button), or right click on the row selector (the shaded gray field to the right of the ISBN's Field Name column) and select Primary Key from the pop-up menu.

5. Save the completed table design. Either click the *Save* button on the toolbar (the second button from the left) or select the Save option from the File menu. When Access opens the Save As dialog, type BOOKS into the Table Name text box and click *OK*.

6. Close the BOOKS table in Design View.

You're now ready to begin entering data into the table. Select the BOOKS table in the database window and click on the *Open* button. Access opens the BOOKS table in Datasheet View, which allows you to input information into the database. Enter the data shown in Table C-3. When you've finished, close the table. Note that you don't have to explicitly save the data that you've entered into the table; Access automatically takes care of writing the records that you've entered to disk.

*Table C-3. Data for the BOOKS table*

| ISBN | Title | PubID | Price |
|---|---|---|---|
| 0-555-55555-9 | Macbeth | 2 | 12.00 |
| 0-91-335678-7 | Faerie Queene | 1 | 15.00 |
| 0-99-999999-9 | Emma | 1 | 20.00 |
| 0-91-045678-5 | Hamlet | 2 | 20.00 |
| 0-55-123456-9 | Main Street | 3 | 22.95 |
| 1-22-233700-0 | Visual Basic | 1 | 25.00 |
| 0-12-333433-3 | On Liberty | 1 | 25.00 |
| 0-103-45678-9 | Iliad | 1 | 25.00 |
| 1-1111-1111-1 | C++ | 1 | 29.95 |
| 0-321-32132-1 | Balloon | 3 | 34.00 |
| 0-123-45678-0 | Ulysses | 2 | 34.00 |
| 0-99-777777-7 | King Lear | 2 | 49.00 |

*Table C-3. Data for the BOOKS table (continued)*

| ISBN | Title | PubID | Price |
|------|-------|-------|-------|
| 0-12-345678-9 | Jane Eyre | 3 | 49.00 |
| 0-11-345678-9 | Moby Dick | 3 | 49.00 |

# *Creating the AUTHORS Table*

To create the AUTHORS table, follow the same basic steps listed in the previous section, "Creating the BOOKS Table." The field definitions for the AUTHORS table are shown in Table C-4.

*Table C-4. Fields of the AUTHORS table*

| Field Name | Data Type |
|------------|-----------|
| AuID | Text |
| AuName | Text |
| AuPhone | Text |

There is only a single property that you need to set:

| Field Name: | AuID |
|-------------|------|
| Property: | Indexed |
| Value: | Yes (No Duplicates) |

When you've finished creating the fields and assigning their attributes, define AuID as the table's primary key. Then save the table, assigning it the name AUTHORS.

Next, enter the author data into the table; it is shown in Table C-5.

*Table C-5. Data for the AUTHORS table*

| AuID | AuName | AuPhone |
|------|--------|---------|
| 1 | Austen | 111-111-1111 |
| 12 | Grumpy | 321-321-0000 |
| 3 | Homer | 333-333-3333 |
| 10 | Jones | 123-333-3333 |
| 6 | Joyce | 666-666-6666 |
| 2 | Meville | 222-222-2222 |
| 8 | Mill | 888-888-8888 |
| 4 | Roman | 444-444-4444 |
| 5 | Shakespeare | 555-555-5555 |

*Table C-5. Data for the AUTHORS table (continued)*

| AuID | AuName | AuPhone |
|------|--------|---------|
| 13 | Sleepy | 321-321-1111 |
| 9 | Smith | 123-222-2222 |
| 11 | Snoopy | 321-321-2222 |
| 7 | Spenser | 777-777-7777 |

# Creating the PUBLISHERS Table

Once again, follow the same basic steps listed in the earlier section "Creating the BOOKS Table" to create the PUBLISHERS table. Field definitions for the PUBLISHERS table are shown in Table C-6.

*Table C-6. Fields of the PUBLISHERS table*

| Field Name | Data Type |
|------------|-----------|
| PubID | Text |
| PubName | Text |
| PubPhone | Text |

Once again, there is only a single property that you need to set:

| Field Name: | PubID |
|-------------|-------|
| Property: | Indexed |
| Value: | Yes (No Duplicates) |

Designate PubID as the primary key, and save the table as PUBLISHERS.

Once you've finished creating the PUBLISHERS table, you can enter data into it. The PUBLISHERS table contains records for only three publishers; these are shown in Table C-7.

*Table C-7. Data for the PUBLISHERS table*

| PubID | PubName | PubPhone |
|-------|---------|----------|
| 1 | Big House | 123-456-7890 |
| 2 | Alpha Press | 999-999-9999 |
| 3 | Small House | 714-000-0000 |

# Creating the BOOK/AUTHOR Table

The BOOK/AUTHOR table is the final table needed for our examples. Once again, create it following the same basic steps described earlier in "Creating the

BOOKS Table." It consists of only two fields, as shown in Table C-8. Once you've entered the field names and data types into the table definition, change the two properties listed in Table C-9 and save the table as BOOK/AUTHOR. When you save the table, Access will open the dialog shown in Figure C-5. The table in fact does not have a primary key, so click on the *No* button; Access will save the table without designating a primary key.

*Table C-8. Fields of the BOOK/AUTHOR Table*

| Field Name | Data Type |
|------------|-----------|
| ISBN       | text      |
| AuID       | text      |

*Table C-9. Nondefault Properties of the BOOK/AUTHOR Table*

| Field Name | Property | Value                 |
|------------|----------|-----------------------|
| ISBN       | Indexed  | Yes (Duplicates OK)   |
| AuID       | Indexed  | Yes (Duplicates OK)   |

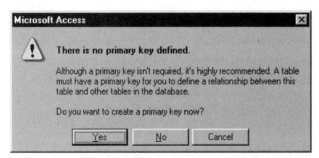

*Figure C-5. The "no primary key" warning dialog*

Once you've created the BOOK/AUTHOR table, you can enter the data shown in Table C-10 into it.

*Table C-10. Data for the BOOK/AUTHOR Table*

| ISBN            | AuID |
|-----------------|------|
| 0-103-45678-9   | 3    |
| 0-11-345678-9   | 2    |
| 0-12-333433-3   | 8    |
| 0-12-345678-9   | 1    |
| 0-123-45678-0   | 6    |
| 0-321-32132-1   | 11   |
| 0-321-32132-1   | 12   |
| 0-321-32132-1   | 13   |

*Table C-10. Data for the BOOK/AUTHOR Table (continued)*

| ISBN | AuID |
|------|------|
| 0-55-123456-9 | 9 |
| 0-55-123456-9 | 10 |
| 0-555-55555-9 | 5 |
| 0-91-045678-5 | 5 |
| 0-91-335678-7 | 7 |
| 0-99-777777-7 | 5 |
| 0-99-999999-9 | 1 |
| 1-1111-1111-1 | 4 |
| 1-22-233700-0 | 4 |

Once you've finished this data entry, you'll still have to define the relationships among the tables. This is discussed in detail in "Setting Up the Relationships in Access," in Chapter 3, *Implementing Entity-Relationship Models: Relational Databases*. Once this detail is taken care of, you can use the tables to create the queries and to run the programs discussed in the text of the book.

# *Backing Up the Database*

Once you've created the BOOKS database, it's a good idea to make a backup copy of each of the tables. That way, you can feel free to make modifications to individual tables, to try out the book's sample programs, and generally to experiment with the data, the tables, and the database, without having to be concerned that you'll corrupt the data. You can make a backup copy by following this procedure for each of the four tables of the Books database:

1. Highlight the table you'd like to back up.

2. Select the Save As option from the File menu. Access opens the Save As... dialog shown in Figure C-6.

3. Select the *Within the current database* button. Access will suggest a filename for your backup copy, such as Copy of BOOKS, as shown in Figure C-6.

4. Click the *OK* button to create the backup copy. It will appear in the Tables property sheet of the Database dialog.

If the data in any of your tables do become lost or corrupted, you can restore the table as follows:

1. Highlight the backup copy of the table in the database window.

2. Select the Save As option from the File menu. Access again opens the Save As... dialog shown in Figure C-6.

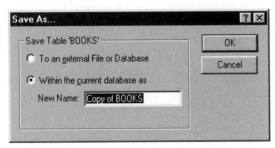

*Figure C-6. The Save As... dialog*

3. Select the *Within the current database* button.

4. Replace Access' suggested filename (Copy of Copy of...) with the name of the original table and click *OK*.

5. Access displays a message warning that the name you entered has already been assigned to another table and asking whether you want to replace it. Click *OK*.

---

NOTE          Before replacing any of the tables that participate in relationships with other tables, you'll have to delete that table's relationships. To do this, select the Relationships option from the Tools menu. When Access opens the Relationships window, right click on the line depicting each relationship in which a table participates, then select the Delete option from the pop-up menu.

---

# Entering and Running the Sample Programs

If you've downloaded the sample file from O'Reilly & Associates, your database already includes a code module, Examples, that contains all of the book's sample VBA programs.  If not, you can create a code module yourself and enter programs into it.  To create the code module:

1. Select the Modules tab when the Library database is open in the Database window.

2. Click on the *New* button to create a new code module.

3. When Access opens a new code module (which it will usually name Module1, unless your database already contains code modules saved with their default names), click on the *Save* button on the toolbar.

4. When Access displays the Save As dialog, enter the name of your new code module, Examples, in the Module Name text box and click *OK*.

You can then begin entering code for each of the program examples. To do this, for each code example:

1. Select the Procedure option from the Insert menu.

2. When Access opens the Insert Procedure dialog, enter the name of the procedure in the Name text box. Since all of the programs listed in the book are subroutines, you don't have to worry about the dialog's other options. Just click *OK*.

To run a program:

1. Select the Modules tab in the Database window, and open the Examples module.

2. Select the Debug Window option from theView menu.

3. When Access opens the Debug window, simply type in the name of the program you'd like to run.

# D

## Suggestions for Further Reading

Here is a brief list of some books on database theory:

Atzeni, P. and De Antonellis, V., *Relational Database Theory*, Benjamin Cummings, 1993, 389 pages. A highly theoretical and mathematical treatment of the subject.

Codd, E.F., *The Relational Model for Database Management: Version 2*, Addison-Wesley, 1990, 538 pages. The classic exposition of the relational model by one of its creators and chief proponents.

Date, C.J., *An Introduction to Database Systems*, 6th Edition, Addison-Wesley, 1995, 839 pages. A less formal and highly readable book.

Simovici, D. and Tenney, R., *Relational Database Systems*, Academic Press, 1995, 485 pages. This is a very mathematical treatment of the subject. Much better written than the Atzeni and De Antonellis book.

Ullman, J., *Principles of Database and Knowledge-Base Systems, Volume 1: Classical Database Systems*, Computer Science Press, 1988, 631 pages. A book with a somewhat different point of view. Not as mathematical as Atzeni or Simovici, but more mathematical than Date.

# *Index*

# About the Author

Steven Roman is a professor of mathematics at the California State University, Fullerton. He has taught at a number of other universities, including MIT, the University of California at Santa Barbara, and the University of South Florida. Dr. Roman received his B.A. degree from the University of California at Los Angeles and his Ph.D. from the University of Washington. Dr. Roman has authored 28 books, including a number of books on mathematics, such as *Coding and Information Theory*, *Advanced Linear Algebra*, and *Field Theory*, published by Springer-Verlag. He has also written a series of 15 small books entitled *Modules in Mathematics*, designed for the general college-level liberal arts student. Dr. Roman has written two other computer books, entitled *Concepts of Object-Oriented Programming with Visual Basic*, published by Springer-Verlag, and *Understanding Personal Computer Hardware*, an in-depth look at how PC hardware works (no publisher yet). He is currently working on a book entitled *Visual Basic 5 and the Component Object Model*. Dr. Roman is interested in combinatorics, algebra, and computer science.

# Colophon

The animal featured on the cover of *Access Database Design & Programming* is a tamandua, one of the three species that comprise the anteater family.

Edie Freedman designed the cover of this book, using a 19th-century engraving from the Dover Pictorial Archive. The cover layout was produced with Quark XPress 3.5 using the ITC Garamond font.

The inside layout was designed by Edie Freedman and Nancy Priest and implemented in FrameMaker 5.0 by Mike Sierra. The text and heading fonts are ITC Garamond Light and Garamond Book. The illustrations that appear in the book were created in Macromedia Freehand 5.0 by Chris Reilley. This colophon was written by Clairemarie Fisher O'Leary.

# More Titles from O'Reilly

## Windows

### Inside the Windows 95 Registry

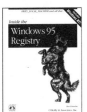

By Ron Petrusha
1st Edition August1996
594 pages, includes diskette
ISBN 1-56592-170-4

This book covers remote registry access, differences between the Win95 and NT registries, and registry backup. You'll also find a thorough examination of the role that the registry plays in OLE, coverage of undocumented registry services, and more. Petrusha shows programmers how to access the Win95 registry from Win32, Win16, and DOS programs, in C and Visual Basic. VxD sample code is also included. The book includes a diskette with registry tools such as REGSPY, a program that shows exactly how Windows applications, libraries, and drivers use settings in the registry.

### Windows NT in a Nutshell

By Eric Pearce
1st Edition June 1997 (est.)
350 pages (est.), ISBN 1-56592-251-4

Anybody who installs Windows NT, creates a user, or adds a printer is an NT system administrator (whether they realize it or not). This book organizes NT's complex 4.0 GUI interface, dialog boxes, and multitude of DOS-shell commands into an easy-to-use quick reference for anybody who uses or manages an NT system. It features a new tagged callout approach to documenting the GUI as well as real-life examples of command usage and strategies for problem solving.

### Inside the Windows 96 File System

By Stan Mitchell
1st Edition May 1997
400 pages, ISBN 1-56592-200-X

This book details the Windows 95 File System, as well as the new opportunities and challenges it brings developers. Over the course of the book, the author progressively strips away the layers of the Win95 File System, which reside in a component named Installable File System Manager or IFSMgr, providing the reader with information crucial for effective File System development. Its "hands-on" approach will help developers become better equipped to make design decisions using the new Win95 File System features.

### Windows Annoyances

By David A. Karp
1st Edition June 1997
300 pages, ISBN 1-56592-266-2

*Windows Annoyances*, a comprehensive resource for intermediate to advanced users of Windows 95 and NT 4.0, details step-by-step how to customize your Win95/NT operating system through tips, tricks, and workarounds.

You'll learn how to customize every aspect of these systems, far beyond the intentions of Microsoft. An entire chapter on the registry explains how to back up, repair, compress, and transfer portions of the registry for personal customization. Win95 users will discover how Plug and Play, the technology that makes Win95 so hardware-compatible, can save time and improve the way you interact with your computer. You'll also learn how to benefit from the new 32-bit software and hardware drivers that support such features as improved multitasking and long filenames.

### Access Database Design and Programming

By Steven Roman
1st Edition June 1997
288 pages, ISBN 1-56592-297-2

When using software products with graphical interfaces, we frequently focus so much on how to use the interface that we forget about the more general concepts that allow us to understand and put the software to effective use.

*Access Database Design and Programming* takes the reader behind the details of the *Access* interface, focusing on the general knowledge necessary for Access users or developers to create effective database applications. In particular, the book focuses on three areas: database design, queries, and programming. This book focuses on the the core concepts, enabling programmers to develop solid, effective database applications.

## O'REILLY™

TO ORDER: **800-998-9938** • **order@ora.com** • **http://www.ora.com/**
OUR PRODUCTS ARE AVAILABLE AT A BOOKSTORE OR SOFTWARE STORE NEAR YOU.
FOR INFORMATION: **800-998-9938** • **707-829-0515** • **info@ora.com**

# C and C++

## C++: The Core Language

By Gregory Satir & Doug Brown
1st Edition October 1995
230 pages, ISBN 1-56592-116-X

*C++: The Core Language* is a first book for C programmers transitioning to C++, an object-oriented enhancement of the C programming language. Designed to get readers up to speed quickly, this book thoroughly explains the important concepts and features and gives brief overviews of the rest of the language. Covers features common to all C++ compilers, including those on UNIX, Windows NT, Windows, DOS, and Macintosh.

## Practical C++ Programming

By Steve Oualline
1st Edition September 1995
584 pages, ISBN 1-56592-139-9

Fast becoming the standard language of commercial software development, C++ is an update of the C programming language, adding object-oriented features that are very helpful for today's larger graphical applications.

*Practical C++ Programming* is a complete introduction to the C++ language for the beginning programmer, and also for C programmers transitioning to C++. Topics covered include good programming style, C++ syntax (what to use and what not to use), C++ class design, debugging and optimization, and common programming mistakes. At the end of each chapter are a number of exercises you can use to make sure you've grasped the concepts. Solutions to most are provided.

## Practical C Programming, Third Edition

By Steve Oualline
3rd Edition July 1997 (est.)
475 pages(est.), ISBN 1-56592-306-5

There are lots of introductory C books, but this new edition of *Practical C Programming* is the one that has the no-nonsense, practical approach that has made Nutshell Handbooks® so popular. C programming is more than just getting the syntax right. Style and debugging also play a tremendous part in creating programs that run well and are easy to maintain.

The third edition of *Practical C Programming* teaches how to create programs that are easy to read, debug, and maintain. It features more extensive examples, offers an introduction to graphical development environments, describes Electronic Archaeology (the art of going through someone else's code), and stresses practical rules. The book covers several Windows compilers, in addition to UNIX compilers. Program examples conform to ANSI C.

## Checking C Programs with lint

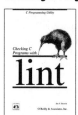

By Ian F. Darwin
1st Edition October 1988
82 pages, ISBN 0-937175-30-7

The lint program checker has proven time and again to be one of the best tools for finding portability problems and certain types of coding errors in C programs. Lint verifies a program or program segments against standard libraries, checks the code for common portability errors, and tests the programming against some tried and true guidelines. Linting your code is a necessary (though not sufficient) step in writing clean, portable, effective programs. This book introduces you to lint, guides you through running it on your programs, and helps you interpret lint's output.

# O'REILLY™

TO ORDER: **800-998-9938** • **order@ora.com** • **http://www.ora.com/**
OUR PRODUCTS ARE AVAILABLE AT A BOOKSTORE OR SOFTWARE STORE NEAR YOU.
FOR INFORMATION: **800-998-9938** • **707-829-0515** • **info@ora.com**

# Java Programming

## Exploring Java, Second Edition

*By Patrick Niemeyer & Joshua Peck*
*2nd Edition June 1997 (est.)*
*500 pages (est.), ISBN 1-56592-271-9*

The second edition of *Exploring Java*, fully revised to cover Version 1.1 of the JDK, introduces the basics of Java, the object-oriented programming language for networked applications. The ability to create animated World Wide Web pages sparked the rush to Java. But what also makes this language so important is that it's truly portable. The code runs on any machine that provides a Java interpreter, whether Windows 95, Windows NT, the Macintosh, or any flavor of UNIX.

## Java in a Nutshell, Second Edition

*By David Flanagan*
*2nd Edition May 1997*
*650 pages, ISBN 1-56592-262-X*

The bestselling Java book just got better. Java programmers migrating to 1.1 find thissecond edition of Java in a Nutshell contains everything they need to get up to speed.

Newcomers find it still has all of the features that have made it the Java book mostoften recommended on the Internet. This complete quick reference contains descriptions of all of the classes in the core Java 1.1 API, making it the only quick reference that a Java programmer needs.

## Java Virtual Machine

*By Troy Downing & Jon Meyer*
*1st Edition March 1997*
*440 pages, ISBN 1-56592-194-1*

This book is a comprehensive programming guide for the Java Virtual Machine (JVM). It gives readers a strong overview and reference of the JVM so that they may create their own implementations of the JVM or write their own compilers that create Java object code. A Java assembler is provided with the book, so the examples can all be compiled and executed.

## Java Language Reference, Second Edition

*By Mark Grand*
*2nd Edition July 1997 (est.)*
*448 pages, ISBN 1-56592-326-X*

The second edition of the *Java Language Reference* is an invaluable tool for Java programmers, especially those who have migrated to Java 1.1. Part of O'Reilly's Java documentation series, this complete reference describes all aspects of the Java language plus new features in Version 1.1, such as inner classes, final local variables and method parameters, anonymous arrays, class literals, and instance initializers.

## Java Fundamental Classes Reference

*By Mark Grand*
*1st Edition May 1997*
*1152 pages , ISBN 1-56592-241-7*

The *Java Fundamental Classes Reference* provides complete reference documentation for the Java fundamental classes.

This book takes you beyond what you'd expect from a standard reference manual. Classes and methods are, of course, described in detail. It offers tutorial-style explanations of the important classes in the Java Core API and includes lots of sample code to help you learn by example.

## Java AWT Reference

*By John Zukowski*
*1st Edition March 1997*
*1100 pages, ISBN 1-56592-240-9*

With AWT, you can create windows, draw, work with images, and use components like buttons, scrollbars, and pulldown menus. *Java AWT Reference* covers the classes that comprise the java.awt, java.awt.image, and java.applet packages. These classes provide the functionality that allows a Java application to provide user interaction in a graphical environment. It offers a comprehensive explanation of how AWT components fit together with easy-to-use reference material on every AWT class and lots of sample code to help you learn by example.

# Java Programming *continued*

## Java Threads

*By Scott Oaks and Henry Wong*
*1st Edition January 1997*
*252 pages, ISBN 1-56592-216-6*

*Java Threads* is a comprehensive guide to the intracacies of threaded programming in Java, covering everything from the most basic synchronization techniques to advanced topics like writing your own thread scheduler.

*Java Threads* uncovers the one tricky but essential aspect of Java programming and provides techniques for avoiding deadlock, lock starvation, and other topics.

## Java Network Programming

*By Elliotte Rusty Harold*
*1st Edition February 1997*
*448 pages, ISBN 1-56592-227-1*

*Java Network Programming* is a complete introduction to developing network programs, both applets and applications, using Java; covering everything from networking fundamentals to remote method invocation (RMI).

It also covers what you can do without explicitly writing network code, how you can accomplish your goals using URLs and the basic capabilites of applets.

## Developing Java Beans

*By Rob Englander*
*1st Edition June 1997 (est.)*
*300 pages (est.), ISBN 1-56592-289-1*

With *Developing Java Beans,* you'll learn how to create components that can be manipulated by tools like Borland's Latte or Symantec's Visual Cafe, enabling others to build entire applications by using and reusing these building blocks. Beyond the basics, *Developing Java Beans* teaches you how to create Beans that can be saved and restored properly; how to take advantage of introspection to provide more information about a Bean's capabilities; how to provide property editors and customizers that manipulate a Bean in sophisticated ways; and how to integrate Java Beans into ActiveX projects.

## Java in a Nutshell, DELUXE EDITION

*By various authors*
*1st Edition June1997 (est.)*
*ISBN 1-56592-304-9*
*includes CD-ROM and books.*

*Java in a Nutshell, Deluxe Edition*, is a Java programmer's dream come truein one small package. The heart of this Deluxe Edition is the Java reference library on CD-ROM, which brings together five indispensable volumes forJava developers and programmers, linking related info across books. It includes: *Exploring Java 2nd Edition*, *Java Language Reference, 2nd Edition*, *Java Fundamental Classes Reference*, *Java AWT Reference*, and *Java in a Nutshell, 2nd Edition*, included both on the CD-ROM and in a companion desktop edition. This deluxe library gives you everything you need to do serious programming with Java 1.1.

## Database Programming with JDBC and Java

*By George Reese*
*1st Edition July 1997 (est.)*
*300 pages (est.), ISBN 1-56592-270-0*

Java and databases make a powerful combination. Getting the two sides to work together, however, takes some effort -- largely because Java deals in objects while most databases do not.

This book describes the standard Java interfaces that make portable,object-oriented access to relational databases possible, and offers arobust model for writing applications that are easy to maintain. It introduces the JDBC and RMI packages and uses them to develop three-tier applications (applications divided into a user interface, an object-oriented logic component, and an information store). Covers Java 1.1.

# How to stay in touch with O'Reilly

## 1. Visit Our Award-Winning Web Site

*http://www.ora.com/*

★ "Top 100 Sites on the Web" —*PC Magazine*
★ "Top 5% Web sites" —*Point Communications*
★ "3-Star site" —*The McKinley Group*

Our web site contains a library of comprehensive product information (including book excerpts and tables of contents), downloadable software, background articles, interviews with technology leaders, links to relevant sites, book cover art, and more. File us in your Bookmarks or Hotlist!

## 2. Join Our Email Mailing Lists

### New Product Releases
To receive automatic email with brief descriptions of all new O'Reilly products as they are released, send email to: **listproc@online.ora.com**
Put the following information in the first line of your message (*not* in the Subject field):
**subscribe ora-news "Your Name" of "Your Organization"** (for example: subscribe ora-news Kris Webber of Fine Enterprises)

### O'Reilly Events
If you'd also like us to send information about trade show events, special promotions, and other O'Reilly events, send email to: **listproc@online.ora.com**
Put the following information in the first line of your message (*not* in the Subject field):
**subscribe ora-events "Your Name" of "Your Organization"**

## 3. Get Examples from Our Books via FTP

There are two ways to access an archive of example files from our books:

### Regular FTP
- ftp to:
  **ftp.ora.com**
  (login: anonymous
  password: your email address)
- Point your web browser to:
  **ftp://ftp.ora.com/**

### FTPMAIL
- Send an email message to:
  **ftpmail@online.ora.com**
  (Write "help" in the message body)

## 4. Visit Our Gopher Site
- Connect your gopher to:
  **gopher.ora.com**

- Point your web browser to:
  **gopher://gopher.ora.com/**

- Telnet to:
  **gopher.ora.com**
  **login: gopher**

## 5. Contact Us via Email

**order@ora.com**
To place a book or software order online. Good for North American and international customers.

**subscriptions@ora.com**
To place an order for any of our newsletters or periodicals.

**books@ora.com**
General questions about any of our books.

**software@ora.com**
For general questions and product information about our software. Check out O'Reilly Software Online at **http://software.ora.com/** for software and technical support information. Registered O'Reilly software users send your questions to: **website-support@ora.com**

**cs@ora.com**
For answers to problems regarding your order or our products.

**booktech@ora.com**
For book content technical questions or corrections.

**proposals@ora.com**
To submit new book or software proposals to our editors and product managers.

**international@ora.com**
For information about our international distributors or translation queries. For a list of our distributors outside of North America check out:
**http://www.ora.com/www/order/country.html**

O'Reilly & Associates, Inc.
101 Morris Street, Sebastopol, CA 95472 USA
TEL   707-829-0515 or 800-998-9938
       (6am to 5pm PST)
FAX   707-829-0104

## O'REILLY™

# Titles from O'Reilly

*Please note that upcoming titles are displayed in italic.*

## WEBPROGRAMMING

Apache: The Definitive Guide
Building Your Own Web
  Conferences
Building Your Own Website
CGI Programming for the World
  Wide Web
Designing for the Web
HTML: The Definitive Guide,
  2nd Ed.
JavaScript: The Definitive Guide,
  2nd Ed.
Learning Perl
Programming Perl, 2nd Ed.
Mastering Regular Expressions
WebMaster in a Nutshell
Web Security & Commerce
Web Client Programming with
  Perl
World Wide Web Journal

## USING THE INTERNET

Smileys
The Future Does Not Compute
The Whole Internet User's Guide
  & Catalog
The Whole Internet for Win 95
Using Email Effectively
Bandits on the Information
  Superhighway

## JAVA SERIES

Exploring Java
Java AWT Reference
Java Fundamental Classes
  Reference
Java in a Nutshell
*Java Language Reference, 2nd
  Edition*
Java Network Programming
Java Threads
Java Virtual Machine

## SOFTWARE

WebSite™ 1.1
WebSite Professional™
Building Your Own Web
  Conferences
WebBoard™
PolyForm™
*Statisphere™*

## SONGLINE GUIDES

NetActivism      NetResearch
Net Law          NetSuccess
NetLearning      NetTravel
Net Lessons

## SYSTEM ADMINISTRATION

Building Internet Firewalls
Computer Crime: A
  Crimefighter's Handbook
Computer Security Basics
DNS and BIND, 2nd Ed.
Essential System Administration,
  2nd Ed.
Getting Connected: The Internet
  at 56K and Up
Linux Network Administrator's
  Guide
Managing Internet Information
  Services
Managing NFS and NIS
Networking Personal Computers
  with TCP/IP
Practical UNIX & Internet
  Security, 2nd Ed.
PGP: Pretty Good Privacy
sendmail, 2nd Ed.
sendmail Desktop Reference
System Performance Tuning
TCP/IP Network Administration
termcap & terminfo
Using & Managing UUCP
Volume 8: X Window System
  Administrator's Guide
*Web Security & Commerce*

## UNIX

Exploring Expect
*Learning VBScript*
Learning GNU Emacs, 2nd Ed.
Learning the bash Shell
Learning the Korn Shell
Learning the UNIX Operating
  System
Learning the vi Editor
Linux in a Nutshell
Making TeX Work
Linux Multimedia Guide
Running Linux, 2nd Ed.
SCO UNIX in a Nutshell
sed & awk, 2nd Edition
*Tcl/Tk Tools*
UNIX in a Nutshell: System V
  Edition
UNIX Power Tools
Using csh & tsch
When You Can't Find Your UNIX
  System Administrator
*Writing GNU Emacs Extensions*

## WEB REVIEW STUDIO SERIES

Gif Animation Studio
Shockwave Studio

## WINDOWS

Dictionary of PC Hardware and
  Data Communications Terms
Inside the Windows 95 Registry
Inside the Windows 95 File
  System
Windows Annoyances
*Windows NT File System
  Internals*
*Windows NT in a Nutshell*

## PROGRAMMING

Advanced Oracle PL/SQL
  Programming
Applying RCS and SCCS
C++: The Core Language
Checking C Programs with lint
DCE Security Programming
Distributing Applications Across
  DCE & Windows NT
Encyclopedia of Graphics File
  Formats, 2nd Ed.
Guide to Writing DCE
  Applications
lex & yacc
Managing Projects with make
Mastering Oracle Power Objects
Oracle Design: The Definitive
  Guide
Oracle Performance Tuning, 2nd
  Ed.
Oracle PL/SQL Programming
Porting UNIX Software
POSIX Programmer's Guide
POSIX.4: Programming for the
  Real World
Power Programming with RPC
Practical C Programming
Practical C++ Programming
Programming Python
Programming with curses
Programming with GNU Software
Pthreads Programming
Software Portability with imake,
  2nd Ed.
Understanding DCE
Understanding Japanese
  Information Processing
UNIX Systems Programming for
  SVR4

## BERKELEY 4.4 SOFTWARE DISTRIBUTION

4.4BSD System Manager's
  Manual
4.4BSD User's Reference Manual
4.4BSD User's Supplementary
  Documents
4.4BSD Programmer's Reference
  Manual
4.4BSD Programmer's
  Supplementary Documents
X Programming
Vol. 0: X Protocol Reference
  Manual
Vol. 1: Xlib Programming Manual
Vol. 2: Xlib Reference Manual
Vol. 3M: X Window System User's
  Guide, Motif Edition
Vol. 4M: X Toolkit Intrinsics
  Programming Manual, Motif
  Edition
Vol. 5: X Toolkit Intrinsics
  Reference Manual
Vol. 6A: Motif Programming
  Manual
Vol. 6B: Motif Reference Manual
Vol. 6C: Motif Tools
Vol. 8 : X Window System
  Administrator's Guide
Programmer's Supplement for
  Release 6
X User Tools
The X Window System in a
  Nutshell

## CAREER & BUSINESS

Building a Successful Software
  Business
The Computer User's Survival
  Guide
Love Your Job!
Electronic Publishing on CD-
  ROM

## TRAVEL

Travelers' Tales: Brazil
Travelers' Tales: Food
Travelers' Tales: France
Travelers' Tales: Gutsy Women
Travelers' Tales: India
Travelers' Tales: Mexico
Travelers' Tales: Paris
Travelers' Tales: San Francisco
Travelers' Tales: Spain
Travelers' Tales: Thailand
Travelers' Tales: A Woman's
  World

# International Distributors

## UK, Europe, Middle East and Northern Africa *(except France, Germany, Switzerland, & Austria)*

**INQUIRIES**
International Thomson Publishing
Europe
Berkshire House
168-173 High Holborn
London WC1V 7AA, United Kingdom
Telephone: 44-171-497-1422
Fax: 44-171-497-1426
Email: itpint@itps.co.uk

**ORDERS**
International Thomson Publishing
Services, Ltd.
Cheriton House, North Way
Andover, Hampshire SP10 5BE,
United Kingdom
Telephone: 44-264-342-832
(UK orders)
Telephone: 44-264-342-806
(outside UK)
Fax: 44-264-364418 (UK orders)
Fax: 44-264-342761 (outside UK)
UK & Eire orders: itpuk@itps.co.uk
International orders: itpint@itps.co.uk

## France

Editions Eyrolles
61 bd Saint-Germain
75240 Paris Cedex 05
France
Fax: 33-01-44-41-11-44

**FRENCH LANGUAGE BOOKS**
All countries except Canada
Phone: 33-01-44-41-46-16
Email: geodif@eyrolles.com

**ENGLISH LANGUAGE BOOKS**
Phone: 33-01-44-41-11-87
Email: distribution@eyrolles.com

## Australia

WoodsLane Pty. Ltd.
7/5 Vuko Place, Warriewood NSW 2102
P.O. Box 935, Mona Vale NSW 2103
Australia
Telephone: 61-2-9970-5111
Fax: 61-2-9970-5002
Email: info@woodslane.com.au

## Germany, Switzerland, and Austria

**INQUIRIES**
O'Reilly Verlag
Balthasarstr. 81
D-50670 Köln
Germany
Telephone: 49-221-97-31-60-0
Fax: 49-221-97-31-60-8
Email: anfragen@oreilly.de

**ORDERS**
International Thomson Publishing
Königswinterer Straße 418
53227 Bonn, Germany
Telephone: 49-228-97024 0
Fax: 49-228-441342
Email: order@oreilly.de

## Asia *(except Japan & India)*

**INQUIRIES**
International Thomson Publishing Asia
60 Albert Street #15-01
Albert Complex
Singapore 189969
Telephone: 65-336-6411
Fax: 65-336-7411

**ORDERS**
Telephone: 65-336-6411
Fax: 65-334-1617
thomson@signet.com.sg

## New Zealand

WoodsLane New Zealand Ltd.
21 Cooks Street (P.O. Box 575)
Wanganui, New Zealand
Telephone: 64-6-347-6543
Fax: 64-6-345-4840
Email: info@woodslane.com.au

## Japan

O'Reilly Japan, Inc.
Kiyoshige Building 2F
12-Banchi, Sanei-cho
Shinjuku-ku
Tokyo 160 Japan
Telephone: 81-3-3356-5227
Fax: 81-3-3356-5261
Email: kenji@ora.com

## India

Computer Bookshop (India) PVT. LTD.
190 Dr. D.N. Road, Fort
Bombay 400 001
India
Telephone: 91-22-207-0989
Fax: 91-22-262-3551
Email: cbsbom@giasbm01.vsnl.net.in

## The Americas

O'Reilly & Associates, Inc.
101 Morris Street
Sebastopol, CA 95472 U.S.A.
Telephone: 707-829-0515
Telephone: 800-998-9938 (U.S. & Canada)
Fax: 707-829-0104
Email: order@ora.com

## Southern Africa

International Thomson Publishing
Southern Africa
Building 18, Constantia Park
240 Old Pretoria Road
P.O. Box 2459
Halfway House, 1685 South Africa
Telephone: 27-11-805-4819
Fax: 27-11-805-3648

O'REILLY™

O'Reilly & Associates, Inc.
101 Morris Street
Sebastopol, CA 95472-9902
1-800-998-9938

*Visit us online at:*
**http://www.ora.com/**
**orders@ora.com**

# O'REILLY WOULD LIKE TO HEAR FROM YOU

Which book did this card come from?

_____

Where did you buy this book?
- ❏ Bookstore
- ❏ Direct from O'Reilly
- ❏ Bundled with hardware/software
- ❏ Computer Store
- ❏ Class/seminar
- ❏ Other _____

What operating system do you use?
- ❏ UNIX
- ❏ Windows NT
- ❏ Macintosh
- ❏ PC (Windows/DOS)
- ❏ Other _____

What is your job description?
- ❏ System Administrator
- ❏ Network Administrator
- ❏ Web Developer
- ❏ Programmer
- ❏ Educator/Teacher
- ❏ Other _____

❏ Please send me O'Reilly's catalog, containing a complete listing of O'Reilly books and software.

Name _____ Company/Organization _____

Address _____

City _____ State _____ Zip/Postal Code _____ Country _____

Telephone _____ Internet or other email address (specify network)

Nineteenth century wood engraving
of a bear from the O'Reilly &
Associates Nutshell Handbook®
*Using & Managing UUCP.*

POST CARD

# BUSINESS REPLY MAIL

FIRST CLASS MAIL   PERMIT NO. 80   SEBASTOPOL, CA

*Postage will be paid by addressee*

**O'Reilly & Associates, Inc.**
101 Morris Street
Sebastopol, CA  95472-9902

║║.║ʼ.║.║ʼ.║.║.║ʼʼ.║.║.║║.║.║.║.║ʼʼʼʼ.║.║.║║║